THE MARK OF CRIMINALITY

RHETORIC, CULTURE, AND SOCIAL CRITIQUE

THE MARK OF CRIMINALITY

RHETORIC, RACE, AND GANGSTA RAP IN THE WAR-ON-CRIME ERA

BRYAN J. MCCANN

THE UNIVERSITY OF ALABAMA PRESS
Tuscaloosa

The University of Alabama Press
Tuscaloosa, Alabama 35487-0380
uapress.ua.edu

Hardcover edition published 2017.
Paperback edition published 2019.
eBook edition published 2017.

Inquiries about reproducing material from this work should be addressed to the
University of Alabama Press.

Typeface: Garamond and Futura

Cover image: Freedesignfile, vector hoody gangsters design set, CC BY 3.0, line
art altered from original
Cover design: David Nees

Chapter 2 and portions of the conclusion are derived in part from an article
posted in *Critical Studies in Media Communication* on August 24, 2012, available
online: http://www.tandfonline.com/doi/abs/10.1080/15295036.2012.676194.
Chapter 4 is derived in part from an article posted in *Cultural Studies ↔ Critical
Methodologies* on August 22, 2013, available online: http://csc.sagepub.com/
content/13/5/408.

Paperback ISBN: 978-0-8173-5948-5

A previous edition of this book has been catalogued by the Library of Congress
as follows:
Library of Congress Cataloging-in-Publication Data
Names: McCann, Bryan J.
Title: The mark of criminality : rhetoric, race, and gangsta rap in the war-on-
crime era / Bryan J. McCann.
Description: Tuscaloosa : The University of Alabama Press, [2017] | Series:
Rhetoric, culture, and social critique | Includes bibliographical references and
index.
Identifiers: LCCN 2016045202| ISBN 9780817319489 (cloth : alk. paper) |
ISBN 9780817391171 (e book)
Subjects: LCSH: Gangsta rap (Music)—History and criticism. | African-
Americans—Social conditions—History—20th century. | Crime in music.
Classification: LCC ML3531 .M3 2017 | DDC 306.4/842490973—dc23
LC record available at https://lccn.loc.gov/2016045202

For Ashley
Especially today . . .

Contents

Figures

Preface

The White Boy Listens to Gangsta Rap

The story goes like this: I perform much of my "research" while riding in my car with my iPod plugged in to the stereo. Music by the likes of NWA, Snoop Doggy Dogg, and Tupac Shakur blares from my car speakers as I mine the songs for insights into this thing I call the "mark of criminality." I come to a stoplight and look to my side. The driver spies the lily-white boy blasting "Fuck Tha Police," "Nuthin' But a 'G' Thang," or "Hit 'Em Up." He and his passengers smile, then chuckle and continue waiting for the light to turn green.

The juxtaposition of white bodies with rap music is problematic and therefore comical. When the music industry began tracking record sales with Nielsen SoundScan in 1991, they discovered something that continues to haunt the hip-hop nation: white kids love gangsta rap.[1] Legions of primarily male, primarily white suburban youth were devouring these sensational tales of black criminality, and they were doing so to such an extent that they constituted a majority of the genre's market share. Affluent white kids became the chief target audience for the marketing of rap music. Their demand for narratives of black-on-black violence, vicious misogyny, copious drug use, and unrepentant capital accumulation ensured that gangsta would rule the hip-hop kingdom in the twilight years of the twentieth century. This commercial reality has inspired many scholars to critique the white appropriation of yet another mode of black vernacular expression. For what else should we call the white consumption of gangsta rap than a latter-day form of minstrelsy?[2]

But this juxtaposition of whiteness and gangsta is also hilarious. One of the most memorable scenes in the beloved cult comedy film *Office Space* features the cubicle laborer Michael Bolton (no relation to the eponymous singer, he insists) blasting a track by Houston-based gangsta rapper Scarface and rapping along with every lyric. Bolton's feeble, if earnest, enactment of gangsta bravado is comic gold.[3] While Eminem maintains a consistent, if fraught, ethos as a white rapper from tough origins, countless wedding receptions, school dances, and other celebratory gatherings of white people continue to partake in the ritual mockery of Vanilla Ice's nostalgia-inspiring "Ice Ice Baby."[4] Indeed, mine is not the only white body that inspires laughter when it shares space with the discourses of the hip-hop nation.

But there is also privilege in being the butt of a joke. If we duplicate my experiences at so many controlled intersections and replace mine with a black masculine body, it is not difficult to anticipate how differently the scene would unfold. The glances from the other car would be brief ("Did he see us look?"), doors would lock and windows would roll up (just as Michael Bolton's did when he spied a black man outside his car during the aforementioned *Office Space* scene), and the occupants would anxiously wait for the red light to turn green. The image of a white guy jamming to gangsta rap is hilarious. A black man doing the same, for too many Americans, is horrifying. The music and image fit perfectly— too perfectly. It is a visual and sonic embodiment of our worst racial fears. My interest in the ways these fears mark certain bodies, and how those bodies themselves appropriate and deploy such fears, motivates this project.

My scholarly interest in gangsta rap, even race and criminality, is always an issue. On one occasion, a black woman enrolled in one of my field's top doctoral programs pointedly asked me, "Why black people?" When I tell my undergraduate students what I study, they almost immediately laugh. When I present my research in academic or activist settings, audience members inevitably ask me to account for my white privilege and its connection to what I study. In other words, why do I study gangsta? Why race and crime? What right do I have to do so? Am I not guilty of the same acts of appropriation that Sound-Scan detected in the early 1990s? I hope to gain an academic thumbs-up, a promotion, and a national reputation as a scholar with this work. How do I justify doing so with the experiences of communities whose members disproportionately fill our prisons?

All I can promise is an unsatisfying explanation. I approach the very prospect of addressing this "elephant in the room" with heavy ambivalence. On one hand, I recognize the ethical imperative of accounting for our relationships to our work and acknowledging, even embracing, the frustrating incompleteness of such accounts.[5] However, such confessional postures also risk leaving structures of privilege intact rather than fostering dialogue and transformation.[6] There is a fine line between thoughtful reflexivity and self-indulgent narcissism. Because I am the author and believe all scholarship contains at least a trace of autobiography, the following story is mine. However, because I have never sat inside a prison cell or had someone on whom I depend for financial or personal stability do so, this book is full of stories that are most certainly not mine. Yet I write them.

Unlike many of my white male peers coming of age in the suburbs during the late 1980s and 1990s, I was not a consumer of the rap artists from whom people like Tipper Gore and Bob Dole hoped to protect me.[7] Instead, I attended punk shows, devoured the work of groups like Nine Inch Nails and The Cure, and wrote horrible emulative poetry. My interest in gangsta rap began later. During the summer of 2007, while living in Austin, Texas, I participated in a grassroots campaign that successfully halted the execution of an African American man named Kenneth Foster Jr. Foster was sentenced to death in 1996 under the law of parties; he was driving a car from which another man, Mauriceo Brown, exited after a night of robberies in San Antonio and shot Michael LaHood to death. Although he did not pull the trigger, Foster was subject to the death penalty under Texas law. The Lone Star State, as most readers will know, is the execution capital of the United States.[8]

Aside from the resonance of a death penalty case in which the defendant, a black man, quite literally did not shoot the victim, Foster was an altogether interesting figure. Born to drug-addicted parents in Austin, he spent much of his childhood living with his grandparents in San Antonio. At the time of his arrest for Michael LaHood's murder (in effect for being an accessory to the murder), Foster's ambition was to be a rap artist. This was one of many factors that sealed Foster's fate in his original trial, as the prosecution read some of his more graphic lyrics aloud to startle the jury during the sentencing phase. He was cast as a "gangsta" unworthy of life in civil society. Such prosecutorial strategies, still used in courtrooms today, exemplify the ways the vernacular practices of black youth can help affirm and entrench fears of black criminality.[9] As a resident of Texas's death row, Foster quickly began establishing connections with the outside world, including a pen-pal relationship with me. He devoured writings by Karl Marx, Frantz Fanon, Malcolm X, and Huey Newton. He identified closely with Black Power/Nationalist tendencies and admired radical activist groups working against the prison system. He also organized his fellow inmates and participated in coordinated acts of nonviolent civil disobedience to protest living conditions on death row. Condemned bodies that had been marked as irredeemable threats to public safety and decency were refashioning themselves to comment on matters of basic human rights. With a provocative case and talent for political analysis, Foster attracted a number of supporters, including his then-wife, Dutch rapper Tasha "Jav'lin" Narez. Tasha composed a rap song about Kenneth's case titled "Walk With Me"; its video spread far and wide across the Internet and was instrumental in bringing attention to the campaign's cause. During that long sum-mer of 2007, we also held a hip-hop benefit for Foster in which several local acts volunteered their talent.[10]

The hip-hop nation loomed large in the Save Kenneth Foster Campaign. As I began listening more closely to rap music, I took note of its embrace and enact-ment of the very discourses of racism and fear that I observed rationalizing capi-tal punishment and mass incarceration in Texas and beyond. Several of the artists who performed at the San Antonio concert valorized drug consumption and vio-lence, whereas a Florida-based group called Dead Prez (a.k.a. dead prez)—which I discuss in more detail in my final chapter—imagined criminality as a source of righteous political resistance. As I looked further into the history of these pro-vocative rhetorical strategies, I revisited the controversies associated with NWA and their antipolice lyrics; the misogynistic discourses of leisure and style de-ployed by Dr. Dre and Snoop Doggy Dogg, as Snoop Dogg was then known; and the voluminous work of Tupac Shakur, whose violent death coincided with my own political development as a high school student.

Stories that unfolded along the periphery of my youth now stood at the center of my academic and activist ambitions as I interrogated anew the politics of race and criminality. I quickly came to recognize that at the precise moments when I was developing my own discursive relationship to the politics of crime and punishment through shows like *America's Most Wanted* and, later, the polariz-ing death penalty case of Mumia Abu-Jamal, an assortment of artists were devel-oping alternative enactments of discourses that had rendered young black men the most feared population in the United States.[11] The musings of gangsta art-ists do not represent the political clarity of seasoned death row activists. But the voices of the marginalized rarely emerge fully formed and capable of cogently speaking to power—at least not in ways that satisfy the rhetorical norms of tra-ditional community organizing. They are more often complex voices that pose as many challenges as they do solutions. In the case of gangsta rap, whose revenue depends on sensationalized discourses of black criminality, the challenges are plentiful. However, we ignore these voices that were able to spark forceful na-tional dialogue on race and crime at the close of the twentieth century at our own peril. For all of its flaws, gangsta rap initially functioned as a way for black voices to produce rhetorics of criminality in ways that complicated the prevail-ing discourses of racialized fear that mobilized white anxieties. I write what fol-lows with an investment in a continuity between the violent rap lyrics of a young Kenneth Foster, and the powerful movement—led by Kenneth and his family—that helped save his life.

Of course, my privileged relationship to the prison-industrial complex also af-fected my ability to establish credibility in the campaign to stop Kenneth's exe-cution.[12] My proximity to matters of incarceration and state-sanctioned death by way of community organizing helps explain my arrival at this project, yet I do not presume to satisfy all curiosities and ambivalences about my relationship to these texts. I know it does not satisfy my own. However, while I am not statistically as likely to enter a prison cell or be profiled by a police officer or shop owner as many African American men my age would be, the criminal justice system has nonetheless played a role in how I imagine my subjectivity. Indeed, I believe this to be the case for all Americans. Those of us invested in challenging the daunting mechanisms of supervision, confinement, and death that compose our criminal justice system must stand prepared to account for our own relationship to criminality. However, those of us who experience such relationships from privileged positions have much to learn from the discourses those most directly targeted for imprisonment have enlisted to reckon with their precarious subject positions. A coherent and unified struggle capable of challenging the prison system and the interests it defends relies on a stubborn commitment to reaching across experiential boundaries by listening to and learning from the "raps" of others.

Acknowledgments

Since finishing my PhD, I have taught at three different institutions in as many states. The result has been no small amount of personal and professional chaos but also the good fortune of connecting with many extraordinary people without whom this project would not have come to fruition. I am undoubtedly leaving some people out, but hopefully they know how much I value them.

Deciding to leave Illinois for the first time in my life to pursue a PhD at the University of Texas was difficult, but ultimately transformative. I chose UT in order to work with Dana Cloud, who quickly became, and remains, one of my dearest friends and comrades. She is family. Her guidance through this project and countless others taught me to be a careful reader of texts and theory. She also continues to motivate me to account for the fact that rhetoric has real consequences for people and their communities. Whatever talents or virtues I currently possess as a professional, activist, and, in many respects, a person would not exist without Dana's influence.

Several other mentors have helped shape this project, including Barry Brummett, Jennifer Fuller, Josh Gunn, and Stephen Hartnett. Other senior scholars inside and outside the communication discipline have provided support in the form of direct feedback on this project or by simply taking me seriously as a scholar early in my career. Thus I am grateful to Harry Cleaver, Dan Brouwer, Rick Cherwitz, Randy Cox, Rod Hart, Chuck Morris, and John Sloop.

Those friends and colleagues who entered this line of work at or around the same time as I did also helped make this book project a reality. Thank you to my Indianapolis writing group, consisting of Casey Kelly, Kristen Hoerl, and

Jonathan Rossing, for their feedback on some of the earliest versions of this project. I am also grateful to Matt May and Jeff Bennett for allowing me to model my book proposal after theirs. Other peers, scattered across the country, whose excellent scholarship, generous engagements with my work, and friendship helped inspire this monograph in various ways, include Jennifer Asenas, Adria Battaglia, Diana Bowen, Karma Chávez, Lisa Corrigan, Amanda Davis-Gatchet, Roger Davis-Gatchet, Johanna Hartelius, Kevin Johnson, Amber Kelsie, Matt Morris, Tiara Na'puti, Kristen Stimpson, Luke Winslow, Jaime Wright, and Amy Young. The members of the Prison Communication, Activism, Research, and Education collective (PCARE), especially Lindsey Badger, Ed Hinck, Karen Lovaas, Eleanor Novek, Emily Plec, Jennifer Wood, and Bill Yousman, have consistently energized my commitment to this project, as well as engaged scholarship and activism regarding crime and public culture in general.

Since 2009, I have taught at Marian University in Indianapolis, Wayne State University in Detroit, and, currently, Louisiana State University in Baton Rouge. Colleagues past and present have supported this project in a variety of ways. I offer deep thanks to Sarah Becker, Dana Berkowitz, Graham Bodie, Jim Cherney, Chris Collins, Gay Lynn Crossley, Renee Edwards, Stephen Finley, Stephanie Houston Grey, Rachel Hall, Jim Honeycutt, Ashley Jones-Bodie, Loraleigh Keishly, Andy King, George LaMaster, John LeBret, Judith Moldenhauer, Loretta Pecchioni, Kashif Powell, Billy Saas (who generously provided feedback on portions of this book), Tracy Stephenson Shaffer, Trish Suchy, David Terry, Sue Weinstein, and Kelly Young. This project also owes much to the energy and talents of students past and present, both graduate and undergraduate. Whether we had a series of conversations about the subjects covered in this book or shared moments that reminded me why I do what I do, I thank Michael Althouse, Nygel Anderson, Minu Basnet, Brandon Bumstead, Savannah Ganster, Raquel Robvais, Cynthia Sampson, Taylor Scott, Matthew Tougas, the students of Marian University's Peace and Justice Studies Program, and my forensics students over the years. Furthermore, I thank the far-too-often unsung heroes of every department where I have ever worked. The work of amazing administrative professionals like Donna Sparks and Tonya Romero make all of our scholarship, teaching, and service possible.

My interest in the cultural politics of race and crime is fundamentally inspired by my encounters with a vast community of activists. The idea for the project emerged during my time doing anti-death-penalty work in Texas and its development benefited from explicit conversations about the subject matter with fellow activists and, crucially, from the plain fact that doing grassroots work has helped keep me honest and focused on the very real consequences of mass incarceration and other forms of state and corporate violence. I am, therefore, grateful for the influence of people like Matt Beamesderfer, Mike Biskar, Kelly Booker, Laura

Brady, Marie Buck, Mike Corwin, Lily Hughes, Randi Jones-Hensley, Matt Korn, Stuart Mora, and Aaron Petcoff, as well as families like the Fosters, Reeds, and Scotts, whose bravery in the face of the worst excesses of state violence should humble and inspire all of us.

This book's completion also owes a great deal to Alvin Carter III and other staff members of the Hiphop Archive and Research Institute at Harvard University. The archive's staggering collection of hip-hop journalism and other artifacts helped transform my research into a book worthy of publication. Such archival work and other steps toward this project's completion were largely possible due to the financial generosity of Louisiana State University's College of Humanities and Social Sciences and Wayne State University's College of Fine, Performing, and Communication Arts.

I am also, of course, indebted to the people at the University of Alabama Press for their faith in this project, especially to series editor John Louis Lucaites, Dan Waterman and his staff, the editorial board, and the two anonymous reviewers.

And then there is my family, both chosen and biological. Clark Bernier, Katie Feyh, David Supp-Montgomerie, and Robert McDonald helped sustain me throughout this project, as well as through so many transitions, joys, and tribulations. My canine children, Harvey Milk and Cap'n Jack, in their most hyperactive and tender moments, keep me grounded most days. I am fortunate to consider my sister, Megan McCann, one of my best friends. She has influenced this project in more ways than she probably realizes. My parents, John and Julie McCann, are responsible for this book in so many fundamental ways. Aside from the obvious (making me), they allowed me to discover the world of culture and politics in ways many other parents would not. By allowing and trusting me to watch movies that were off limits to many of my peers, raid their record collection, and read all kinds of subversive literature, they taught me to engage public life with breadth and depth. The path that led me to this project was long and laden with detours, but begins with their love and sacrifices.

Lastly, my partner and the love of my life, Ashley Mack, falls into every category I have listed. She is my confidante, colleague, ally, and fiercest advocate. From reviewing my work to providing inspiration, laughter, and patience during even my darkest moments, I would not be whole, let alone the author of a book, without her. I sincerely hope I provide for you even a measure of what you give to me. You came into my life at precisely the right time and continue to be my favorite. I love you.

THE MARK OF CRIMINALITY

Introduction

Rhetoric, Race, and Gangsta Rap in the War-on-Crime Era

While the United States has always, to one degree or another, waged war against crime, the period comprising the late 1980s and 1990s was a watershed of racialized moral panic regarding the perceived threats that criminality posed to civil society.[1] At that time, politicians in both the Republican and Democratic Parties increasingly staked their political destinies on their capacity to be "tough on crime" by pursuing unprecedentedly harsh penal policies that led to staggering increases in the nation's prison population. Activists often refer to the resulting network of tough-on-crime policies, sensationalistic rhetorics of fear, and private corporate interests as the *prison-industrial complex*. Political leaders and culture warriors justified such policies by enlisting a range of rhetorical strategies that almost always appealed to public fears of racialized bodies and communities. Young black men were distinctly singled out as a threat to civilization in need of constant surveillance and frequent confinement.[2]

This cultural politics of law and order delivered staggering electoral fortunes to those officials who staked their political capital on their predominantly white voting base's fears of a savage, racialized criminal threat. However, the devastating collateral consequences of the war on crime are manifest to this day. As I write, the United States incarcerates a higher percentage of its adult population than any other nation on earth. Increasingly, states and the federal government are coming to terms with the cold truth that the overcrowding of prisons places paralyzing strains on government budgets and violates many inmates' human and civil rights. Furthermore, while the nation's prison population has increased by 500 percent since the 1970s, such growth does not correspond to fluctuations in crime rates. A recent study by the Bureau of Justice Statistics found that more than three-quarters of prisoners released in thirty states were arrested again within five years. This is in no small part attributable to the fact that individuals with prison records experience what legal scholar Gabriel Chin describes as *civil death*; they are often denied employment, lose their right to vote, and are generally stigmatized in spite of even the sincerest efforts to reenter society. In short, the American prison system is an unmitigated disaster.[3]

While the prison-industrial complex impacts all Americans in important ways, the racial dimensions of mass incarceration are particularly troubling. According to the Pew Center on the States study that reported the United States' status as the world's leading jailer, ethnic minorities remain particularly vulnerable to imprisonment today. For instance, one in thirty-six Latinos ages eighteen or older are behind bars, whereas one in fifteen black men of the same age group are incarcerated (compared to one in 106 white men). The study also found that the nation imprisons one of every nine black men between the ages of twenty and thirty-four. While the United States imprisons fewer women than men, similar racial disparities exist among female inmates.[4] Studies of capital punishment reveal that cases involving white victims are significantly more likely to result in a death sentence than those involving a minority victim, suggesting that prosecutors and juries are less sympathetic toward victims of color.[5] Furthermore, in her highly influential book *The New Jim Crow: Mass Incarceration in the Age of Colorblindness*, Michelle Alexander documents the numerous ways incarceration haunts ethnic minorities after their release. A conviction for even a nonviolent felony virtually erases one's job prospects; limits access to welfare, student loans, and other services; and, in most states, results in a temporary or permanent loss of voting rights. Because black Americans are so overrepresented in the prison system, the collateral consequences of mass incarceration on black communities are especially damaging. As I demonstrate in the following pages, the prison-industrial complex in particular and the cultural politics of criminality in the United States in general are fundamentally racialized.[6]

The Mark of Criminality: Rhetoric, Race, and Gangsta Rap in the War-on-Crime Era attends to the rhetorical dynamics that helped figure blackness as an inherently criminal category in American public discourse. Carol Stabile writes, "No other ethnic or racial group has been singled out for the wholesale criminalization to which African Americans have been subjected during the last four decades of the twentieth century."[7] There can be no denying the devastating consequences of the war on crime for poor and working-class people, and especially people of color, in the United States. However, the narrative of a unidirectional imposition of racialized discourses of criminality on the disproportionately black male bodies that came to fill the nation's jails and prisons in staggering numbers offers too facile an account of the cultural dynamics of this period in our history, as well as the broader cultural history of crime. Criminality is not a static site of meaning, but highly contingent. While discourses of crime and criminality serve the interests of those occupying the upper echelons of power, they also provide resources for those very subjects deemed criminal in a particular context. Although rhetorics of law and order inscribe markers of fear on racialized bodies to justify their surveillance and confinement, those same bodies are capable of deploying and refashioning those markers. The logics of racialized fear that motivate tough-on-crime rhetorics compel affective investments from primarily white constituencies, but other expressions of black criminality generate affective investments for criminalized communities of color.

In order to illuminate the complex and contingent nature of criminality during a period of heightened national discourse regarding law and order, I advance the "mark of criminality" as a generic regime of discourses of blackness. In short, the mark of criminality is a rhetorical genre of performative blackness that privileges hypermasculinity, hyperviolence, and hypersexuality as central characteristics of black subjectivity. By describing the mark of criminality as a genre, I attend to its formal consistencies across time, as well as its malleability. In other words, the mark of criminality possesses structured and recurrent themes that remain consistent in important ways, while also shifting in the hands of different rhetors and in response to changing historical circumstances. Attending to the mark of criminality allows critics to examine the ways dominant cultural discourses criminalize black bodies and communities, as well as the ways those very bodies and communities make use of criminality as resources for cultural and political performances of blackness. To illustrate the highly contingent nature of the mark of criminality during the 1980s and 1990s, I turn to the work of gangsta rap artists who produced incendiary albums in and around South Central Los Angeles during this period. While politicians and culture warriors relied on a bricolage of campaign speeches and commercials, popular culture, and legislation to advance their tough-on-crime agendas, hip-hop artists who traded in gangsta rap set rhymes to beats to weave sensationalistic tales of crime in the inner city. Michael Quinn describes it as "a genre based on the construction of an urban mise-en-scène of drugs, rape and murder."[8] Imani Perry elaborates: "It would be simple if hip hop simply provided sociological analyses of black urbanity. However, numerous hip hop artists instead exploit the white fear of the black assailant as a source of power. In so doing, they mimic and adopt the very American construction of the black monster."[9] Rather than challenging, as some other hip-hop artists did, the prevailing discourses of crime and punishment, gangsta artists like Niggaz With Attitude (NWA), former NWA member Dr. Dre, Snoop Doggy Dogg, and Tupac Shakur, not to mention many savvy and opportunistic music moguls, eagerly refashioned the mark of criminality as a source of masculine bravado and profit. This central characteristic of gangsta rap has made it an object of intense criticism, even contempt, in both intellectual and popular circles.

In the following pages, I argue that an attention to gangsta rap's circulation from 1988 (the year NWA released their hugely influential album *Straight Outta Compton*) to 1996 (the year iconic rapper Tupac Shakur died in a hail of bullets) illuminates the contingent nature of the mark of criminality. While gangsta rap became one of the most widely consumed and controversial musical genres of the twentieth century by drawing on many of the same themes that prevailed in mainstream law-and-order discourses, its artists revised many of these themes to suit their own ends. Gangsta's ambitions included explicit critiques of law enforcement, enactments of hypermasculinity, celebratory narratives of leisure and conspicuous consumption, vitriolic declarations of superiority over industry rivals, and, above all else, accrual of monetary gain from the cultural reproduction of the mark of criminality. My goal here is not to romanticize gangsta rap as a resistant alternative to the hegemonic iterations of the mark of criminality that predominated in political and popular discourses in the late twentieth century. On the contrary, much of what I describe in the following pages helped reify notions of the black criminal as an existential threat to all that "good Americans" held near and dear, while also inflicting significant symbolic violence on women, members of the LGBTQ+ community, and other marginalized people. I argue that gangsta rap played as much a role in shaping how many Americans made sense of criminality during this era as the rhetoric of elected officials or cultural elites by, in the words of Eric King Watts, "re-inscribing the rules of a spectacular game."[10] I deliberately reject neat delineations of repressive and emancipatory deployments of the mark of criminality in favor of a rhetorical and cultural history that illuminates the kind of work the mark of criminality did for a range of interested parties. Through a triangulation of the politics of law and order, gangsta rap, and discourses of black criminality, I argue that attending to the mark of criminality's formal consistencies and fluctuations illuminates how rhetorics of criminality, particularly black criminality, provide a broad repertoire of cultural and political resources for the mobilization of affects across a range of communities. By dispensing with the notion that the mark of criminality possesses an a priori essence, scholars and activists are better suited to tell complex histories of criminality in the United States and to imagine new ways of challenging the prison-industrial complex.

Before proceeding any further, I must account for my own limitations in endeavoring to draw on a musical genre, gangsta rap, to advance new ways of understanding race and criminality. As a rhetorician, I am trained to interrogate the suasive functions of symbols to find, constitute, and mobilize audiences. While, as I shall demonstrate throughout this book, gangsta rap is thoroughly rhetorical in this regard, I am not a musician or ethnomusicologist. Rhetorical critics typically privilege language in their studies of popular and political texts.[11] Even those scholars who study sonic phenomena like music generally focus on visible components like lyrics, music videos, audience, and political economy.[12] This tendency is problematic because music possesses distinctly affective qualities that function outside the boundaries of what Roland Barthes called "the poorest of linguistic categories: the adjective."[13] George Lipsitz claims music and other culture forms can function as "a repository of collective memory, a site of moral instruction, and a mechanism for bringing communities into being through performance."[14] Furthermore, popular music presents itself to many audiences in myriad forms, including the original recording, the television commercial, the live concert, the music video, and as "background music in public spaces."[15] Emphasizing these various contexts is key to discerning the rhetorical character of music. It is, therefore, essential to treat music as something other than mere epiphenomena in relation to lyrics or images. This is especially vital for the study of music and politics, for, as John Street argues, "Music does not just provide a vehicle of political expression, it *is* that expression."[16]

The successful musical critic is one who follows Greil Marcus's lead in "looking into the corners" of a song or album's historical moment, accounting not only for the convergence of lyrical and tonal qualities but also considering how both operate within a multitude of concurrent, even contradictory contexts.[17] Music is best understood as a product of history, as well as a participant therein. I agree with Tony Kirschner that in the study of music, "A good map is one that provides the most useful explanation, which opens political possibilities for those who are affected by power—it provides us with a theoretical basis for struggle."[18] Such maps help us place the conjuncture of lyrical, visual, and tonal characteristics in conversation with historical forces that may illuminate salient elements residing even in those musical texts that are, on face value, vacuous in their pop sensibilities or destructive in their content. In addition to spying such latent content, reading music in a way that emphasizes context also illuminates potential linkages across communities of struggle that would otherwise remain hidden absent the broadest possible method of contextualization.[19]

Attending to gangsta rap as music, therefore, is vital to encapsulating the formal patterns and fissures of the mark of criminality. Because music is itself formal, its persuasive power resides in its capacity to repeat and revise ways of being. Joshua Gunn and Mirko Hall describe how music is able to create the illusion of "losing" oneself because it "has the uncanny ability to involve, construct, and energize the body in accordance with rhythms, gestures, surfaces, and desire . . . [causing] listeners to experience their body and its social identity in new ways."[20] The tonal characteristics of gangsta rap, therefore, play as central a role in deploying the mark of criminality as the lyrics or other political and cultural discourses that more conspicuously employ the mark of criminality.

(Re)mapping the Mark of Criminality

My goal in *The Mark of Criminality: Rhetoric, Race, and Gangsta Rap in the War-on-Crime Era* is to revisit the meaning of "crime" in an era whose discourses and policies helped make the American prison system one of our great contemporary human rights catastrophes. To this end, the book proceeds with a conceptualization of the mark of criminality as a pervasive and unstable genre associated with the state's ability to name, surveil, and contain public enemies and their communities, as well as the tendency of those communities and others to employ the mark of criminality to various ends. I then offer readings of key texts of 1980s and 1990s gangsta rap to explain how those texts participated in the meaning systems of the war on crime by repeating and refashioning the mark of criminality in ways that transgressed the prevailing logics of law and order, even while reinforcing many stereotypes about poor communities of color for unabashedly profit-driven reasons. The focal point of these readings is the genre's iconic albums released from 1988 to 1996, with a particular focus on their most popular and controversial tracks. In addition to dwelling on the textual, visual, and sonic dimensions of these recordings, I contextualize them in a broad tapestry of other recordings and associated media from the era; commentary from artists, producers, politicians, and culture warriors; and mainstream and hip-hop journalism. My goal, in other words, is to meditate on the ways key musical texts of 1980s and 1990s gangsta rap operated in a complex and ever-moving constellation of meaning associated with criminality.

Chapter 1 elaborates the mark of criminality's status as a genre of blackness that comprises discourses of race, gender, class, and nationhood. I begin by noting the central role of black folklore, music, and other cultural forms in sustaining and challenging shifting meanings of racialized criminality throughout US history. Most of the chapter documents the emergence of the mark of criminality as a key resource for political rhetoric beginning in the 1960s. As large social movements began to make major gains in the public square in the post–World War II era, many prominent political figures began crafting messages that framed law and order as a matter of great national concern, arguing that crime control must be a federal priority to calm the tumult of the period.[21] Such discourses almost always appealed to racialized fears associated with criminality, as much of this shift in political rhetoric came in direct response to the growing strength and militancy of the civil rights movement. Concluding with the ascent of Ronald Reagan to the White House in 1980, the chapter offers a foundation for interrogating the contested rhetorical norms of criminality at the close of the twentieth century.

Chapter 2 contains the book's first case study. While some rap groups from the late 1970s and early 1980s employed gangsta themes of criminality in their work, the Compton-based group NWA was, by acclamation, responsible for introducing the nation to gangsta rap.[22] This chapter reads their double-platinum debut album, *Straight Outta Compton* (1988), as a parodic intervention in the politics of space and violence at a historical moment when Compton and other sectors of South Central Los Angeles were objects of surveillance, confinement, and sensationalistic fear. I focus primarily on readings of two key recordings from *Straight Outta Compton*: its title track and the controversial single "Fuck Tha Police." Both, I argue, engage in a reformulation of the mark of criminality. The lyrical, visual, and sonic components of "Straight Outta Compton" troubled the contemporary spatial politics upon which racialized South Central residents waged battles with Los Angeles police across Compton's postindustrial urban terrain. In addition to challenging law enforcement's right to infiltrate urban communities of color, the single "Fuck Tha Police" contained explicit lyrics about doing physical violence to police officers. The widely popular song generated unprecedented backlash from law enforcement, suggesting police officers viewed the song's reconfiguration of the mark of criminality as a viable threat to their monopoly over space and violence in the inner city.

Chapter 3 begins in 1992, the year of the devastating Los Angeles riots and the election of Democratic president Bill Clinton on a "tough-on-crime" platform. Because this was a period of such palpable racial tension, one might have reasonably expected the hip-hop nation to adopt a more explicitly political tone as mainstream political and cultural figures increasingly deployed the mark of criminality in ways that stigmatized the bodies and communities of young African Americans. However, hip-hop's greatest commercial successes and notoriety came from the heralding of the so-called g-funk era. This period was best embodied in its two best-selling albums of the immediate post-riot era: Dr. Dre's *The Chronic* (1992) and his collaborator Snoop Doggy Dogg's *Doggystyle* (1993). Former NWA member Dr. Dre produced both albums; perfecting a distinctive style drawing heavily from samples of late 1960s and early 1970s funk tracks. The result was a profoundly smooth, often lackadaisical aesthetic that complemented lyrical themes of drinking malt liquor, smoking marijuana, engaging in promiscuous sex, and participating in house and street parties. Violence was strictly limited to the black-on-black variety. Many musical and cultural critics of this period regarded g-funk as a tragic abandonment of black music's emancipatory promise. That both *The Chronic* and *Doggystyle* were staggering commercial successes only aggravated this concern. The result was a confrontation between two visions of black publicity: one that exalted the iconic imagery of Dr. Martin Luther King Jr. and other civil rights giants in hopes of challenging the mark of criminality's ubiquity in public culture, and another intent on capital accumulation through the production and circulation of discourses of violence and pleasure. My position in this chapter is that by reading g-funk in the context of the mark of criminality's circulation in the post-Los-Angeles-riots era, critics can appreciate it as a salient cultural challenge to the norms of law-and-order politics. In the wake of the riots, South Central Los Angeles and other urban sectors enacted incredibly restrictive policies that coded black youth leisure and style practices, particularly those associated with hip-hop, as criminal. The mark of criminality, in other words, adapted to the changing dynamics of black communal being in ways that sustained the state's prerogative of violence, space, and surveillance. Read in this context, I argue that those who ferociously attacked g-funk neglected to appreciate its political character vis-à-vis the concurrent dynamics of law and order. Through a reading of the lyrical, sonic, and visual components of *The Chronic* and *Doggystyle*, as well as discourses from key mainstream and hip-hop media, I demonstrate the ways g-funk, even in its deeply troubling renditions, constituted a distinct deployment of the mark of criminality by circulating and celebrating the criminalized leisure practices of black youth.

Chapter 4 chronicles the work of one of hip-hop's most important and complex icons, the late Tupac Shakur. My discussion of Shakur emanates primarily from the central theme of his work: "Thug Life." Adopted early in his career, "Thug Life" expressed Shakur's espoused belief that the mark of criminality (although he never used the term) overdetermined young black Americans' (especially men's) place in civil society. The status of the criminal, for Shakur, was one of resistance by which he and his brethren might express black rage and realize success in spite of the structural determinants he believed inhibited it. The relevance of "Thug Life" for this project is that it represents one of the first explicit attempts by a widely successful rap artist to leverage the mark of criminality toward conspicuously political ends. However, Shakur's story is also a cautionary one, as it reveals the mark of criminality's vulnerability to the structures of musical commerce, in which Shakur became deeply entrenched following a near-fatal shooting and rape conviction. He continued to circulate the mark of criminality, but rather than expressing rage in the interest of critique and political mobilization, he did so to advance a coastal feud largely predicated on the commercial calculations of those who stood to profit handsomely from such sensationalistic vitriol. Ultimately, I argue that the malleability of "Thug Life" provides concrete evidence of the mark of criminality's capacity to serve explicitly political purposes, as well as the perilous consequences of channeling the mark of criminality through the treacherous demands of music capital.

In closing this book, I reflect on the project's political traction. If readers accept my central claim that gangsta rap is best understood as comprising a range of deployments of the mark of criminality and, therefore, most faithfully read alongside the concurrent political and popular discourses of crime and punishment of the late 1980s and 1990s, they may rightfully ask if such insight is of any political consequence. I argue that gangsta rap's mobilizations of the mark of criminality are undeniably perilous, but nonetheless instructive for an anti-prison and antiracist politics. In a nation with as staggering an incarceration rate as ours, scholars and activists invested in pursuing alternatives to mass impris-onment require a posture of imagination toward criminal discourses, even those that make us most uneasy. By contextualizing the ascent of gangsta rap at the close of the twentieth century, we stand not only to gain a more nuanced rhe-torical history of a period largely defined by law and order, but also to recognize and generalize the vernacular strategies of communities whose intimate relation-ships to the criminal justice system make them indispensable participants in the movement to change it.

I

The Horrors and Heroics of Crime; or, Mapping the Mark of Criminality

A whip of fear broke through the heart chambers as soon as you saw a Negro's face in a paper, since the face was not there because the person had a healthy baby, or outran a street mob. Nor was it there because the person had been killed, or maimed or caught or burned or jailed or whipped or evicted or stomped or raped or cheated, since that could hardly qualify as news in a newspaper. It would have to be something out of the ordinary—something whitepeople would find interesting, truly different, worth a few minutes of teeth sucking if not gasps.

—Toni Morrison, *Beloved*

And you are not the guy and still you fit the description because there is only one guy who is always the guy fitting the description.

—Claudia Rankine, *Citizen: An American Lyric*

Nigger, I told you. I *told* you not to touch my hat.

—Derek McCulloch and Shepherd Hendrix, *Stagger Lee*

To understand how the mark of criminality developed coherent generic characteristics that enabled the public vilification and containment of America's black urban working class and poor at the close of the twentieth century, and functioned as a resource for cultural production for gangsta rap artists, we must go back ("waaaaay back!").[1] Such an investigation brings us to the dawn of Emancipation, the collapse of Reconstruction, and the accompanying horrors of Jim Crow, as well as the social tumult of the 1960s and 1970s. Situating the genre and its political context within a wider historical tapestry of cultural discourses on race, gender, violence, and crime is a precondition for appreciating the rhetorical gestures and political stakes associated with the meanings of crime and criminality in the United States. Doing so illuminates the nimble character of the mark of criminality. This chapter works toward a theorization of the mark of criminality as a distinct genre of blackness. To clarify how discourses of criminality acted upon and were enacted by black, mostly masculine bodies in the United States, I offer a genealogy of the mark of criminality. By tracing the definitional struggles that helped propel the development of law-and-order politics following the end of slavery, we will be better positioned to situate gangsta rap therein. Gangsta, I shall explain, functioned as a participant in a far grander narrative of criminality whose meanings, while often relatively stable, have always been subject to refashioning and, at times, rupture.[2] To begin, I further develop my understanding of the mark of criminality as a genre.

Genre, Affect, and Criminalized Bodies

In public culture, crime is widely associated with genres. Hollywood has generated billions of dollars in revenue by producing action films and dramas that chronicle the experiences of law enforcement officers pursuing villainous criminals. Police procedurals are among the most popular programs on television. Mystery novels and "true crime" books are lucrative industries in their own right. Gangsta rap itself is a subgenre of a broader musical genre, rap, and draws heavily on discourses of criminality. However, for the purposes of this project, I see genre as encompassing more than a particular type of cultural artifact. One of my central claims is that all of these examples from popular culture draw heavily on generic iterations of blackness that induce attention, affective investment, and action.

Human symbol use is premised on form. The structures of daily interactions, oratory, various kinds of narratives, and modes of popular culture imbue such practices with coherence and predictability. Kenneth Burke wrote that "form is the creation of an appetite in the mind of the auditor, and the adequate satisfying of that appetite."[3] As Burke's larger body of work argued, humans crave order and rely on language to create it. Form, in other words, satisfies an appetite for order.[4] When similar forms repetitiously emerge in response to recurrent situations, they become a genre. Crucially, genre is not something that a dutiful critic simply spies lingering under the surfaces of a set of texts. Rather, as Joshua Gunn writes, genres are "patterned forms that reside in the popular imaginary."[5] Genres cohere around audience desires and expectations, or appetites. Rhetors employ genres to suasive ends, even as genres themselves constrain and enable rhetorical action. We use genres and genres use us.[6]

Because genres reside in the public imaginary, they are fundamentally unstable. Gunn writes, "Owing to the dynamism of the formal repetitions that give rise to generic norms, there is simply no way to stabilize human affective response; by definition, genres cannot keep pace."[7] Affect describes the inherently unstable prelinguistic intensities residing in bodies and emerging in encounters between different bodies. Robert Seyfert writes, "Affect Studies captures the situational nature of affect in conceptualizing affects, as *emerging* at the moment when bodies meet, *affecting* the bodies involved in the encounter, and *marking the transformation/s of the bodies.*[8] Affect, in other words, is fundamentally social. Brian Massumi writes, "[Individuals and societies] might be seen as differential emergences from a shared realm of relationality that is one with becoming—and belonging."[9] While affect precedes its expression through rhetoric, its character nonetheless varies across different situations. Gilles Deleuze explains, "We should notice at this moment that, depending on culture, depending on the society, men [*sic*] are not all capable of the same affects."[10] For example, affect emerges when black bodies encounter white bodies, but those respective bodies are affected differently because of their relationships to distinct communities, histories, and social institutions. I agree with Seyfert that we should not limit our notion of bodies to sentient human bodies but should also account for physical space like the city of Compton, nonlinguistic aesthetic forms like music, and social structures like the prison-industrial complex. In other words, while the social expression of affect requires rhetoric, or what Deleuze calls "ideas," the materiality of bodies produces a multiplicity of affects.

While the expression of affect as joy, fear, or any other emotion necessitates its containment in something like a genre, affect is also capable of escape. Nonetheless, any sort of political or cultural practice requires the capture and deployment of affect.[11] Therefore, genres require persistent repetition and refashioning if they are to remain useful for mobilizing such intensities. While genres retain certain formal characteristics in common, they are also highly contingent. Furthermore, different rhetors will employ genres to different ends, just as different audiences will respond to genres in distinct ways. While genres can undeniably help keep prevailing meaning systems in check, they are also subject to disruption, or what Charles Bazerman calls "textual mischief."[12] The payoff of genre criticism, therefore, is not engaging in brittle taxonomies of public discourse. Rather, because genres, as Carolyn Miller writes, "help constitute the substance of cultural life," they offer rich insights into public practices and affective investments; they are suggestive of the ways form allows people to comprehend, accept, and transform their social lives.[13]

Genre is an invaluable heuristic for charting the contingent nature of criminalized black bodies in public culture. Gunn argues for a turn toward the body when studying genre, writing, "A genre is not merely the label for a text, but the signature of an affective apparatus that both presumes and produces bodies-in-feeling."[14] In other words, genre organizes and produces affect, and, consequently, moves bodies. This is not to suggest that bodies are blank slates upon which rhetors inscribe meaning. Bodies are unwieldy, capable of creating and transforming meaning in their own right.[15] While they are subject to discipline, bodies can also participate in the circulation and reinvention of genres. This is certainly true of the black body, whose very constitution in the United States is founded on racial subjugation. Indeed, the existence of the black body is predicated on slavery and its aftermath, for there would be no black body as such if not for the need to codify racial difference to help rationalize the slave economy and other forms of racialized violence.[16] In her highly influential work on black identity and subjection, Saidiya V. Hartman documents consistent patterns of black subjugation that stretch beyond slavery into more contemporary forms of subordination. Reflecting on post-Emancipation regimes of racial domination, Hartman writes, "Bound by the fetters of sentiment, held captive by the vestiges of the past, and cast into a legal condition of subjection—these features limn the circumstances of an anomalous, misbegotten, and burdened subject no longer enslaved, but not yet free."[17] The black body, in other words, remains constrained by the sentiments, or affective investments, that have mobilized white supremacy during and after chattel slavery. The key change, Hartman argues, is not the abjection of black life, but the forms such abjection takes.

As I detail in this book, the mark of criminality emerged as a generic enactment of white supremacy from the ashes of chattel slavery. While one system of discourses helped rationalize involuntary servitude on the plantation, the mark of criminality comprised a new set of meanings inscribed on the black body. While these iterations of white supremacy differed in form, they remained relatively consistent in function; they marked black bodies as subordinate to white ones. Again, my argument is not that the black body under slavery or after was or is passively subject to subordination, or that alternative performances of blackness are unequivocally heroic. While there can be no denying the profoundly imposing limitations of the slave economy, transgressive enactments of blackness nonetheless took place. Reflecting on performances of blackness under slavery, Hartman writes, "[Such performances] are enactments of social struggle and contending articulations of racial meaning."[18] Other scholars have also noted the liminal character of black performance, noting its entrenchment in regimes of racial domination while also affirming blackness's ability to circulate in new and often unpredictable ways.[19]

The mark of criminality emerged as a generic assemblage of discourses associated with blackness that mobilized "social struggle and contending articulations of racial meaning."[20] Those who wished to sustain white supremacy employed it to subordinate black populations through surveillance and incarceration. Many black communities refashioned the mark of criminality after Emancipation to weave dramatic tales of criminal virtuosos who mercilessly pursued their ends through violence and hypersexuality. Still others fashioned the mark of criminality in ways that motivated them to wage cultural warfare against it in favor of alternative meanings of blackness. While these dynamics changed in important ways during the twentieth century, they retained key formal characteristics that helped the mark of criminality remain a central generic force in public discourse regarding race in the United States. I dedicate this chapter's remaining pages to historicizing the mark of criminality and extrapolating its key characteristics. Specifically, the mark of criminality possesses three generic components: (1) privileging masculinity as an essential characteristic of blackness, (2) portraying black masculinity as inherently violent, and (3) portraying black masculinity as hypersexual. As we shall see throughout this book, while these components have remained remarkably consistent across time, they have also proved flexible and polysemic.

The Origins of the Mark of Criminality

The rhetorical dimensions of crime in public culture are salient and of considerable interest to scholars and activists interested in crime and criminality, urban issues, race and racism, the politics of gender and sexuality, neoliberalism, and related subjects. As the members of the Prison Communication, Activism, Research, and Education (PCARE) writing collective argued in a 2007 article, "We are so saturated with images of crime and criminality that incarceration has become a routine part of our daily consumerist practices and political assumptions, yet actual prisons and prisoners remain virtually invisible in television news and entertainment. Contemporary US popular culture has thus become a spectacular carousel of fantasies about crime and criminals, meaning that the prison-industrial complex has become the stuff of our escapist frivolities and our political consciousness."[21] Drawing broadly from Foucauldian approaches to disciplinarity and power, as well as cultural studies' understandings of racial signification, most writers in rhetorical and critical/cultural studies investigate the criminal justice system as a site of domination.[22] In addition to detailing the ways racialized and otherwise ostracized communities become labeled as threats to civil society who must be contained and surveilled, critics interested in the carceral state argue that discourses of crime and punishment condition the subjectivities of all citizens, even if they have never set foot inside a jail or prison. Inundated with arguments for harsher penal policies by politicians and culture warriors, and the reification of such logics in popular culture, average citizens, the argument goes, come to monitor their own behavior in ways that correspond to the demands of law and order. The policies and logics of mass incarceration become naturalized.[23]

While most inquiries into the rhetorical and cultural dynamics of the criminal justice system emphasize the critique of domination as their chief site of intervention, others engage the resistant practices associated with mass incarceration. For example, some scholars address how public discourses on the carceral state function as vibrant sites of contestation upon which subjects craft notions of citizenship and develop strategies of resistance.[24] Furthermore, critics invested in challenging mass incarceration often note the practices of resistance and survival employed by those languishing behind bars, whether in the form of pedagogical practices like competitive debate or writing classes, or more explicit forms of activism.[25] A growing number of scholars also draw on various theoretical traditions to engage in applied antiprison politics.[26] In short, there exists a vibrant and emergent tradition of critical practice geared toward theorizing the prison-industrial complex as a site of rhetorical and cultural struggle.

Indeed, those we identify as criminal become our public enemies, and the justificatory rhetorics accompanying their punishment tend to reinforce prevailing norms of nation, race, class, gender, sexuality, and religion. When we speak of crime in the dominative sense, then, we are describing who "we" are and are not. A public enemy is no mere episodic purveyor of dastardly deeds, but synecdoche for a range of social anxieties. Rhetorics of criminality, in short, function to prevent and address potential ruptures in the social fabric.[27] But what is lacking from previous literature, and what this book seeks to provide, is a consideration of how the rhetorical parameters of criminality as such provide resources for political and cultural practice. While crime and criminality certainly function as topoi for repressive regimes of governance and social exclusion, history records a far more dynamic interplay between the carceral state and the citizens and communities it deems "criminal."

The very meaning of the criminal subject is a long-standing object of vernacular revision among populations most violently impacted by shifts in the social relations and the accompanying changes in the norms of jurisprudence. When bodies come to occupy different social arrangements, new affects emerge and often find expression in discourses of criminality. For example, Eric Hobsbawm argued that narratives of *social banditry* were ubiquitous and astonishingly uniform across precapitalist societies. Social bandits were distinct from other criminals in that they rarely, if ever, targeted common folk. Rather, they robbed from the lords and became heroes to commoners.[28] Tales of social banditry persisted into the nineteenth and twentieth centuries in the United States, often as sensationalized narratives associated with real-life criminals such as Jesse James, Billy the Kid, "Pretty Boy" Floyd, and Bonnie and Clyde. These stories helped poor and working-class members of white civil society reckon with times of social tumult. Like other genres, social banditry was both nimble in its ability to respond to specific contexts and remarkably consistent in advancing arguments about freedom when the tide of history seemed to drown it.[29]

Such tales were highly gendered and racialized. One only finds a handful of female social bandits in the annals of American folklore. Rather, as we shall see in ample detail in the context of the 1980s and 1990s, both the heroics and horrors of criminality in America have long been coded as masculine.[30] Equally salient is the emergence of America's most prominent outlaw bandits in the post–Civil War South. While giving expression to the economic woes of the devastated region, figures like Jesse James and Billy the Kid also embodied affective investments in post-Emancipation white supremacy.[31] As Hobsbawm explains, "Insofar as [social] bandits have a 'programme,' it is the defence or restoration of the traditional order of things 'as it should be.'"[32] In the South, this meant deploying heroic rhetorics of white criminality while the region was dragged, kicking and screaming, into the industrial age and Emancipation.

As the nation's reliance on incarceration grew throughout the nineteenth century and the promises of Reconstruction subsided, the carceral state in both the North and the South increasingly focused on the surveillance and containment of black bodies. Former Confederate states turned to prisoner leasing programs to reinstate unwaged black labor in the South. Such programs allowed employers to lease prisoner labor for work on plantations and other spaces. Because local and state criminal statutes were deliberately discriminatory, leased prisoners were almost always black. The result was a dynamic of confinement and unwaged labor that was, by many measures, identical to slavery. Given the Thirteenth Amendment's qualification that involuntary servitude remained legal "as a punishment for crime whereof the party shall have been duly convicted," such programs functioned within post-Emancipation legal confines.[33] With the expansion of industrialization, the birth of Jim Crow, and the migration of many black people to northern urban areas, African Americans disproportionately found themselves relegated to impoverished urban sectors where employment was low and the prospects of incarceration ever increasing.[34] While these conditions certainly made crime for many poor and working-class blacks a matter of survival, the discourses that framed black bodies as somehow predisposed toward criminal activity were grossly out of step with post-Emancipation crime statistics.[35]

It is at this time that we witness the emergence of the mark of criminality as a distinctly racialized genre in discourses of law and order. While rhetorics of criminality were obviously sites of domination and resistance prior to the end of slavery, at this juncture in US race politics we see the tethering of blackness to criminality in such a way as to make the two nearly synonymous. W. E. B. Du Bois lamented in his influential study of Reconstruction, "Wherever a black head rises to historic view, it is promptly . . . put out of view by some quite unproven charge of bad moral character."[36] Khalil Gibran Muhammad concludes, "The idea of black criminality was crucial to the making of modern urban America," and that, as the nineteenth gave way to the twentieth century, black criminality "stood as an almost singular reflection of black culture and humanity."[37] Public discourses of criminality increasingly characterized black citizens, and men in particular, as unfit for participation in civil society. Political discourses, news media, and popular culture characterized the black male as shiftless and always already violent. Such discourses were also deeply gendered. Commenting on the cultural legacy of race lynchings, Kobena Mercer writes, "the primal fantasy of the big black penis projects the fear of a threat not only to white womanhood, but to civilization itself, as the anxiety of miscegenation, eugenic pollution and racial degeneration is acted out through white male rituals of racial aggression—the historical lynching of black men in the United States routinely involved the literal castration of the Other's strange fruit."[38] Black men in the late nineteenth and early twentieth centuries were highly vulnerable to often-false accusations of raping white women. Exemplified in white supremacist texts like D. W. Griffith's *The Birth of a Nation* and chronicled in novels like Harper Lee's *To Kill a Mockingbird* and Richard Wright's *Native Son*, white civil society often regarded the black masculine body as irrationally and violently sexual—the living embodiment of social anxieties about the "mixing" of races.[39] As we proceed into the later years of the twentieth century, it becomes clear that discourses of African American men as "booty call-seeking rapists" adopted new characteristics, but remained consistent with the generic characteristics that emerged following Emancipation.[40] The mark of criminality, in other words, has always been profoundly imbued with a gendered politics of racialized fear.

Amid the joy of Emancipation, blacks in the late nineteenth and early twentieth centuries quickly found themselves subject to the legal violence of a changing criminal justice system, as well as the extrajudicial excesses of the lynch mob. Their bodies bore the burden of changing affective intensities emerging from white bodies coming to terms with a new racial and economic order. This required that black people seek new ways to survive amid white supremacy under this peculiar new status called freedom. While there can be no diminishing the savagery of slavery, Emancipation made African Americans vulnerable in new ways. To do violence to a black body was no longer to damage a piece of property but a mere subordinate whose labor power, while still important to economic development, was replaceable. Whereas African Americans throughout the country were themselves increasingly likely to be arrested, imprisoned, and leased, law enforcement was rarely inclined to respond to crime between or against people of color. The forces of white supremacy, in other words, quickly replaced slavery with new strategies for figuring blackness as an abject category.[41]

In this context we witness the first evidence that the mark of criminality was a highly mobile and flexible genre. With the emergence of "badman" folklore (which fashioned black criminal figures into cultural icons) following the end of the Civil War, many black Americans made use of the mark of criminality even as it made use of them. The genre gave expression to new affects emerging amid changing times. During slavery, one of the most important folk heroes of the African Diaspora was the trickster. Anthropomorphic animal figures like the Signifyin(g) Monkey and Brer Rabbit employed various strategies of linguistic and intellectual high jinks to outwit more physically powerful members of the animal kingdom. Such tales were especially meaningful for American slaves, whose physical domination by slaveholders was essentially absolute. Stories of wise animals who pitted two powerful beasts against each other or duped a vicious hunter out of a meal served as models for moral behavior on the plantation. In addition to portraying the plantation as a skewed moral landscape requiring inventiveness on the part of the slave, folklorist John Roberts explains that the trickster tale "served as an expressive mechanism for transmitting a perception of cleverness, guile, and wit as the most advantageous behavior options for dealing with the power of the slavemasters in certain generic situations."[42] Whereas open rebellion against enslavement was rare, less conspicuous acts of theft and slacking on the job enabled slaves to transgress the norms of slavery and imagine themselves as wiser, more enlightened foils to the hated slave master.[43]

The heroic trickster quickly wore out his use to many African Americans after Emancipation, for neither avoiding work in the context of waged labor nor theft of white property in an increasingly ferocious context of law and order served the interests of African Americans. Folklorists note the subsequent emergence of the black badman as a distinct folk type and, I am arguing, an iteration of the mark of criminality. Whereas the trickster used intellect to emerge triumphant in the face of adversity, the badman used sexual prowess, gambling, and especially violence to have his way. In other words, badman stories adopted, refashioned, and deployed the chief elements of the mark of criminality. Tales of badmen, like those of social bandits, were typically based on actual crime stories but were rewritten to include grander acts of transgression and, in many cases, supernatural components. Whereas the social bandit spared members of his community, the badman's transgressions occurred almost exclusively among other African Americans. Thus the badman came to represent freed blacks' ambivalent relationship to law and community. The looming threat of the law and the lynch mob precluded most criminal activity against whites. However, law enforcement often neglected black communities themselves, making it possible to engage in criminal enterprises among other African Americans with relative impunity.[44] In what remains a mainstay of the American criminal justice system, black criminality was most feared when it appeared to threaten the property and bodies of white citizens.

The badman's entrenchment in the black community, however, posed important challenges. Criminal acts against other African Americans threatened communal welfare. Thus, through collective finessing, badman tales sought to reconcile the various tensions implicit in romanticizing criminal activity. A badman's victims were themselves rotten people deserving of violent retribution and, in many tales, the badman hero met a violent end by the gun or the gallows. Such stories would change in specifics to reflect the needs and norms of those who uttered them, but all came to reflect refashioned deployments of the mark of criminality. A populace that had no reasons to trust the legitimacy of law and order reinvented the mark of criminality in the service of cohesion and empowerment. The most iconic badman hero was Stagger Lee (or Stackolee), who infamously shot and killed Billy Lyons in a St. Louis, Missouri, bar. Lee's motives vary from Lyons stealing Stagger Lee's Stetson hat, cheating in a game of cards (or craps), or some combination thereof. In some versions, Stagger Lee possesses supernatural, even demonic powers, and is prolifically sexual (typically favoring women, but in Australian rocker Nick Cave's telling, would "crawl over fifty good pussies just to get to one fat boy's asshole").[45] The tale would typically end with some form of reckoning for Stagger Lee, ranging from execution to eternal damnation wherein he must wage battle with Billy Lyons in the pits of hell.[46]

The story of Stagger Lee, adapted from an actual 1895 murder, thrived in turn-of-the-century juke joints before enjoying more mainstream success. Black musicians including Lloyd Price and Wilson Pickett as well as white artists such as Woody Guthrie, the Grateful Dead, and Pat Boone recorded successful musical versions of this badman tale. The mobility of Stagger Lee across racial lines reflected the anxieties associated with white appropriation of black cultural expression that also weighed heavily on the cultural politics of gangsta rap.[47] The mark of criminality, in other words, was part of an ongoing and fraught cultural exchange that manifested in seemingly infinite forms. In spite of the tale's grim content, musical renditions of Stagger Lee were almost universally sung over cheerful melodies. When we ignore the lyrics in Lloyd Price's version, it is virtually indistinguishable from other doo-wop classics of the late 1950s and early 1960s. The Grateful Dead's 1978 rendition featured Jerry Garcia's relaxed vocals accompanied by the band's country-infused blues style that made them acid rock pioneers. One can picture a dance floor full of twisting bodies while listening to Wilson Pickett's high-energy chronicle of Billy Lyons's bloody demise. With few exceptions, the musical legacy of Stagger Lee anticipated the celebratory telling of hyperviolent narratives that characterizes gangsta rap.[48]

Badmen like Stagger Lee, Railroad Bill, Devil Winston, and John Hardy played the role of the "crazy motherfucker" well before the likes of NWA made such boasts in a Los Angeles recording studio. For an audience of African Americans, many of whom had just escaped the bonds of slavery, such figures provided equipment for living in the context of a changing criminal justice infrastructure that subordinated black bodies to the demands of capital and the fears of white civil society. Whereas a majority of white Americans' affective investments with the mark of criminality stemmed from anxieties associated with threats to white privilege and, they believed, the fate of civilization, tales of black badmen mobilized affect in ways that addressed the changing contours of racial subjugation. As Adam Gussow argues in his study of Mississippi Delta blues in the late nineteenth and early twentieth centuries, the ability to fantasize about and even enact crime in relatively autonomous black cultural enclaves functioned as a joyful, if fraught, source of resistance against new regimes of white supremacy. Tales of violence against other black bodies amounted to an enactment of freedom unavailable when in white society. One could express masculine prowess, exact revenge, and channel one's rage against white supremacy through a black substitute. To do bad, in other words, felt good.[49]

In the context of such black icons of the early twentieth century as Marcus Garvey and W. E. B. Du Bois, it is tempting to dismiss badman folklore just as firmly as many African American activists did gangsta rap while invoking the legacy of Martin Luther King Jr. in the 1980s and 1990s.[50] However, such uneasy texts enabled disempowered populations to reimagine their affective relationships to shifting social relations. To contextualize the badman within the violence of law and order (both judicial and extrajudicial) reveals a world of limited possibilities for most black Americans. To confront directly the cruelty of prison leasing programs, lynch mobs, or unjust police forces was to risk one's life. The development of vernacular practices like the badman enabled black Americans to co-create new meanings for the mark of criminality and deploy them through the spoken and written word, as well as through music.

Recognizing the pleasures associated with such enactments of the mark of criminality cannot, however, prompt us to ignore their collateral consequences. In addition to directing violence against other black bodies, the heroes of badman folklore behaved in ways highly degrading to women. In one telling of the Stagger Lee myth, the badman boasts, "now me and this broad we started to tussle / and I drove twelve inches a dick through her ass before she could move a muscle."[51] In an invective against a prostitute named Nell, Pimping Sam declares, "And, anyhow, whore, shut up talkin' to me / 'fore I tell the people your past pedigree. / Like rotten wood, your ass ain't no good, all beat and clappy, / get your kicks from suckin' dicks and fuckin' your bald-headed pappy."[52] Another legendary badman named Dolomite, whose name lives on in blaxploitation cinema and gangsta rap, spent his years on earth ravaging both women and animals. His sexual prowess was such that at his funeral, one narrator recalls, "Dolomite was dead, but his dick was still hard."[53] In ways that anticipate gangsta's own degradation of the female body, badman folklore rarely saw use for women outside heroes' sexual exploits. Thus badman tales function as an early exemplar of the mark of criminality's troubled gendered politics. Whereas many iterations of the mark of criminality helped rationalize mass incarceration through the stigmatization of black masculinity, others exalted the black masculine body in misogynistic and heteronormative ways.

However, we must resist too facile an assessment of gender politics intrinsic to badman folklore and similar versions of the mark of criminality. As bell hooks notes, "Negative stereotypes about the nature of black masculinity continue to overdetermine the identities black males are allowed to fashion for themselves."[54] While hooks writes in the twenty-first century, such stereotypes also overdetermined the performance of black masculinity in the decades following the Civil War. In her studies of blues culture, Angela Davis notes that sexuality factored significantly into the fashioning of post-Emancipation selves for black men and women. She writes, "Sovereignty in sexual matters marked an important divide between life during slavery and life after emancipation."[55] Much like violence in the juke joint and other cultural enclaves, sexually charged vernacular practices allowed African Americans to constitute themselves anew. For many black men, however, sexuality bore white supremacy's albatross of the archetypical sexual sadist. Thus while badmen like Stagger Lee and Dolomite wielded their sexual prowess in ways unavailable during chattel slavery, they did so within the generic contours of the mark of criminality.[56]

The mark of criminality thus emerged in the wake of Emancipation primarily as a system of meanings associated with black bodies and, especially, black masculinity. The end of slavery required black and white bodies to encounter each other in new ways and, consequentially, produced new affective intensities. Its deployment throughout white civil society helped justify the shifting parameters of law and order and naturalized the criminalization of African Americans. However, vernacular practices like badman folktales, the blues, and, later, blaxploitation cinema and gangsta rap, deployed the mark of criminality in alternative and ambivalent ways. The genre both protected the interests of white supremacy following the end of slavery and mobilized new subjectivities for certain sectors of the post-Emancipation black community as its members began to experience blackness in new ways. It was not until the post–World War II era, and specifically the tumultuous years of the civil rights movement and the Vietnam War, however, that the mark of criminality would become a chief building block of national politics.

The Mark of Criminality and National Crime Policy in the Postwar Era

By the end of 2011, nearly 1.6 million adults resided in US federal and state penitentiaries. In 1987, the year before NWA released *Straight Outta Compton* and George H. W. Bush succeeded in his bid to replace Ronald Reagan in the White House, that figure was a comparatively modest 585,084. As staggering as this nearly threefold increase in incarcerated bodies is, the trend is all the more alarming when we look to the early 1970s, when the prison population stood at about 200,000. In other words, in both spans of time represented here, the United States nearly tripled its adult prison population. At every turn, a disproportionate number of these incarcerated individuals have been people of color. Black men, in particular, were and remain the single most likely demographic to spend time behind bars in America. How did this happen?[57] While the mark of criminality has consistently been a powerful force in the surveillance and containment of black bodies, and crime in general has functioned as a political wedge issue for national politicians throughout the centuries, I argue subsequently that the period beginning in the mid-1960s was a particularly consequential period in law-and-order politics and the evolution of the mark of criminality.[58]

Beginning, arguably, with Lyndon B. Johnson's landslide electoral victory over Republican Barry Goldwater in the 1964 presidential race, elected officials in federal government increasingly addressed urban crime as a symptom of major social disorder. While the nation's violent crime rates during this period were actually relatively low, members of both major parties appealed to law and order as a mainstay of stability.[59] Speaking before Congress specifically on the issue of crime, Johnson conjured dystopian visions, describing a crime epidemic that "can turn us into a nation of captives imprisoned nightly behind chained doors, double locks, barred windows" and "make us afraid to walk city streets by night or public parks by day."[60] He proceeded to advocate funneling millions of dollars into local law enforcement efforts through the auspices of the Law Enforcement Assistance Act of 1965. Prior to this piece of legislation, although national leaders often leveraged law and order to achieve political ends, law enforcement was generally understood to be a local concern. Now the federal government was taking an active role in expanding the reach of the carceral state.[61]

While Johnson was militant on matters of law and order, as well as the spread of communism, such issues were especially central to conservative politics from the 1960s onward. In his nomination acceptance speech at the 1964 Republican National Convention, Barry Goldwater—a senator from Arizona and a conservative icon—advanced a vision of government that largely defines the Grand Old Party to this day. Goldwater said, "We Republicans seek a government that attends to its inherent responsibilities of maintaining a stable monetary and fiscal climate, encouraging a free and a competitive economy, and enforcing law and order."[62] Governing on domestic matters, in other words, should be concerned solely with allowing the free market to thrive and leveraging the tools of the carceral state to maintain order. Goldwater's emphasis on market ideology and harsh crime policies portends the policies of economic liberalization and austerity that shaped the final decades of the twentieth century. His speech also anticipated a turn away from rehabilitative theories of punishment toward punitive models. In short, as the gap between rich and poor widened in the subsequent decades, those without jobs or means to live a decent life often turned to crime and, therefore, found themselves behind bars.[63] Goldwater added, "Security from domestic violence, no less than from foreign aggression, is the most elementary and fundamental purpose of any government."[64] Crucially, Goldwater tethers the role of the state in exercising military might abroad to its responsibility to leverage police power against "bullies and marauders."[65]

Although Goldwater lost to Johnson in what was, at that point, the most devastating presidential electoral defeat in American history, his appeal to law and
order resonated with voters and helps explain Johnson's willingness to incorpo-
rate stricter crime policies into his Great Society agenda.[66] As I previously noted,
this moral panic concerning disorder in the streets had little to do with actual
crime rates. Rather, many of the anxieties fueling this drive to incarcerate concerned a civil rights movement growing in influence and militancy and, by the
end of Johnson's first and only full term in the White House, a vibrant and angry
movement against the US presence in Vietnam. These were affectively charged
times that mobilized bodies in a variety of ways. Just as they had done during the
rise of market capitalism, following the abolition of slavery, and through so many
other crises of the Republic, political and cultural elites sought to leverage rhetorics of criminality to silence dissent.[67] Whereas many activists filled the streets
to direct outrage toward imperialism abroad and various modes of oppression at
home, more conservative bastions of white civil society's affective energies found
expression in elected officials' new deployments of the mark of criminality.[68]

While figures like Johnson and Goldwater deployed the mark of criminality
in ways that corresponded with distinct historical exigencies, the genre retained
its key racialized characteristics vis-à-vis gender and violence. The centrality of
law and order in institutional responses to activism was especially acute amid
the growing Black Power movement. While figures like Stokely Carmichael and
Malcolm X served as radical flanks to Martin Luther King Jr.'s nonviolent activism during the early 1960s, such militant antiracist politics attracted more ad-
herents near the end of the 1960s and dawn of the 1970s. Although King's and
others' work in the South put significant dents in Jim Crow's armor, African
Americans throughout the United States understood that white supremacy ran
deeper than the ballot box, classroom, or lunch counter. Rather, it was entrenched
in the very structures of the economy, urban planning, and law enforcement.[69]
Before his 1968 assassination, even King had begun linking American racism to
capitalism and empire.[70] Following his death, numerous urban sectors exploded
in riots fueled by anger over the assassination and entrenched racial disparities in
America's cities. During the postwar era, as growing numbers of African Americans left the rural South for metropolitan areas like New York, Los Angeles, Chicago, and Detroit, many black activists grew more radical in their critiques of
white supremacy and more militant in their approaches to defying it.[71]

By far the most iconic representation of the growing Black Power movement
in the late 1960s was the Black Panther Party for Self Defense. Formed in 1966
in Oakland, California, the Panthers espoused a desire to protect black city residents in ways the state, due to what they saw as entrenched white supremacy,
could not. While the party's initiatives included independent community services like free breakfast programs, party members also took up arms. Espousing a

deep distrust of law enforcement, claiming police officers were more inclined to terrorize African American communities than protect them, party members organized armed military patrols of predominantly black neighborhoods. Party co-founder and Minister of Defense Huey Newton explained, "By patrolling the police with arms, we would see a change in their behavior."[72] The Panthers were also central to catalyzing an acute wave of prisoner activism, as they and their supporters deemed incarcerated African Americans like George Jackson, Assata Shakur, and Angela Davis "political prisoners" serving unjust sentences due to their involvement with the Black Power movement.[73] The strategies of the Panthers and other Black Power activists were inextricably bound to their opposition to the carceral state. Furthermore, highly circulated images of primarily black masculine bodies taking up arms and confronting law enforcement constituted a distinctly activist version of the mark of criminality, for they deployed discourses of black masculinity that remained deeply tethered to violence and, as evident in such organizations' investment in normative gender roles, sexual virility.[74] Furthermore, by refiguring incarcerated individuals such as George Jackson as freedom fighters, the Panthers advanced alternative meanings of the mark of criminality. The Panthers and other members of the Black Power movement theorized the mark of criminality as a tool of racist domination and an epistemological standpoint for emancipatory politics.[75]

Along with the rise of the Black Panthers and urban uprisings during the late 1960s and early 1970s came a new form of black cinematic expression that also traded in new deployments of the mark of criminality. Blaxploitation films gave expression to the changing racial dynamics of the period by offering alternative portrayals of black life at a time when the movie industry was content to portray blackness as apolitical, asexual, and generally palatable to white audiences. These blaxploitation films varied significantly in their political content. While Melvin Van Peebles's germinal *Sweet Sweetback's Baadasssss Song* (1971) concluded with the message "A BAADASSSSS NIGGER IS COMING TO COLLECT SOME DUES," Gordon Parks's *Shaft* (1971) subordinated explicit political critique to the norms of the Hollywood action film. Nonetheless, the several dozen blaxploitation films released during the genre's greatest period of activity (identified by Ed Guerrero as spanning from 1969 to 1974) engaged in distinct deployments of the mark of criminality by featuring highly sexualized, usually male, protagonists on various sides of the law who engaged in violence and other illegal acts to secure victory over an enemy. Ed Guerrero writes that the standard blaxploitation formula told "the story of a 'bad nigger' who challenges the oppressive white system and wins."[76] Like the badman folklore that preceded it, and the gangsta rap it helped inspire, blaxploitation was an ambivalent account of the mark of criminality that inspired intense deliberation among black political and cultural leaders. While more conservative voices complained that films like *Sweetback*, *Shaft*, and *Superfly* only reinforced negative stereotypes associated with the black community, Huey Newton claimed that such films constituted a militant and virile black masculine subject that resonated deeply with the Black Power zeitgeist.[77]

Black militants' brandishing of weapons and open advocacy of violence, as well as blaxploitation's unapologetic cinematic enactments of black violence and sexuality transgressed institutional interpretations of the mark of criminality that, in the wake of urban riots and growing militancy, attracted strong affective investments from most sectors of white civil society. For its part, blaxploitation cinema faded from prominence before the second half of the 1970s. Guerrero attributes its decline to backlash from conservative black audiences and a realignment of Hollywood marketing toward "constructing black stories to accommodate white sensibilities and values."[78] While Newton and his allies hoped their deployments of the mark of criminality through deliberately confrontational threats of racialized violence would galvanize the masses and prompt law enforcement to reevaluate their treatment of African Americans, they paid dearly for their gamble. In a wave of covert operations that make more recent scandals surrounding the National Security Agency appear modest in comparison, the Federal Bureau of Investigation used a number of strategies to delegitimize and fracture the Black Power movement. These included the distribution of counterfeit Black Panther Party propaganda depicting members savagely murdering anthropomorphic pigs in police uniforms (offering yet another version of an already refashioned deployment of the mark of criminality), and infiltration by moles. Some party members paid with their lives, including Chicago-based Panther leader Fred Hampton, who, by most credible accounts, was shot to death by Windy City police officers while he slept. In short, the Panthers' aggressive tactics posed too great a challenge to the state's monopoly on violence at precisely the time when national elected officials turned to law and order to quell the social tumult of the late 1960s and 1970s. Such confrontations, I am arguing, were largely predicated on competing iterations of the mark of criminality. While the generic themes of race, violence, and masculinity remained central to the rhetorical strategies of all participants, they situated the black masculine body in ways that mobilized different audiences and affective investments. Figures like LBJ and Goldwater enlisted the mark of criminality to organize white civil society's anxieties over black militancy and public disorder. Those invested in Black Power and Black Nationalism, as well as those who produced and enjoyed blaxploitation films, drew upon and refashioned the same rhetorical resources to mobilize escalating black anger toward white supremacy.[79]

When I discuss the death of Fred Hampton and other federal strategies of

control directed toward Black Power activists, undergraduate students in my social movements classes often wonder why such egregious cases of state overreach
did not prompt stronger resistance. After all, Hannah Arendt argued that violent displays of state power typically betray an utter lack thereof.[80] To be sure,
men like Hampton became martyrs to many radicals in the 1960s and 1970s but,
by and large, the FBI and its partners in local law enforcement proceeded with
impunity. To understand what kind of political climate tolerated such abuses of
power, one must appreciate the concurrent political ascent of Richard Nixon.
Narrowly elected to the White House in 1968 amid the implosion of a Democratic Party divided over the Vietnam War, Nixon premised his political identity on the restoration of law and order and deployed the mark of criminality
to that end.[81] Channeling Goldwater's 1964 address to the Republican National
Convention, Nixon said the following in 1968 as he accepted his party's nomination: "Let those who have the responsibility to enforce our laws, and our judges
who have the responsibility to interpret them, be dedicated to the great principles of civil rights. But let them also recognize that the first civil right of every
American is to be free from domestic violence. And that right must be guaranteed in this country."[82]

Whereas the racialized character of Goldwater's 1964 comments lingered
enthymematically in his pledge to protect citizens from "the license of the mob
and the jungle," Nixon in 1968 openly appropriated the vocabulary of civil rights
that had defined so much of the contemporary political climate.[83] Yes, reasonable people can agree that civil rights matter, but demands for racial justice pale
in comparison to defending ordinary (that is, white) people against the forces of
instability sweeping the nation at that time. Nixon expropriated the language of
civil rights from black communities and affixed a version of the mark of criminality upon those communities that refigured the role of government. Rather
than protecting the interests of marginalized populations, the state would now
defend what Nixon later called his "silent majority" against the cacophony of racialized communities that threatened the status quo.[84]

In addition to elevating the war against disorder above demands for racial justice, Nixon shrewdly infused the mark of criminality with appropriations of the
era's war metaphors deployed typically in the interest of progressive causes. During his 1970 State of the Union address, Nixon declared: "We have heard a great
deal of overblown rhetoric during the sixties in which the word 'war' has perhaps
too often been used—the war on poverty, the war on misery, the war on disease,
the war on hunger. But if there is one area where the word 'war' is appropriate it
is in the fight against crime. We must declare and win the war against the criminal elements, which increasingly threaten our cities, our homes, and our lives."[85]
The "overblown" war rhetoric Nixon targeted typically emphasized the need to
address racial and class inequities through targeted social welfare programs, yet

the president wanted his congressional and national audience to understand with perfect clarity that one domestic war mattered, and that was the war on crime. Such a war, of course, targeted the very communities that disproportionately relied on social welfare programs. Nixon, in other words, drew upon the mark of criminality to direct governmental war rhetoric away from the systemic forces that marginalized black communities and, instead, waged war on poor and working-class black people themselves.[86] While American soldiers waged battles in the jungles of Vietnam against communism, law enforcement officers would protect the home front from those racialized bodies residing in urban "jungles" where they would murder, rape, steal, and trade in deadly narcotics.[87]

A consummate opportunist on matters of race and racism, Nixon understood that the mark of criminality could mobilize white anxieties about social disorder in the service of expanding the carceral state and blaming social inequities on those who experienced them most intensely. For it was in predominantly black neighborhoods that they witnessed horrific urban riots, and it was men and women of color who espoused the most militant rhetorics amid the most tumultuous period in American history since the Great Depression.[88] Criminologist Markus Dubber writes, "The crime war is fought on behalf of the community of actual and potential victims against a community of actual and potential offenders, where the boundaries between the two communities track familiar, and politically potent, American socioeconomic friend-foe distinctions of race and class."[89] The Nixon administration experienced numerous political defeats and even oversaw some important progressive reforms, but Nixon's appeals to fear through racialized rhetorics of crime were among his most successful strategies. His ability to speak on behalf of the "silent majority" against the unruly mobs helped cement his historic landslide victory in the 1972 election and entrench the mark of criminality as a key generic resource in the arsenal of political and cultural warfare.[90]

Waging War on Crime in an Age of Neoliberalism

The rise of the war on crime and the accompanying circulation of the mark of criminality across American political discourse came in the wake of great social tumult. Many antiracist activists interpreted the period's riots and social movements as expressions of communal anger against entrenched white supremacy, but most political and cultural elites regarded them as unwelcome threats to social order.[91] Accordingly, figures like Nixon deployed the mark of criminality to mobilize affect in ways that emphasized the fearsome threats posed by primarily black masculine bodies. Whereas earlier deployments of the mark of criminality emerged from desires to protect white supremacy following the end of slavery, its uses during the 1960s and 1970s served to subordinate growing mobilizations of resistance by turning white civil society against them. Racialized criminal threats, not poverty, white supremacy, and war, were to be understood as the true threats to stability in the United States.

The proliferation of crime as a central issue in national politics also coincided with major shifts in world economic policy. The postwar era was largely characterized by Keynesian policies exemplified by the New Deal and Great Society programs of the Roosevelt and Johnson administrations, respectively.[92] Even the Republican Nixon advocated economic and health care policies, including wage and price controls, which resonated deeply with the fiscal common sense of the era.[93] However, when a crisis of stagflation (that is, high inflation amid recession) led to soaring prices in the United States and across the globe during most of the 1970s, economic elites doubted the capacity of familiar Keynesian models of state intervention to solve the problem. Rather, thinkers like Friedrich Hayek and Milton Friedman, who were longtime advocates of relatively unfettered free market capitalism, gradually emerged as prophets of a new economic age. With the 1979 election of a conservative government led by Margaret Thatcher in Great Britain, and the presidential victory of Republican Ronald Reagan the following year, free market orthodoxy became the new modus operandi of global capital.[94]

Neoliberalism describes the ideologies that rationalize policies of reduced state regulations on commerce, trade liberalization, austerity measures, and attacks on organized labor. David Harvey writes that political and economic leaders justify such policies, which are often deeply corrosive to the well-being of poor and working-class citizens, by claiming "that human well-being can best be advanced by liberating individual entrepreneurial freedoms and skills" through market forces.[95] The individual citizen, or neoliberal subject, thus becomes a self-contained entrepreneurial enterprise, presumably free to thrive or fail within the infinitely enabling marketplace. Look no further than book titles like Hayek's *The Road to Serfdom* and Friedman's *Capitalism and Freedom* to understand neoliberalism's investment in the free market as the quintessential site of personal freedom. Government intervention, on the other hand, was a "road to serfdom" that stifled potential.[96] Reagan invoked precisely this logic in a 1986 White House press conference, where he declared, "I've always felt the nine most terrifying words in the English language are: 'I'm from the government, and I'm here to help.'"[97]

However, neoliberalism does not resist all modes of governmental intervention. Its proponents staunchly advocate monetarist policies by the Federal Reserve that adjust interest rates in response to various market fluctuations (mainly inflation). Furthermore, Harvey notes, neoliberalism's argumentative foundations are very nimble and have "primarily worked as a system of justification and legitimation for whatever needed to be done to achieve" its ultimate ends of maximizing private accumulation.[98] It is in this utilitarian context that the concurrent expansion of America's law-and-order apparatuses, as well as its military, during the rise of neoliberalism makes sense. To be sure, increasing federal spending on law enforcement and building more prisons constitutes an expansion of governmental influence, rather than a reduction. However, as I will show, such measures corresponded to the shifting realities of neoliberal life in the late twentieth century. The mark of criminality also shifted at this time in order to better rationalize the ethics of neoliberalism.

While neoliberalism created staggering gains for the private sector and political successes for its advocates in Washington, DC, London, and elsewhere, it was a source of intense misery for many working-class and poor people in the United States and around the world. Global poverty rates skyrocketed during the 1980s and 1990s, as well-paying, typically unionized industrial jobs left the United States and many European countries for more impoverished nations with less stringent or nonexistent wage controls, and equally weak workplace safety and environmental regulations. Organizations like the International Monetary Fund and World Bank helped propel such strategies by tethering global finance to austerity and privatization—in other words, implementing neoliberal economics became a precondition for receiving a loan. For the developing world, neoliberalism entailed environmental upheaval and often-dangerous low-wage labor. In the United States and other wealthy nations, it meant rapid deindustrialization, the rise of a nonunion and low-wage service sector economy, and the rapid dismantling of New Deal and Great Society social safety nets.[99]

Reagan and his allies consistently targeted public assistance programs, public schools, and other arteries of the welfare state for debilitating cuts. Such policies were especially damaging to urban areas where poor and working-class African Americans disproportionately bore the impact of capital divestment and austerity.[100] In South Central Los Angeles during the 1980s—the metropolitan area that contextualizes so much of the proceeding story of race, crime, and culture—131 industrial plants closed their doors.[101] Service sector employment replaced these unionized jobs but rarely remained in predominantly black areas like Watts or Compton. Rather, it moved to mostly white suburban sectors. Nationally, at least one-third of African Americans lived below the poverty line, and black unemployment was more than double that of whites by the end of the 1980s.[102]

This precarious relationship to the market led many young inner-city African Americans to participate in activities marked as criminal.[103] One particularly destructive opportunity for profit and employment was the introduction of crack cocaine to inner-city streets. This cheaper and highly addictive freebased form of cocaine spread particularly quickly among poor African Americans.[104] Mike Davis wrote at the time, "the deafening public silence about youth unemployment and the juvenation of poverty has left many thousands of young street people with little alternative but to enlist in the crypto-Keynesian youth employment program operated by the cocaine cartels."[105] As Davis's words suggest, these criminal practices mimicked the legal business enterprises of capitalism. Labor was still exploited and profits still emerged. The economy of drugs and other illicit commodities of the inner city became a shadow economy for those left with precious few alternatives.[106] This important fact of inner-city African American life would not only lead to the enhanced criminalization of such practices but also to their often celebratory deployment by gangsta rap artists. While we cannot dismiss the deadly consequences of the drug trade and the ruthlessness of gang life, it is difficult not to observe a strong historical resonance with emerging working classes of the eighteenth and nineteenth centuries, for whom crime was a way of reckoning with new regimes of exchange, labor, and crime.[107] However, while the workers of early capitalism were forced to engage in waged labor, the black youth of South Central and other urban sectors joined the ranks of what Davis calls a "surplus humanity."[108] There were no jobs for these young people. The choice for so many young African Americans, it seemed, was between crime and suffocating under a new economic regime.

Put in plain terms, with their schools crumbling and job prospects vanishing, these young people had to go somewhere. For Reagan, a reinvigorated war on crime fueled by new deployments of the mark of criminality not only offered an avenue for warehousing the growing number of poor and racialized bodies languishing under a new neoliberal order but also helped him justify the very policies that devastated America's most vulnerable communities. In his 1985 State of the Union address, Reagan struck a tone unmistakably inspired by the Arizona senator for whom he aggressively campaigned in 1968: "Of all the changes in the past 20 years, none has more threatened our sense of national well being than the explosion of violent crime. One does not have to be attacked to be a victim. The woman who must run to her car after shopping at night is a victim. The couple draping their door with locks and chains are victims; as is the tired, decent cleaning woman who can't ride a subway home without being afraid."[109] Invoking images of crime victimization, Reagan declared his own war on crime. He also blamed the social programs he would slash from his presidential budgets for creating a "new privileged class" of lazy welfare cheats who would prefer to stay home, use drugs, and parasitically live on taxpayer dollars.[110] By associating crime and victimization with the degraded lives of inner-city minorities, rather than their political militancy, Reagan refashioned the mark of criminality to justify both his tough-on-crime policies and his neoliberal market agenda.[111]

At this time, Reagan also declared war on illegal narcotics. When crack cocaine began circulating in minority urban areas, his administration aggressively publicized (and by many measures embellished) the social costs of the drug on civil society. During Reagan's second term, Congress passed the Anti-Drug Abuse Act of 1986, which classified drugs as a matter of national security and instituted federal mandatory minimum sentences. In other words, the act legally codified the militarized surveillance of poor communities of color and the mass incarceration of black and brown bodies into federal law.[112] The political and media discourses accompanying such policies included specters of inner-city "crack babies" languishing in neonatal units, First Lady Nancy Reagan's televised ride-alongs during drug busts in South Central, and aggressive antidrug marketing campaigns directed at suburban white youth. While Reagan and his allies coded their agendas in race-neutral terms, such a media spectacle helped reconstitute young African Americans and their communities—once epicenters of black cultural production and political activism—into sources of crime and depravity.[113] Doing so was central to Reagan's broader agenda of securing his own political fortunes and entrenching the logics of neoliberalism. Doris Provine writes, "A punitive drug war would play well among middle-class suburban voters concerned that their children might be attracted to drugs. The human costs of enforcement would be borne by people with whom they did not identify or sympathize."[114] From 1985, the year preceding the Anti-Drug Abuse Act, to 2000, the number of adult Americans incarcerated for drug offenses increased by 546 percent.[115] Illegal drugs, and especially crack cocaine, became scapegoats for a range of social ills. Thus while closer analysis of the era reveals that the policies of neoliberalism were themselves largely responsible for urban decay during the 1980s, Reagan and his allies circulated the mark of criminality in a way that blamed inner-city minorities for such problems. In other words, the war on drugs helped produce a new iteration of the mark of criminality that instilled in mostly white citizens fears of racialized narco-bogeymen and welfare cheats, and indifference toward the skyrocketing number of black bodies filling America's jails and prisons. Furthermore, by adopting optimistic narratives of American ingenuity and progress, Reagan invited his mostly white supporters to invest in an affectively charged vision of America as a "shining city on a hill."[116] The criminalized communities that increasingly filled the nation's penitentiaries were parasitic remainders with no place in this utopic, if also fictive, vision of the Republic.

By the end of his second term in the White House, Ronald Reagan not only helped make neoliberalism the centerpiece of an era's economic common sense but also helped solidify a national war on crime that began as a response to the radicalism of the 1960s. With the movements of that era now all but decimated, the twin forces of neoliberalism and mass incarceration faced relatively little substantive resistance from the grass roots. However, much like the newly freed slaves of the late nineteenth and early twentieth centuries, many African Americans, who remained disproportionately targeted by the drive to incarcerate in the 1980s and 1990s, found in their vernacular practices ways to engage and re-deploy the mark of criminality. The result, we shall see, was rarely tidy and inspires more dissonance than inspiration. Nonetheless, as we turn to the close of the 1980s and a new chapter of the war on crime, we see the mark of criminality functioning as a profoundly malleable genre at the nexus of mass incarceration and black cultural production.

2

Parody, Space, and Violence in NWA's
Straight Outta Compton

L.A. is probably the most mediated town in America, nearly unviewable
save through the fictive scrim of its mythologizers.

—Michael Sorkin, "Explaining Los Angeles," in *California
Counterpoint: New West Coast Architecture*

"You must not know where Bop comes from," said Simple, astonished at
my ignorance.
"I do not know," I said. "Where?"
"From the police," said Simple.
"What do you mean, from the police?"
"From the police beating Negroes' heads," said Simple. "Every time a cop
hits a Negro with his billy club, that old club says, 'BOP! BOP! . . .
BE-BOP! . . .
MOP! . . . BOP!'"

—Langston Hughes, *The Best of Simple*

1989!

—Public Enemy, "Fight the Power"

If the 1980 presidential election was, in part, a referendum on the viability of
Keynesian economics, the campaign of 1984 was undoubtedly an appraisal of so-
called Reaganomics. During his first four years in office, Reagan championed and
implemented a slew of neoliberal economic policies. For example, during his first
year in office, Reagan summarily fired over 11,000 members of the Professional
Air Traffic Controllers Organization for unlawfully striking. His unprecedented
move is still regarded as a climactic moment in the decline of organized labor
since the late twentieth century.[1] Such actions, coupled with aggressive policies
of deregulation and austerity, help explain why Reagan, to this day, remains the
quintessential American icon of neoliberalism.[2]

Democratic candidate Walter Mondale's campaign aimed to recapture the
spirit of the New Deal and Great Society by emphasizing the consequences of
Reagan's tenure for poor and working-class people. Arguably, no figure better

expressed Mondale's theme than New York governor Mario Cuomo during his keynote address at the 1984 Democratic National Convention. In what is widely regarded as one of the finest orations in American history, Cuomo chastised Reagan for his failure to recognize the struggles of ordinary Americans "from the portico of the White House and the veranda of his ranch." He spoke ominously of a national economic landscape where citizens struggled to pay mortgages, could not afford a college education, and "middle-class parents watch the dreams they hold for their children evaporate." Mondale aimed to defeat Reagan on the basis of a widening gap between the rich and the poor. The story of America circa 1984, as Cuomo's speech argued, was a tale of two cities.[3]

In a staggering repeat of what Walter Fisher described as the triumph of a materialistic rendering of the American dream over a moralistic one in Richard Nixon's 1972 defeat of George McGovern, Reagan surpassed his Republican predecessor in securing what still stands as the largest number of electoral votes in American history.[4] Whereas Mondale, like McGovern, asked Americans to face the brutality of the world around them, Reagan made no such demands on voters. Rather, as his campaign slogan proclaimed, it was "morning in America." Noting rising employment rates (in spite of diminishing real wages and union protection) and home purchases (part of a growing system of credit that caused so many of today's economic ills), Reagan told Americans they should be proud of their nation and reject McGovern's and Cuomo's tales of gloom. Americans listened.[5]

The 1988 presidential election served, yet again, as a battle between Reagan's contribution to the creation of neoliberalism and the liberalism of FDR and LBJ. Embodying this dichotomy were the presidential candidates, Republican vice president George H. W. Bush and Democratic governor of Massachusetts Michael Dukakis. After securing the Democratic Party nomination, Dukakis was performing well in national polls, often leading Bush by double digits. However, the governor's campaign sustained an irreparable blow when a conservative political action committee aired its "Weekend Passes" ad. The television spot told the story of Willie Horton, an African American prisoner released in 1986 on a weekend furlough in Massachusetts while Dukakis was governor.[6] The ad used a blue background, white text, and still photographs of Bush, Dukakis, and Horton. After distinguishing Bush's pro-death-penalty stance from Dukakis's opposition to the sanction, the segment reveals an ominous picture of Horton and describes his original incarceration for murder. The male narrator—speaking in a deep, stern voice—explains how Horton used his furlough to kidnap a young couple, "stabbing the man and repeatedly raping his girlfriend." The words "Kidnapping," "Stabbing," and "Raping" appear on the screen below Horton's image in cadence with the narrator's lurid account of the horrific night.[7] Thus, potential voters can contemplate the juxtaposition of these horrible deeds with the cool-eyed, black Horton and, in turn, tether his transgressions to the permissive Dukakis. While the Bush campaign never publicly released an advertisement mentioning Horton by name, the Massachusetts convict figured significantly in a rejuvenated campaign offensive that staked much of its fortunes on the war on crime in general and the mark of criminality in particular. Bush's campaign manager, Lee Atwater, bragged, "By the time we're finished, they're going to wonder whether Willie Horton is Michael Dukakis' running mate."[8] Dukakis had allowed a violent black man to rape a white woman. The conservative Bush promised to protect the citizenry from the inherent violence of the "big black penis."[9]

The Dukakis campaign never recovered from Willie Horton, and Bush comfortably secured a third consecutive term for the Reagan agenda.[10] As president, he committed significant political rhetoric and federal resources to an accelerated war on drugs. Like Reagan and Nixon before him, Bush understood crime was a winning policy. For example, officials in the Bush administration once orchestrated a drug deal across the street from the White House so that the president could use a bag of crack cocaine as a prop in an upcoming speech. Such was the nature of the Bush administration's rhetorics of criminality. Amid this spectacle of racialized fear that emphasized the threat of a deadly narcotic issuing forth from predominantly black urban sectors and the savage violence of the street gangs who dealt it, Bush continued the Reagan era's policies of austerity and deregulation.[11] While the consequences of neoliberalism provided working Americans of all races reasons to fear for their economic well-being, manifestations of the mark of criminality like the Horton ad invited affective investment in fearsome gendered black bodies and the seemingly anarchic drug economies of typically isolated racialized urban spaces. Willie Horton, however, was not the sole embodiment of black criminality circa 1988. Rather, a group of five rappers in South Central Los Angeles were, at this precise moment, perfecting an emergent style in the growing world of hip-hop: gangsta rap.

The release of NWA's 1988 album *Straight Outta Compton* was a watershed moment in black popular culture that coincided with the devastating consequences of austerity, surveillance, and scapegoating associated with the Reagan and Bush years. The album sold over three million copies and was certified double platinum by the Recording Industry Association of America.[12] Due to its staggering success, the album introduced the entire country to gangsta rap. As journalist Terry McDermott wrote several years following the album's release, "Hide the women and children; bar the doors. Too late. Gangsta rap was in the house."[13] As McDermott's ironic prose suggests, the political and cultural mainstream of the 1980s regarded gangsta rap as a genuine threat to the social order rather than a playful destabilization of the period's law-and-order discourses. After all, these were people who staged crack cocaine deals across the street from the White House with serious resolve. To regard gangsta rap as anything other than a deadly threat to the social order, as previously stated, would be to acknowledge the mark of criminality as a contingent genre rather than a natural representation of looming criminal threats against civil society. Indeed, a seismic cultural force had emerged with the collaboration of Eric "Eazy-E" Wright, O'Shea "Ice Cube" Jackson, Lorenzo "MC Ren" Patterson, Andre "Dr. Dre" Young, Kim "Arabian Prince" Nazel, and Antoine "DJ Yella" Carraby. NWA's iconic album became a popular window into black inner-city life by enacting, exaggerating, and celebrating the practices and locales at the heart of 1980s law-and-order politics. In other words, the album represented an alternative, and business-savvy, rendition of the mark of criminality. To be clear, NWA was not alone in their celebratory deployment of the mark of criminality. Rap artists including Schooly D, Boogie Down Productions, Ice T, and Toddy Tee adopted a gangsta ethos before NWA, while acts like King Tee, DJ Pooh, Compton's Most Wanted, and Above the Law were dropping gangsta records as well. However, NWA's staggering commercial success makes them unrivaled icons of gangsta rap whose reinventions of the mark of criminality served as a popular counterpoint to the prevailing logics of law and order in the 1980s and 1990s. The success of the 2015 film *Straight Outta Compton*, which chronicles the group's rise and eventual dissolution, indicates that NWA's iconic status remains secure in popular public memory.[14]

The mark of criminality circulated in white civil society in ways that mobilized affect as fear of racialized bodies and communities, but NWA attracted affective investments from audiences with playful, even joyful performances of black criminality. In this chapter, I argue that *Straight Outta Compton* used a parodic deployment of the mark of criminality that advanced alternative interpretations of violence and place in the late 1980s. By parodic, I mean those socially symbolic acts that contest prevailing orders of meaning by reconstituting them in alternative, subversive, and still problematic ways. Indeed, to engage in parody is fundamentally criminal. In his influential work on the subject, Henry Louis Gates Jr. defines Signifyin(g) as a distinctly African American vernacular practice that engages in linguistic indirection and tropological play, and exploits the conceptual space between denotative and figurative meaning. Signifyin(g) disrupts the coherence of Euro-American meaning systems, although it is also intertwined with such systems. Playful, humorous, and parodic reversals of meaning and power relationships characterize many enactments of Signifyin(g). The most dominant contemporary manifestation of these vernacular practices is rap music. *Straight Outta Compton* represents a particularly salient example of a parodic reconfiguration of the dominant discourses that composed the mark of criminality in late twentieth-century political and popular culture. It also reveals how an utter lack of humor from the upper echelons of law enforcement fol-

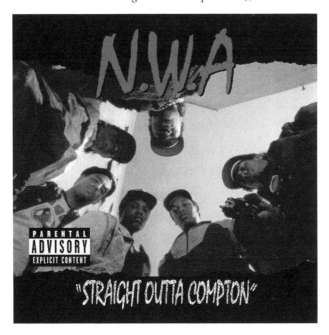

Figure 1: *Straight Outta Compton* album cover. Priority Records, 1988.

lowing the release of *Straight Outta Compton* betrayed both the mark of criminality's vulnerability to revision and its indispensable role in sustaining power relations in the 1980s. However, before engaging the album proper, we must turn to the geographies of race and criminality to appreciate what it meant to come straight outta Compton.[15]

How Los Angeles Became the Land of Racial Nightmares

As Michael Sorkin's opening provocation suggests, Los Angeles is a land of hyperreality. One searches in vain for an authentic cityscape amid a tapestry of simulation. Since its inception, the City of Angels and its surrounding municipalities like Long Beach, Compton, and Watts have served as blank screens upon which others project their fantasies about American exceptionalism, white supremacy, scientific discovery, and just about any other domain of meaning. Edward Soja writes, "The visible aggregate of the whole of Los Angeles churns so confusingly that it induces little more than illusory stereotypes or self-serving caricatures—if its reality is ever seen at all."[16] Los Angeles's champions posit it as an experimental wonderland of innovation. By such measures, it is a metropolis overflowing with creative energies. Others dismiss it as a carnival of simulation—a hollow, plastic urban nightmare. It is a city equally loved and loathed by politicians, artists, filmmakers, intellectuals, and ordinary citizens.[17]

To understand how Los Angeles became, among other things, the geographical epicenter for meaning making during the war on crime of the late twentieth century, we must historicize "Black Los Angeles," as Darnell Hunt has coined the term.[18] Such inquiry necessitates mindfulness toward what Katherine McKittrick and Clyde Woods call "black geographies." They write, "Black geographies disclose how the racialized production of space is made possible in the explicit demarcations of the spaces of *les damnés* [the damned] as invisible/forgettable at the same time as the invisible/forgettable is producing space—always, and in all sorts of ways."[19] In other words, Los Angeles County municipalities such as Compton, Watts, and Long Beach became spaces of segregation and impoverishment for many of their black inhabitants, while also functioning as incubators for the creative energies that produced gangsta rap. Such areas simultaneously provided spatial frames of reference for deployments of the mark of criminality that advanced the law-and-order politics of the late twentieth century and served as a locus for the fidelity to place expressed on an album like *Straight Outta Compton*. In short, encounters with Los Angeles during the 1980s and 1990s generated a multiplicity of affects that found expression through diverse political and popular modalities. But like all spaces, urban or otherwise, the meanings of Black Los Angeles experienced numerous revisions across history.

During the eighteenth and nineteenth centuries, when Californians lived under Spanish and Mexican rule, individuals of Afro-Caribbean descent often thrived as participants in civic culture and economic development. However, when the United States seized California from Mexico in 1846, life for black residents changed in abrupt and damaging ways. While California entered the union as a free state, many slaveholders migrated there and kept their slaves with impunity. Furthermore, a combination of discriminatory laws and white terrorism made life for black Californians difficult and often dangerous. While the abolition of slavery following the Civil War improved conditions for many Afro-Californians, white supremacy remained entrenched in the structures of governance and daily life.[20]

In the early twentieth century, Los Angeles experienced rapid urban development. Subdivisions emerged at a staggering rate, which imposed downward pressure on housing prices. Thus from the 1880s to early 1900s, Los Angeles was an attractive destination for many poor and working-class African Americans seeking stable employment and housing. However, like in so many other metropolitan areas across the nation, black residents faced housing discrimination that forced them into concentrated areas where commerce, employment, and police protection were sparse. Even after such practices became illegal, white migration away from central Los Angeles created identical conditions of segregation. Whereas South Central had previously been a region of distinct black neighborhoods with their own regional identities, the "white flight" of the mid-twentieth century created "one contiguous black residential space."[21] While the emergence of majority-black space is obviously not inherently problematic, the accompanying flight of white bodies and capital from such areas posed significant challenges for Black Los Angeles. Furthermore, the merging of poor black residents with those who enjoyed middle-class status lessened the desirability of predominantly black areas in South Central. The result was a complex matrix of intraracial class relations in which those African Americans with means were unwelcome by white Los Angeles and those without continued to languish under the ever-present burdens of poverty and class immobility. Both suffered immensely as the white middle and upper classes sought to forge ahead without them. The American dream remained a dream deferred.[22]

We have already surveyed the various ways American norms of law and order function to sustain white supremacy, and this was undeniably the case in Los Angeles County. So pronounced was the role of law enforcement in protecting racial segregation and subordination in the city and its surrounding municipalities that Los Angeles became the quintessential spatial signifier for the politics of race and criminality during the second half of the twentieth century. Prior to the 1950s, the Los Angeles Police Department (LAPD) was notorious less for its toxic relationships with minority communities than for its entrenched culture of corruption. In the wake of a particularly embarrassing prostitution racket within the department, the city sought new leadership, appointing William H. Parker to the position of chief in 1950. A former marine, Parker moved quickly to impose a military-style culture of professionalism on the department. The result was an army of officers increasingly detached from the communities they served. The prototypical "beat cop" became a thing of the past as Parker deployed swarms of radio cars around the city and ordered his officers to strictly enforce laws "without exception."[23]

Exceptions, however, remained and they followed distinctly racial logics. Throughout its postwar history, the LAPD made few if any distinctions between ordinary minority citizens and those who may be involved in criminal activity. Rather, residents of color, particularly African Americans, were always and already criminal. In other words, dominant iterations of the mark of criminality shaped police engagement with black people. Because the LAPD was disproportionately white in composition and, by hierarchical edict, detached from the day-to-day lives of the citizenry, officers increasingly surveilled, harassed, confined, and, in some cases, brutalized black bodies with little dissension. Music journalist Brian Cross claims that the post-Parker LAPD was "a modern autonomous army of occupation."[24] This status of the city's law enforcement apparatus, which patrolled all of Los Angeles County, as gang of outsiders invading black urban space became a central motif in gangsta rap's redeployments of the mark of criminality.

The affect that emerged from these encounters between law enforcement and Los Angeles's black communities found expression through a variety of channels. The most explosive expression of local anger came in 1965 in Watts when a crowd of neighbors formed around a seemingly routine police traffic stop. A melee unfolded and Watts gradually became a war zone. The riot lasted four days, covered forty-six square miles, caused thirty-four deaths, over one thousand injuries, led to nearly four thousand arrests, and produced $40 million in property damage. Out of the riots emerged a potent culture of political radicalism in Watts, including a powerful Nation of Islam and Black Panther presence, and a robust avant-garde of poets, actors, and other political artists. However, the uprising also inspired a deep paranoia in the upper echelons of Los Angeles law enforcement, prompting the LAPD to invest heavily in their intelligence division. For over a decade, the department's investigators monitored and infiltrated a range of left and liberal organizations, provoking several lawsuits and vocal anger from civil rights and civil liberties organizations.[25]

In 1978, department veteran Daryl Gates became the police chief and began fashioning the LAPD in a way that corresponded perfectly with the ascendant national political culture of racialized law and order. Empowered by a fresh cache of federally funded military-grade vehicles and other equipment, Gates launched Operation Hammer, a sustained raid on South Central that began in 1987 and extended into the early 1990s. Consider Mike Davis's description of a standard Gates-style police raid in South Central: "Kids are humiliatingly forced to 'kiss the sidewalk' or spread-eagle against police cruisers while officers check their names against computerized files of gang members. There are 1,453 arrests; the kids are processed in mobile booking centers, mostly for trivial offenses like delinquent parking tickets or curfew violations. Hundreds more, uncharged, have their names and addresses entered into the electronic gang roster for future surveillance."[26] Gates's indiscriminate searches and detentions effectively turned an entire generation of primarily male Los Angeles African American youth into targets for a militarized law enforcement apparatus. So sensationalistic were these sweeps of predominantly black neighborhoods that, on one occasion, First Lady Nancy Reagan donned a department flak jacket and watched a raid unfold from the comfort of an adjacent mobile home. Thus, Gates's operation helped entrench the criminalization of black youth in two respects. First, unprecedented numbers of young people, many of whom had no gang affiliations whatsoever, were now embedded in the criminal justice system. They became criminalized objects occupying the backs of police cars and prison cells, and were interpellated as criminal subjects whose association with urban crime increasingly overdetermined their already tenuous place in civil society. Second, Gates's flair for militarized drama played remarkably well with the broader sensationalism of the war on crime. In other words, the LAPD became a central collective actor in mainstream iterations of the mark of criminality. If places like Compton and Watts were to be seen as cesspools of villainous criminality, then those empowered to surveil such places were heroes in this Manichean drama.[27] It was in this context that five young black men from Compton found a resource for cultural production in these discourses of criminality.

NWA and the "Strength of Street Knowledge"

Scenarios like those Davis outlines signaled a spatial confrontation at the heart of the war on crime that rap was particularly equipped to express. Murray Forman documents the ways "minority youth use rap in the deployment of discourses of urban space and more proximate scales of urban locality, or place."[28] He writes, "Identities forged in the 'hood are products of spatial compression and are deeply influenced by locally sustaining bonds cohering within the more narrowly defined social parameters of space."[29] In other words, Forman understands hip-hop as the production of subjectivities vis-à-vis different types of locale. By parodying hegemonic representations of Compton and other criminalized municipalities of South Central, the members of NWA mocked the state's infiltration of their urban space and exalted themselves as hypermasculine heroes.

Throughout most of the 1980s, the West Coast rap scene was, at best, marginal to the already well-established artistry issuing from the boroughs of New York City and other parts of the East Coast. By most accounts, Jamaican-born Clive "DJ Kool Herc" Campbell originated rap in South Bronx during the early 1970s. At this time, the Bronx was sustaining the collateral consequences of the Cross Bronx Expressway. The brainchild of urban planner Robert Moses, the expressway was designed to efficiently link Manhattan to the New Jersey suburbs. It cut directly through South Bronx, displacing many residents and local businesses. It also served as a kind of separation wall from the rest of the borough and city. Steadily, life for the largely African American, Latinx, and Afro-Caribbean residents began to disintegrate.[30] Property values plummeted and, along with them, the quality of public schools. In fact, the absence of expensive musical instruments for extracurricular activities in the public schools was one of the motivating factors for the emergence of rap—a genre dependent on the use of records and turntables to produce new sounds out of recorded music.[31]

Campbell's family moved to New York from Jamaica at a time when the Caribbean nation was increasingly ravaged by political violence.[32] They were one of many refugee families who left their homeland for major urban sectors in the United States during this time. With them, they brought various cultural practices from Jamaica. One that deeply inspired a young Campbell and provided part of the foundation for rap was the dub genre. Typically void of lyrics, dub performances employed prerecorded music and rearranged it to produce new, danceable tracks (that is, sampling). Dub was wildly popular at Jamaican dance halls just as its streets and tenement yards exploded with political violence.[33]

As a young man in the South Bronx, Campbell began raiding his parents' blues, soul, gospel, country, and reggae albums in hopes of making a name for himself as a DJ. In addition to incorporating the sampling techniques of dub, Campbell began to zero in on the part of a song that most excited the dancers at South Bronx house parties. Jeff Chang explains, "The moment when the dancers really got wild was in a song's short instrumental break, when the band would drop out and the rhythm section would get elemental. Forget melody, chorus, songs—it was all about the groove, building it, keeping it going. Like a string theorist, Herc zeroed in on the fundamental vibrating loop at the heart of the record, the break."[34] Identifying the break as the key sonic component of popular music that mobilized bodies on his dance floors, Campbell began experimenting with strategies for focusing on, repeating, and prolonging this key percussive moment in the recording. This was the piece that enraptured the crowd in what sound scholars call a "sonorous envelope."[35] Tricia Rose argues that rap's emphasis on rhythm, rather than melody or harmony, distinguishes it from other Western forms of music and situates it instead in the cultural legacies of the African Diaspora. While Western music typically relies on structured melodies and harmonic resolution, African and African-derived musical expressions emphasize repetition and rhythmic layering. Thus the sampling of recorded music functions as a technological innovation of a long-standing musical practice that allowed for cultural continuity and revision in various renditions of black musical expression. Campbell's sampling of his parents' record collection enabled him to both pay reverence to artists who came before him and refashion their work to resonate with the specific desires of his South Bronx community.[36]

The other key half of rap performance is, of course, the lyrics. At the same parties where he discovered the break beat, Campbell routinely uttered rhymes and general bravado into the microphone. This technique, judged by the rapper's ability to keep pace with the sampled rhythms, came to be known as *flow*. However, just as the sampling of beats from other artists' work has its origins in Jamaican dub, the lyrical content of rap also has deep roots in African American vernacular traditions. Henry Louis Gates Jr. writes that Signifyin(g) functions as "a discursive reversal of historically prevailing power relationships" through methods of spontaneity, exaggeration, mimicry, punning, and other tools of linguistic and tonal trickery.[37] Cheryl L. Keyes explains that rap invokes other black vernacular practices associated with Signifyin(g), including elaborate "tonal contouring" and "vivid gesturing."[38] Such oral and gestural strategies, as well as the rhythmic tonality of rap's sampled beats, are broadly rooted in traditions with origins in both Africa and the Caribbean, situating rap in what Paul Gilroy calls the "black Atlantic."[39] However, Imani Perry insists that scholars should not mistake the strong presence of Afro-Diasporic influences in rap for "a united ideology in the Afro-Atlantic world manifest through fluid musical forms."[40] To do so, she argues, risks neglecting rap's status as a distinctly black American phenomenon, shaped by the experiences of individuals who must operate at the fraught intersection of black ethnic and American national identities.

Campbell's sampled rhythms and virtuoso lyricism influenced legions of other DJs, most notably Afrika Bambaataa and Joseph "Grandmaster Flash" Saddler. Both these artists envisioned rap and other elements of hip-hop (that is, graffiti, break-dancing) as mechanisms for cultivating community solidarity among black youth (for example, Bambaataa's Zulu Nation) and engaging in social critique (for example, Grandmaster Flash and the Furious Five's iconic track "The Message").[41] Rap evolved into a musical genre defined by the techniques that these and other young artists helped create and refine. In 1979, the Sugarhill Gang recorded the hugely successful single "Rapper's Delight" and helped seal hip-hop's fate as a viable and successful part of American popular culture, rather than as a mere urban fad. Throughout the 1980s, acts such as Run-DMC and LL Cool J, as well as white rappers like the Beastie Boys, grew in popularity, and hip-hop became a pronounced cultural force. The New York–based group Public Enemy flanked such commercial successes with their own brand of politically charged rap. Informed by Black Nationalism and outraged by what the past decades had wrought on the black community, Public Enemy forged a body of work that was both incendiary and popular. Many intellectuals and veterans of the civil rights era began to take hip-hop seriously as a potentially resistant and emancipatory force. Not only had its success across racial boundaries and the proliferation of black-owned record labels helped integrate previously closed sectors of the entertainment industry, but also acts like Public Enemy represented the genre's capacity for pointed political critique.[42]

A combination of historically rooted claims to authenticity and strong commercial instincts helped make New York the kingdom of the hip-hop nation. While the rivalry that contextualized so many of gangsta rap's most destructive excesses in the 1990s had yet to emerge, the seeds of resentment were already present in a prevailing discourse of West Coast inferiority. To be sure, Los Angeles produced important artists whose work anticipated the emergence of the hip-hop nation. For instance, the Watts Prophets, like their East Coast contemporaries the Last Poets, Gil Scott Heron, Nikki Giovanni, and others, combined elements of jazz with spoken poetry. Their politically potent work was popular with many black residents of Los Angeles County and elsewhere. Keyes notes that these juxtapositions of poetry and music both anticipated and influenced early rap artists. These performers also attracted the covert attention of the FBI in the form of surveillance and infiltration during the late 1960s and early 1970s.[43]

As East Coast hip-hop grew in popularity, artists like the Sugarhill Gang, Afrika Bambaataa, and Run-DMC began touring in Los Angeles and other western locales. Gradually, rhyming became a popular vernacular practice in South Central schoolyards, parks, and other popular youth spaces. However, what the West Coast came to call hip-hop was significantly different from its "purer" New York counterpart. East Coast groups drew their ethos from a rugged urban aesthetic characterized by heavy sampling of soul and funk tracks, abrasive yet danceable break beats, and lyrics contemplating various aspects of black urbanity. When hip-hop made its presence known in California, many black youths were also attracted to electropop artists like the German band Kraftwerk. Characterized by heavy use of synthesizers and sound effects, such groups anticipated the techno and industrial work of popular 1990s acts like Nine Inch Nails or KMFDM. Whereas improvisational break-dancing embodied the tonal characteristics of East Coast hip-hop, many West Coast rappers produced sounds that were conducive to more orchestrated, disco-inspired dances like "popping" and "locking." While New York hip-hop was widely understood as an urban corrective to the vapid commercialism of disco, the emerging West Coast scene seemed to embrace such tendencies hook, line, and sinker. The accompanying lack of "street cred" haunted the West Coast even after the explosion of gangsta rap.[44]

While the electropop brand of West Coast rap was inspiring mockery from the more complex and politically conscious virtuosity taking place in New York, other black Los Angeles artists were experimenting with more rugged and inflammatory styles. After several years of making a living through small-time drug dealing, Eric "Eazy-E" Wright decided to put his money and energy toward starting a record company. Founded in 1987 by Eazy and future NWA manager Jerry Heller, Ruthless Records provided a space for Wright to assemble local rap talents into a "South Central supergroup." He eventually recruited rappers Ice Cube, MC Ren, and Arabian Prince, as well as DJs Dr. Dre and DJ Yella.[45] Other than Eazy, none of the young men in the group lived a life of crime or even abject poverty. Rather, all of them, Eazy included, came from middle-class backgrounds. Ice Cube, for example, was bussed to a suburban high school and earned a degree in architectural drafting from the Phoenix Institute of Technology in Arizona. However, the fact that NWA's lived experiences did not perfectly correspond with the yarns they weaved in their songs does not justify dismissing their rhetoric as simple opportunism or posturing. All six original members lived in close physical proximity to the gangs, drugs, and violence that permeated their neighborhoods. Even if they had not seen the inside of a prison cell, taken part in a drive-by, or any of the other deeds they valorized in their records, they undoubtedly knew people who had. To be African American at the end of the twentieth century, especially in South Central Los Angeles, was to be thoroughly familiar and affectively engaged with the contours of the mark of criminality regardless of one's immediate relationship to the prison-industrial complex. Thus while NWA's claims to authenticity were suspect, they were not altogether fictive.[46]

Before releasing *Straight Outta Compton* in 1988, Compton-based NWA recorded the eleven-track *N.W.A. and the Posse*. Less a coherent album than a collection of tracks produced by those affiliated with NWA, the recording anticipated the cultural force of the album to follow. Tracks such as "8-Ball," "A Bitch Iz a Bitch," and "L.A. Is the Place," coalesced to produce a gangsta ethos grounded in crime, hypermasculinity, and fidelity to South Central Los Angeles as a site of community and agency. In other words, the album deployed the mark of criminality to cultivate a distinct aesthetic that reveled in, rather than apologized for, the symbolically rich cityscape Los Angeles had become in the context of the war on crime. The album's most popular single was "Boyz-N-The-Hood," which Ice Cube penned and Eazy performed. Much of the track—which Eazy raps over a relatively simple drum machine beat and synthesizers from the New York rap group Whodini's 1986 track "I'm a Ho"—exemplifies the themes that came to typify popular gangsta rap. Consider the third verse: "Bored as hell and I wanna get ill / So I went to a place where my homeboys chill / The fellows out there, making that dollar / I pulled up in my 6-4 Impala / They greet me with a 40 and I started drinking / And from the 8-ball my breath start stinking / Love to get my girl, to rock that body / Before I left I hit the Bacardi / Went to her house to get her out of the pad / Dumb hoe says something stupid that made me mad / She said somethin' that I couldn't believe / So I grabbed the stupid bitch by her nappy ass weave / She started talkin' shit, wouldn't you know? / Reached back like a pimp and slapped the ho / Her father jumped out and he started to shout / So I threw a right-cross cold knocked him out."[47] A brief sample of Jean Knight's chart-topping 1971 release "Mr. Big Stuff" suggests that Eazy-E and his gang make no apologies about their hubris and hedonism. It is as if the track is an unambiguous response to Knight's rhetorical question, "Who do you think you are?" Eazy-E is a boy from the hood and, as the song's chorus suggests, "the boyz in tha hood are always hard." Ice Cube's lyrics and Eazy's easily identifiable nasal voice exude a peculiar kind of bravado that exalts the very locales, practices, and discourses of black masculinity that in other sectors of national meaning-making were objects of sheer terror. NWA was reformulating the mark of criminality as a source of pride and profit.[48]

Protecting Black Space in "Straight Outta Compton"

If hip-hop is, in part, an expression of spatial fidelity among minority youth, such discourse in South Central Los Angeles inevitably dealt with law enforcement. Since at least the 1950s, the LAPD deliberately alienated itself from the black residents of Los Angeles County. In the era of Daryl Gates, this alienation evolved into a bona fide military operation in the name of fighting gangs and drugs. Although their presence in Compton, Watts, and other black municipalities was undeniable, the police were outsiders—colonizers in the parlance of Frantz Fanon and other twentieth-century theorists of black struggle. Thus gangsta rap's valorization of criminalized urban locales operated in a broader discursive regime of affectively charged spatial politics in which Gates, Reagan, and other powerful individuals deployed the mark of criminality to stigmatize and police South Central. To celebrate Compton *because of* its status as the single most feared urban space in America was an unavoidably political provocation. *Straight Outta Compton* engaged in such a politics from its opening titular track.[49]

The song "Straight Outta Compton" is simplistic by contemporary hip-hop standards. The members of NWA rap over a basic drum machine beat with various samples woven throughout.[50] They take turns reciting their respective verses with brief interludes consisting of sound effects and spoken dialogue. In the first verse, Ice Cube introduces himself as a "crazy motherfucker named Ice Cube / From the gang called Niggaz With Attitude." His is an exercise in violent hypermasculine bravado, as he brags, "When I'm called off, I got a sawed off / Squeeze the trigger, and bodies are hauled off / You too, boy, if ya fuck with me / The police are gonna hafta come and get me / Off yo' ass, that's how I'm goin' out / For the punk motherfuckers that's showin' out." He adds, "Here's a murder rap to keep yo' dancin' / With a crime record like Charles Manson." Ice Cube, in other words, imagines himself as California's new "crazy motherfucker" par excellence, replacing Manson as the state's most notorious criminal figure. And just as Manson's murderous cult provided a grim conclusion to the idealistic 1960s, NWA's gangsta verses represented for many hip-hop purists and African American elders the death knell of virtuous black cultural production in the United States.[51]

Ice Cube also establishes his hip-hop virtuosity (that is, his capacity to dispense "murder raps") through fantasies of frantic, artillery-packing violence. The mark of criminality thus functions as an expression of both hypermasculinity and lyrical talent. Similarly, in the second verse, MC Ren declares, "More punks I smoke, yo', my rep gets bigger / I'm a bad motherfucker and you know this / But the pussy ass niggaz don't show this / But I don't give a fuck, I'ma make my snaps / If not from the records, from jackin' or craps." For Ren, recording violent rhymes ("records") and criminal activity ("jackin'") amount to sensationalistic registers for expressing strength and talent.[52] This proud posture of the "crazy motherfucker" functions as a form of badman folklore for the late twentieth century. Whereas mythical figures like Stagger Lee and Dolomite were distinct products of post-Emancipation black life, NWA's tough-talking personas were unmistakably organic to the law-and-order politics of the Reagan and Bush era. The song, thus, reads like a hyperbolic proclamation of masculinity and virtuosity written with the guns, drugs, and sex of the Compton the United States had already come to know and fear, while also operating within the well-established parodic norms of the black vernacular tradition. And like other generations' tales of badmen, NWA's iterations of the mark of criminality compelled affirmative, if fraught, affective investments from black (and white) listeners that differed, but also derived potency from, prevailing discourses of fear and loathing that circulated in the upper echelons of 1980s public culture.[53]

However, the rhetorics of criminality at play in "Straight Outta Compton" are not limited to commerce or talent. Indeed, by parodying the politically explosive discourses associated with the mark of criminality, NWA creates the conditions of possibility for critiquing the surveillance and incarceration of poor people of color. The song's video is particularly helpful in illuminating this potential by contextualizing the lyrics within the era's crushing poverty and enhanced surveillance.[54] Rose explains that rap is distinct from other American musical genres because it came of age alongside the mass production of music videos. The artistry and commerce of rap, therefore, always accounted for its visual expression on the nation's television screens. Rose notes that rap videos during the 1980s and 1990s were typically filmed at the artist's or group's urban point of origin, or 'hood. She writes, "Rappers' emphasis on posses and neighborhoods . . . satisfies poor young black people's profound need to have their territories acknowledged, recognized, and celebrated."[55] Rappers and their local fans experienced deep affective investments with the 'hood, and rap expressed such investments. Gangsta rap videos, in particular, adopted what Ed Guerrero calls a "ghettocentric" aesthetic, emphasizing the poverty, crime, and other tribulations of places like Compton.[56] Rose explains that while the prominent role of the ghetto in black cultural production at this time affirmed mainstream assumptions about black urban space, it also enabled artists to offer affirmations of their communities.

The music video for "Straight Outta Compton" highlights the economic malaise that saturated Compton at the time, including shots of boarded-up storefronts and quick zoom shots of bail bond establishments and crisis centers. Furthermore, the video's opening scenes alternate between images of NWA rapping directly to the camera as they roam Compton's streets with their posse, and patrolling, highly caricatured, Los Angeles police officers donning aviator sunglasses and sporting large mustaches reminiscent of the most clichéd 1970s cop shows. The band's walking, indeed *strutting*, through Compton corresponds with Dr. Dre's opening declaration to listeners that, "You are now about to witness the strength of street knowledge." Throughout the video, it is clear that NWA and their posse know South Central like the back of their hands. Their walking becomes an embodied epistemological practice for their distinct enactments of the mark of criminality, resonating deeply with Michel de Certeau's argument that "walking in the city" can "elude discipline without being outside the field in which it is exercised."[57] In spite of a robust and militarized police presence,

Figure 2: Malaise in Compton. "Straight Outta Compton" music video. Priority Records, 1988.

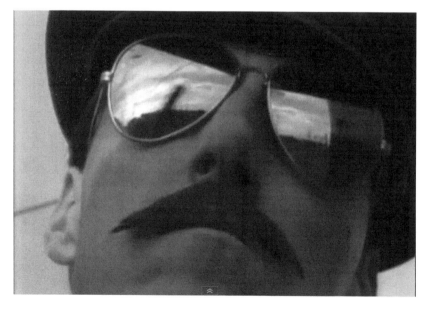

Figure 3: Cliché invaders. "Straight Outta Compton" music video. Priority Records, 1988.

Figure 4: "Crazy motherfuckers" strutting through Compton. "Straight Outta Compton" music video. Priority Records, 1988.

Compton remains the rightful home of NWA and the young black bodies they, willingly or not, have come to represent.[58]

By the song's second verse, rapped by MC Ren, the cruising police officers have arrested NWA and their posse, placing them inside a paddy wagon. However, as the video enters the third verse, we realize that Eazy-E was not among the arrested, and he quickly comes to the rescue. Riding alongside the paddy wagon in a convertible, Eazy mocks the police, stating, "I see a motherfuckin' cop I don't dodge him / But I'm smart, lay low, creep a while / And when I see a punk pass, I smile." Eazy, in other words, roams the streets of Compton with no fear of Daryl Gates and his officers. A subsequent external shot of the vehicle reveals the band members and their posse inexplicably standing at the curb, as if Eazy's stealth rhymes had liberated them. To reiterate the plain point that the occupiers in blue are not welcome in Compton, the group hurls stones at the departing vehicle. The episode comes to a close as the oblivious police drive their wagon out of the area and the posse proceeds to patrol *their* streets. The music video for "Straight Outta Compton," in effect, reimagines the relationship between the 'hood and law enforcement, deploying rhymes as weapons against cops. Coupled with its visual articulation, the track represents an enactment of the mark of criminality that parodies dominant cultural narratives expressed in the

Figure 5: Eazy-E saves the day. "Straight Outta Compton" music video. Priority Records, 1988.

upper echelons of political and popular culture. In NWA's Compton, the police are invasive buffoons, mocked and expunged by a criminal(ized) vanguard.

The Political Violence of "Fuck Tha Police"

The second track on *Straight Outta Compton*, "Fuck Tha Police," continues this critique of law enforcement but ups the ante by centralizing police officers as the sole focus of NWA's mockery and violent fantasizing.[59] No longer one of many in a series of potential enemies or the visual accompaniment of an otherwise apolitical toast, law enforcement officers function as the quintessential villain in NWA's cultural universe. The track begins with many familiar tropes associated with the mark of criminality. A satirical courtroom scene both opens and structures the entire song. In a reversal of the prevailing dynamics of law and order, the criminalized members of NWA place the police on trial for their transgressions against the black communities of Los Angeles County. The group delivers this opening portion over a soulful sample of brass horns, creating a sonic aesthetic reminiscent of 1950s- and '60s-era crime shows (for example, *Dragnet*), as if to parody such romantic portrayals of law enforcement saving the day. In short, "Fuck Tha Police" invites alternative affective encounters with one of mainstream law-and-order politics' most revered spaces. The courtroom becomes a site for vengeance and mockery directed toward law enforcement.

Rapper and NWA affiliate The D.O.C. begins by announcing, "Right about now, N.W.A. court is in full effect / Judge Dre presiding / In the case of N.W.A. versus the Police Department; / Prosecuting attorneys are: MC Ren, Ice Cube, / And Eazy-motherfuckin'-E." Apparently unfazed by his bailiff's crass disregard for courtroom conduct, Dr. Dre "enters the courtroom" and declares, "Ice Cube, take the motherfuckin' stand / Do you swear to tell the truth, the whole truth / And nothin' but the truth so help your black ass?" Ice Cube responds with an affirmative, "You god damn right!" and lays into the incendiary verbiage that would light a cultural fuse: "Fuck the police comin' straight from the underground / A young nigga got it bad cause I'm brown / And not the other color so police think / They have the authority to kill a minority / Fuck that shit, cause I ain't the one / For a punk motherfucker with a badge and a gun / To be beatin' on, and thrown in jail / We can go toe to toe in the middle of a cell / Fuckin' with me cause I'm a teenager / With a little bit of gold and a pager / Searchin' my car, lookin' for the product / Thinkin' every nigga is sellin' narcotics." Critiquing law enforcement was nothing new in black popular culture at the end of the twentieth century.[60] However, after his initial take on the LAPD's overzealous surveillance procedures, Ice Cube threatens to "Beat a police out of shape / And when I'm finished, bring the yellow tape / To tape off the scene of the slaughter." Images of yellow tape, another powerful visual trope associated with the mark of criminality, typically adorn scenes of ghastly crimes that heroic police officers intend to solve and prosecute. But in Ice Cube's hands, it denotes a scene of righteous vengeance against those very officers.

Not content with forthright acts of violence, Ice Cube also desires to castrate the hypermasculine expression of state power by affixing homophobic epithets to routine search procedures. He raps, "I don't know if they fags or what / Search a nigga down, and grabbin' his nuts." This lyric, to put it mildly, is alarming. To be sure, we should resist the kind of apologia for such content that Henry Louis Gates Jr. offered in defense of 2 Live Crew's misogynistic lyrics during their 1989 obscenity trial. Whereas Gates testified that the group's lyrics were merely playful expressions of the black vernacular tradition, Kimberlé Crenshaw's critique of Gates's defense argued that such a reading of 2 Live Crew's lyrics subordinates legitimate feminist concerns about gendered violence.[61] Equally problematic, however, would be a denial of this invective's location in a broader affective matrix of race, crime, and masculinity. To be clear, many scholars and activists have challenged homophobic rap lyrics and located them in the broader hypermasculine logics that frame so much hip-hop artistry.[62] However, many authors have also cautioned against too-facile a reading of homophobia in hip-hop or other black cultural practices. For example, Chandan Reddy claims that essentialist notions about "black homophobia" homogenize black politics and culture through the erasure of queer black subjectivities in particular, and the complexities of black life in general.[63] Indeed, Ice Cube's invective against the LAPD, while homophobic, is best read within the matrices of its historical moment. The mark of criminality is infused with gendered politics. D. Marvin Jones argues that rap music functions as an important, if often flawed, resource for recuperating marginalized masculinity. He writes, "These performances . . . are intended at a deep level as counternarratives, as resistance in the context of marginalized people attempting to represent themselves as potent, large, and in charge: predators rather than victims in a society where they have found themselves jobless, powerless, social victims languishing on street corners and in jails."[64] Viewed through such a prism, Ice Cube's "emasculation" of law enforcement becomes something more than outright homophobia—although it certainly qualifies as such. Instead, it constitutes a parodic reversal of the gendered roles associated with the mark of criminality that had for far too long allowed his brethren to be humiliated, "spread-eagle," by the likes of the LAPD. While those of us invested in feminist and queer political projects rightfully trouble the very notion of masculinity, black or otherwise, a gesture of intersectional openness is essential for productively attending to this and other lyrical content in the gangsta rap catalog. We should not excuse, bracket, ignore, or categorically malign Ice Cube's words, but understand that they function as equipment for living in an age when the black male was public enemy number one. The lyric is a flawed but nonetheless salient deployment of the mark of criminality.

NWA also deploys the mark of criminality in ways that resonate strongly with the currents of black and pan-African nationalisms that circulated in many activist communities during the postwar era, and enjoyed some renewed popularity with the emergence of the Nation of Islam's Louis Farrakhan as a polarizing public figure during the late 1980s and 1990s.[65] MC Ren raps, "Fuck the police and Ren said it with authority / Because the niggaz on the street is a majority." This declaration echoes a central ethic of Black Nationalism: the belief that colonized people of color can find comfort and encouragement in the fact that they outnumber their oppressors.[66] By imagining oneself as part of an urban majority, the listening black youth can, through MC Ren, assert, "Readin' my rights and shit, it's all junk." The track, in other words, reveals the potential of parody to express a proto-nationalist politics by mocking and, therefore, reversing the discursive power dynamics of Compton. Like Ice Cube, MC Ren highlights the artificiality of law enforcement authority. Mocking the police, he raps, "Pullin' out a silly club, so you stand / With a fake-assed badge and a gun in your hand / But take off the gun so you can see what's up / And we'll go at it punk, and I'm-a-fuck you up!" Elaborating upon this theme Eazy-E joins with a third verse, rapping, "Without a gun and a badge, what do ya got? / A sucker in a uniform waitin' to get shot." Eazy insists that the police possess no authentic authority in the 'hood. Rather, they are invaders rightfully vulnerable to the mockery and weaponry of NWA. As I explain subsequently, such a highly publicized parodic reversal of law enforcement's prerogative of violence posed an intolerable threat to the state's institutional authority and cultural hegemony in the war on crime. Instead of attempting to sanitize the public image of the fearsome black male, NWA enacts the mark of criminality as a playful generic tool for recasting black urban violence as righteous vengeance, supplanting the ethical police officer with the savvy, Signifyin(g) gangsta guerrilla.

The tracks "Straight Outta Compton" and "Fuck Tha Police" intervened at a political and cultural moment when most Americans were exposed to a particular narrative of the inner city that was void of irony—one where law enforcement cleans the streets of drug dealers and violent gangsters. Such versions of the mark of criminality invited affective investments from a predominantly white middle-class constituency whose racialized anxieties fit neatly into discourses of constabulary heroics. NWA's work inverted this dynamic not by refuting the criminal deeds that Reagan, Bush, and other figures crafted policy to supposedly combat, but by redeploying the mark of criminality as a resource for heroic, playful masculinity and artistic mastery, while vilifying the colonizer police officer as an unwanted fool in the streets of Compton. But if *Straight Outta Compton* gave expression to the affective intensities that emerged from black communities' encounters with state violence and economic hardship, it also provided a fearsome validation of the anxieties that motivated and rationalized the mass surveillance of black communities in places like Compton. Because NWA's was a multiplatinum album inaugurating a new phase in music history, it represented a very potent threat to the discourses of criminality on which many had staked their political careers. The fallout following the record's release revealed precisely how unamusing this challenge was.

Crime Control and the Prerogative of Violence

By 1988, black cultural producers in the United States and elsewhere had been mocking, and sometimes figuratively killing, cops for generations. For example, the nineteenth-century badman Railroad Bill allegedly shot the local sheriff, but only after he "Shot all de buttons off de Sheriff's coat."[67] In Melvin Van Peebles's germinal blaxploitation film, *Sweet Sweetback's Baadasssss Song*, our hero's odyssey begins when he assaults a pair of racist officers who were beating a black militant named Moo Moo.[68] Possibly the most relevant text to understanding the social force of NWA's antipolice lyricism is the legendary Nigerian musician Fela Kuti's 1977 single "Zombie." Directed toward the abusive Nigerian military, "Zombie" framed the soldiers as mindless robots, or zombies, violently imposing the government's will on the public. Dorian Lynskey explains, "Instead of earnestly denouncing soldiers, Fela dances around them, poking fun, each blurting trumpet

line or darting chant representing another knock to their macho pride."[69] Such an
attack inspired vicious military retaliation against Fela Kuti and his comrades.[70]

If Kuti's experience following the release of "Zombie" reflects a repressive military's lack of humor where their monopoly on violence is concerned, the political fallout surrounding *Straight Outta Compton* in general, and "Fuck Tha Police" in particular, reveals the dour state of law-and-order politics in the age of Willie Horton. Whereas the prevailing narrative of criminality in popular and political culture distinguished the righteous violence of law enforcement from the vindictive criminal deeds of gangs and drug dealers, NWA transformed the noble police officer into a colonizing goon and the inner-city gangsta into a militant trickster. They had, in other words, disrupted sacred tropes of law and order—tropes whose ability to capture and mobilize public affect helped sustain the war on crime. While the members of NWA downplayed the seriousness of their work, describing "Fuck Tha Police" as a simple "revenge fantasy," those who attacked *Straight Outta Compton* took it very seriously and were invested in recuperating the mark of criminality and reasserting the state's prerogative of violence.[71]

In the summer of 1989, the Fraternal Order of Police adopted a resolution boycotting the shows of any artist who "advocates assaults on police officers."[72] This made it incredibly difficult for venues hosting NWA to provide security for their shows and purchase insurance. Owners began insisting that NWA refrain from performing "Fuck Tha Police." These tensions between law enforcement and the group intensified on August 6, 1989, when NWA performed at Detroit's Joe Louis Arena. Although they agreed to omit the offensive track from their set list, the group relented to an insistent crowd chanting, "Fuck the police!" No sooner did the song open, than a legion of police officers stormed the stage.[73] NWA's experiences with law enforcement and music venues were part of wider discourses of racialized fear associated with rap shows. During the late 1980s and early 1990s, many rap artists found it incredibly difficult to secure concert venues. Insurance and permit rates for rap shows were significantly higher than those for other, mainly white, musical acts. Rap's already strong association with racialized masculine violence, coupled with mass mediated fixations on violent incidents at some rap shows, created an environment in which the site of assembled black bodies in concert halls or arenas resonated with white anxieties that found expression through the affective registers of the mark of criminality. Rose writes, "The way rap and rap-related violence are discussed in the popular media is fundamentally linked to the larger social discourse on the spacial control of black people."[74] She adds, "The fact that rap-related concert violence takes place outside the invisible fence that surrounds black poor communities raises the threat factor."[75] In other words, because rap concerts often placed black artists and fans' enactments of the mark of criminality outside the parameters of already-criminalized black space, they made the perceived danger of such assemblies more immediate to white civil society. Coupled with tough-on-crime rhetoric from politicians, sensationalism from television news and other media, and the proliferation of gangsta rap in the homes of white suburban youth, rap concerts figured naturally into dominant deployments of the mark of criminality.

The law enforcement backlash against NWA reached its boiling point when Milt Ahlerich, the FBI's assistant director for the Office of Public Affairs, sent a letter to the distributor of *Straight Outta Compton*, Priority Records. He noted, "a song recorded by the rap group N.W.A. on their album entitled *Straight Outta Compton* encourages violence against and disrespect for the law enforcement officer and has been brought to my attention." As if to inoculate against any constitutional red flags, Ahlerich claimed he was simply "writing to share my thoughts and concerns with you." He then proceeds with the injunction, "Advocating violence and assault is wrong, and we in the law enforcement community take exception to such action." Citing statistics on law enforcement officer deaths and injuries in 1988, Ahlerich condemned NWA for pouring salt in the collective wounds of those who swore to protect and serve. In the letter's conclusion, he writes, "music plays a significant role in society, and I wanted you to be aware of the FBI's position relative to this song and its message." He adds, "I believe my views reflect the opinion of the entire law enforcement community."[76] In other words, this high-ranking official at the nation's most powerful law enforcement entity had simply taken it upon himself to share his thoughts on the controversial new album Priority Records was bankrolling. Oh, and by the way, the rest of the law-and-order community felt precisely the same way.

The FBI's intervention, the first of its kind, raises numerous concerns regarding free expression.[77] However, the letter also highlights a more fundamental tension at the intersection of race and criminality in the 1980s. Particularly telling is Ahlerich's claim that "advocating violence and assault is wrong." This deceptively straightforward comment illustrates a central antagonism at the heart of "Fuck Tha Police" and NWA's work in general—arguably the very enterprise of gangsta rap and other vernacular deployments of the mark of criminality. Between each verse in "Fuck Tha Police" are comical vignettes of NWA members encountering racial profiling and police brutality. For example, the following scene precedes MC Ren's verse:

Cop: Pull your goddamn ass over right now!
Ren: Aww shit, now what the fuck you pullin' me over for?
Cop: 'Cause I feel like it! Just sit your ass on the curb and shut the fuck up!
Ren: Man, fuck this shit!
Cop: A'ight smart ass, I'm takin' your black ass to jail!

NWA may very well have agreed that violence and assault are wrong (if not also profoundly lucrative). The question is, whose violence and assault? Within the domain of NWA's Compton, slaying a police officer becomes a playful, heroic act, and law enforcement aggression a crime. It is a reconfiguration of the prevailing rhetorical norms of criminal justice in America that mobilize primarily white public anxieties about crime through the criminalization of the black masculine body. Ahlerich's letter, *recognizing the significant role music plays in society*, sought to reclaim the prerogative of violence from NWA's trickery and reify dominant, starkly serious notions of racialized justice and law enforcement culture. The true threat of "Fuck Tha Police," in other words, was not the risk of dead police officers (even Ahlerich knew of no police deaths inspired by the song), but of those officers being laughed out of the 'hood and losing their authority to provide punitive leverage to the moral panic circulating through the political and popular culture of the era.[78] Rather than challenging the very foundations of the mark of criminality, NWA threatened to beat the state on its discursive home turf.

"My Identity by Itself Causes Violence"

When Public Enemy trickster Flavor Flav screamed "1989!" to open his group's beloved 1989 track "Fight the Power," many listeners knew precisely what he meant.[79] Race relations in the United States were, by many measures, reaching a climactic point. Reaganomics was now entrenched in the circuitries of American capitalism, and neoliberal logics continued to shape public attitudes and policies. Incarceration and poverty rates for African Americans were rapidly rising and, if one believed the popular and political discourses of the day, they only had themselves to blame. Furthermore, a series of racially charged and violent events fomented distrust and anger between African Americans, the police, and white America. For example, in 1984, police fatally shot an arthritic sixty-seven-year-old black woman while she resisted eviction from her Bronx apartment. The following year, in Philadelphia, police firebombed the residence of the black radical group MOVE, destroying an entire neighborhood and killing eleven adults and children. In 1986, a white mob killed a young black man in the predominantly white Howard Beach neighborhood in Queens, New York. One year later, an African American woman named Tawana Brawley claimed a gang of racist white men brutally raped her, only to have her story quickly dismissed by many public officials, mainstream media, and a grand jury. Amid these events, polarizing African American figures like Jesse Jackson, Al Sharpton, and Louis Farrakhan grew in visibility and popularity. The movement to end apartheid in South Africa was also capturing the imagination of many young black activists. While the 1980s were not a decade of mass mobilizations like the 1960s and 1970s, they were nonetheless a time of excitement and sheer terror for American racial politics. Thus, Flavor Flav's cry registers as a release and acknowledgment of a racially suffocating decade.[80]

The perceived promise of Public Enemy's incendiary political raps, as well as director Spike Lee's perfectly contextual 1989 meditation on race relations, *Do the Right Thing*, led many hip-hop progressives to regard NWA as a threat to hip-hop's emancipatory potential. At a time of crisis for many sectors of the African American community, did anyone really need Eazy-E and his crew glorifying images of blackness that were helping justify austerity and mass incarceration? Following the release of *Straight Outta Compton*, many hip-hop DJs and writers boycotted the album because they were, as Chang explains, "outraged at the crew's belligerent ignorance, and privately ambivalent about the music's visceral heart-pounding power."[81] While outrage was certainly an understandable response to the swagger of the "crazy motherfucker," I have aimed in this chapter to advocate on the side of ambivalence.

Again, to be clear, NWA was not a "political group" in any traditional sense of the term. They lacked the political clarity or ambition of black activist musicians like Stevie Wonder, Bob Marley, Nina Simone, or Public Enemy.[82] While there are important virtues associated with the rap industry's status as a site for black cultural production and commercial success, NWA was not in the business of heroism.[83] In an interview with Brian Cross, Dr. Dre explains the group's fidelity to Compton as a business decision and adds, "I wanted to go all the way left, everybody trying to do this black power and shit, so I was like let's give 'em an alternative, nigger, niggernigger niggernigger fuck this fuck that bitch bitch bitch bitch suck my dick, all this kind of shit, you know what I'm saying."[84] Dr. Dre and his collaborators, in other words, were wary of what they regarded as political bombast and instead wanted to trade in the commodities of black criminality. They wanted to sell America its "worst racial nightmares."[85] Furthermore, figures like Wonder, Marley, or Simone were at their most politically creative during affectively charged periods of political upheaval and social movements confronting issues of racism, poverty, gender inequality, and national liberation.[86] NWA, on the other hand, came of age amid the ashes of antiracist movements that collapsed under their own contradictions and due to state suppression. This is not to suggest that the 1980s were void of antiracist political activism, but such work, as Mark Anthony Neal and others have argued, was constrained by the impacts of neoliberalism—specifically, the fragmentation of a coherent black public sphere and increasing entrenchment of black political leadership in the political and corporate mainstream.[87] Consequentially, NWA's own intentions notwithstanding, the potential of their work to help mobilize public affect against mass incarceration and other forms of institutional racism was significantly lessened in a period of relative grassroots demobilization.

The profoundly well-organized forces of law enforcement and music capital, however, were more than willing to act upon NWA's ascent and the emergence of gangsta rap as a major cultural force. While the humorless law-and-order establishment succeeded in convincing many of their constituents to fear gangsta and regard it as the sinister superstructure of a racialized criminal base, the music industry absorbed the humor of gangsta and transformed it into what became, in the eyes of many activists and scholars, a lucrative minstrel show marketed to poor African American youth and affluent suburban whites.[88] Thus, NWA's political potency and that of their gangsta offspring were neutralized in two respects: as an object of sheer terror and a commodified, if still humorous, expression of the mark of criminality. Blackness, as has historically been the case in the wake of slavery, was to be feared or mocked.

To conclude that NWA was subsumed by its own commercial ambitions and their fateful location at the close of the twentieth century should not result in an abandonment of gangsta's political salience. To do so would be to relegate the weapons of parody to the humorless structures of mass incarceration—to, in other words, lack a sense of humor. M. Lane Bruner argues that humorous protest functions as a site for utopian imagination where social roles are reversed and injustices corrected.[89] While a far cry from social activists, NWA nonetheless offered resources for imagining the 'hood anew as part of a proto-nationalist fantasy. While NWA's parodic use of the mark of criminality helped reify public investments in the fear and incarceration of young African Americans, their disruption of the meaning systems that sustained such a project left the syntax of law and order forever changed and, therefore, vulnerable. Furthermore, NWA resides in twenty-first-century public memory as a profoundly politically salient force in black popular culture. For example, promotional media surrounding the release of the 2015 film *Straight Outta Compton* conspicuously locates the group's legacy in more recent mobilizations around police violence and other forms of institutional racism.[90]

It should come as no surprise that NWA did not play a role in exploiting the discursive vulnerabilities they helped create. In addition to lacking the motivation to do so, the group called Niggaz With Attitude barely outlasted the decade whose politics of criminality they disrupted. Shortly after the group released *Straight Outta Compton*, Ice Cube, widely considered the group's most talented rapper and lyricist, left NWA over a financial dispute with Eazy and Heller. In addition to slinging vitriol at his former bandmates, Ice Cube's first solo albums, 1990's *Amerikkka's Most Wanted* and 1991's *Death Certificate*, reflected the young rapper's growing interest in Black Islam and embodied a more politically explicit sensibility than in his work with NWA. Ice Cube also starred in John Singleton's 1991 Compton-set film *Boyz N The Hood*, which is still considered among the most important pieces of ghettocentric black cinema from the late twentieth century.[91]

Following Ice Cube's departure, NWA released its final album, *Efil4zaggin (Niggaz4Life)*. Shortly thereafter, Dr. Dre and Eazy became embroiled in a financial dispute that, according to Eazy, culminated in Dr. Dre's bodyguard, Marion "Suge" Knight, forcing him to release Dr. Dre from his contract with Ruthless Records under threat of physical harm. Dr. Dre and Knight formed the label Death Row Records in 1991. Aside from making obvious allusions to the criminal justice system through its name, Death Row helped transform gangsta rap into a coherent industry and remained its most important label throughout most of the 1990s. As the remainder of this book demonstrates, Knight and the artists he employed were the chief architects of rap's continuing iterations of the mark of criminality.[92]

With NWA's disintegration, DJ Yella and MC Ren faded into relative obscurity. Eazy remained a high-profile figure in the hip-hop nation, even if his recording efforts received little enthusiasm from critics. He sparked significant backlash from some members of the African American community after attending a Republican fund-raising dinner where George Bush was the featured speaker. Eazy also drew the ire of hip-hop opinion leaders when he publicly declared support for one of the Los Angeles police officers charged in the videotaped beating of black motorist Rodney King. Ironically, one of the founders of a musical style whose reconfigurations of the mark of criminality drew equal parts enthusiasm and backlash increasingly found himself aligning with forces most frequently associated with dominant versions of law-and-order politics. On the other hand, if we take Eazy and other members of NWA at their word, perhaps there is no irony at all. They were, after all, in it for the money.[93]

Eazy-E proceeded to make minor waves in the hip-hop nation until March 16, 1995, when he announced he was HIV positive; he died from AIDS complications ten days later. Eazy's death provoked strong responses from hip-hop and other black media outlets, as it became a testament to African Americans' vulnerability to HIV/AIDS. Frank Williams wrote in the *Source*'s obituary for Eazy, "Hopes are that the fear and gossip surrounding him and the deadly disease will translate into discussion analyzing the disease's effect on the hip-hop and Black communities—two groups who are widely under attack from the disease but who have not strongly mobilized around this issue."[94] Eazy-E spent most of his adult life inaugurating a form of rap that reveled in and redeployed criminalized discourses of black masculinity, but his death located his legacy in a disease whose various racialized public iterations, both inside and outside communities of color, further entrenched the policing of black sexuality.[95]

The following year, Tupac Shakur, the rapper whose life and work is covered in this book's fourth chapter, died in a drive-by shooting at the height of a bicoastal rap feud. Thus, if this volume's chosen timeline is any reflection, Eazy-E was present at the beginning and nearly made it until the end of the period when gangsta rap engaged most directly with the ever-shifting contours of the mark of criminality. However, well before becoming one of a legion of victims to HIV/AIDS, Eazy ceased to be a relevant actor in the mark of criminality's circulation in the 1980s and 1990s. Rather, with the union of Dr. Dre and Suge Knight, the West Coast rap scene grew into a lucrative and, eventually, dangerous behemoth.

3

Leisure, Style, and Terror in the G-Funk Era

I'm just, you know, relatin' to my people the best way I know; bringing them what they know and what they see out there in the streets, but I'm bringing it to them in a musical way, a way of partying rather than, you know what I'm sayin', through violence. Now they can party their way through their problems.

—Snoop Doggy Dogg

This morning. We got reports from down here that people were doing "stupid sensual things," were in a state of "uncontrollable frenzy," were wriggling like fish, doing something called the "Eagle Rock" and the "Sassy Bump"; were cutting a mean "Mooche," and "lusting after relevance."

—Ishmael Reed, *Mumbo Jumbo*

Here I am, about [to] embark on a journey with Governor Bill Clinton and his running mate, Senator Al Gore—the Democratic "dream team," America's best hope to finally put the Gipper (former President Ronald Reagan) and his lapdog (current President George Bush) to bed. Once and for all. But Clinton is also the man who recently fried a mentally-impaired convicted murderer in the electric chair, a method of punishment disproportionately used against people of color. He is also the coward who attacked Sister Souljah to show white America that he knows how to keep the darkies in check.

—James Bernard, *The Source*

Do the Right Thing, director Spike Lee's cinematic meditation on the racial politics of the late 1980s, ended with prophecy. Following the death of the film's Public Enemy–playing, silent black militant Radio Raheem at the hands of New York City police officers, a black Brooklyn crowd explodes in anger. Mookie throws a trash can through Sal's pizzeria window and, as the situation disintegrates, the Italian American patriarch's local business goes up in flames. The crowd screams "Burn it down!" as Sal's eldest son watches assembled black bodies burn his family's livelihood and place in the neighborhood to ashes. He quietly utters, "Niggers." Mother Sister, a black neighborhood matriarch, breaks into tears as she watches the violence unfold. The police and fire department eventually disperse the crowd. The next morning, Radio Love Daddy wonders aloud on his radio show, "Are we ever going to live together?" Mookie and Sal reach a tenuous truce outside the ruined storefront, and the film fades to black. As if to encapsulate the tensions that propelled the film's diegesis and the decade as a whole, Lee leaves viewers with two quotations from the perennial counterpoints of the civil rights era: Martin Luther King Jr. and Malcolm X. King insists, "violence as a way of achieving racial justice is both impractical and immoral. It is a descending spiral ending in destruction for all." And the more militant Malcolm X counters, "I don't even call it violence when it's self-defense, I call it intelligence." The credits role as it befalls us to find some semblance of truth in the aporia between their words.[1]

The 1980s ended without the racial apocalypse prophesied by Lee and so many other culture producers, politicians, and social commentators. Instead, judgment day came in 1992. On March 3, 1991, five Los Angeles police officers savagely beat black motorist Rodney King after he eluded them in a high-speed pursuit. Unbeknownst to the officers, a resident videotaped the entire episode from his nearby apartment. The video received extensive media coverage and inspired outrage from activist organizations and African American residents. The King beating was not a particularly shocking affair for Black Los Angeles, but instead a rare concretization of postwar LAPD excesses. It represented, many hoped, an opportunity to force law enforcement accountability. The five officers were indeed charged with assault and excessive force. However, the judge agreed to a change of venue, and a majority white jury tried them in affluent Simi Valley, forty-five minutes northwest of Los Angeles.

On April 29, 1992, the jury delivered "not guilty" verdicts on all charges. News of the acquittal spread quickly and black bodies began filling the streets of South Central. Angry protests turned into looting, property damage, and physical violence. While the LAPD went to great lengths to protect wealthy, predominantly white neighborhoods like Beverly Hills, they had virtually abandoned South Central. When most of the violence ended on May 4, fifty-three people were dead, thousands of others arrested, and $1 billion in property was destroyed. In spite of much-heralded exceptions like the beating of white truck driver Reginald Denny, the victims were overwhelmingly black, Latinx, and Asian.[2]

Given its status as the most visible mode of black vernacular expression in the United States, the hip-hop nation seemed like an obvious resource for meaningful political expression after the affectively charged riots. Artists like Public Enemy, KRS-One, and Ice Cube spent much of the late 1980s and early 1990s expressing outrage about racial stratification in America, and even forecasting events like the 1992 riots. Ice Cube's 1992 album *The Predator* broadly functioned as a meditation on the King beating and riots. On the track "We Had to Tear This Muthafucka Up," the former NWA member fantasized aloud about murdering the five acquitted officers, the Simi Valley jury, and the judge. He also rapped over an ominous jazz bass, "Don't fuck with the black-owned stores, but hit the Foot Lockers," to express racial solidarity through the looting of businesses in South Central.[3] While Ice Cube critiqued police brutality and other arteries of white supremacy, he also unapologetically waxed nostalgic about looting and other practices that so dominated mainstream news media following the riots. As if to place himself in conversation with those very representations, Ice Cube sampled heavily from news coverage of the King verdict and riots, drawing on them as evidence of the woefully inadequate discourses of race and crime spewing forth from white civil society. At a time when black affective energies in South Central Los Angeles were finding expression in various modalities of outrage, Ice Cube fashioned the mark of criminality in a way that framed the riots as righteous violence.[4]

While Ice Cube had already cemented his post-NWA reputation as possibly the most controversial rapper in the United States, the Los Angeles riots also coincided with Dr. Dre's nascent solo career. His 1992 debut album, *The Chronic*, quickly became one of the best-selling LP's in the country and is now widely regarded as among the best and most influential rap albums ever. It ushered in a period in gangsta rap called the gangsta funk, or "g-funk" era. Characterized by lackadaisical tonality and lyrical tales of violence, misogyny, copious drug and alcohol use, and unapologetic materialism, g-funk constituted a further departure from the more political pretenses of many East Coast artists, as well as the more abrasive gangsta rhymes of NWA.[5]

Although Death Row released the album the same year the riots occurred, only one track on *The Chronic* explicitly engages the fallout surrounding the Rodney King verdict. Sandwiched between more prototypical g-funk standards, "The Day the Niggaz Took Over" is visceral in its angry tonality and lyrics. Like Ice Cube's "We Had to Tear This Muthafucka Up," the track draws heavily on television coverage of the riots, including news anchors reporting on the unfolding tumult and black citizens reflecting on the King verdict ("That's what they told us today. In other words, you still a slave"). The heavy bass sampled from Boogie Down Productions' "Love's Gonna Getcha" produces an ominous aesthetic, as if to say, "We're pissed and we're coming to get you." In the second verse, Dre raps, "Sittin' in my livin' room calm and collected / Feelin' mad, gotta get mine respected / Cuz what I just heard broke me in half." In addition to frankly expressing his disappointment following the verdict, Dr. Dre invokes visions of intergang solidarity in the face of the verdict, boasting, "Bloods, Crips on the same squad." However, while "The Day the Niggaz Took Over" sounded like a perfect expression of the outrage of 1992, the rest of *The Chronic* struck a decidedly different tone. Jeff Chang writes, "It could be heard as a guiltless, gentrified gangsta—no Peace Treaties, rebuilding demands, or calls for reparations, just the party and the bullshit."[6] As its title's reference to potent marijuana makes clear, *The Chronic* was chiefly a musical document celebrating leisurely abandon and masculine bravado in the ashes of the riots. Such Dionysian excess, however, was every bit as political as the album's lone polemic.

I argue in this chapter that the artists of the g-funk era enacted a rendition of the mark of criminality that valorized black style and leisure practices at a time when blacks were objects of institutional criminalization and intergenerational suspicion.[7] Such valorization constituted both a problematic commodification of black criminality and an expression of utopian desire in post-riot Los Angeles. To this end, I dedicate the remainder of this chapter to contextualizing the works of g-funk's founding fathers, Dr. Dre and Snoop Doggy Dogg (born Cordozar Calvin Broadus Jr.), in the fraught landscape of post-LA-riot law and order. Specifically, I demonstrate the ways the g-funk aesthetic drew on various expressions of black style and leisure to refigure the black criminal subject as one capable of violence, but primarily invested in communal and sensual pleasure. This version of the mark of criminality reflected the changing contours of the rap industry and state surveillance of communities like South Central Los Angeles, and amplified generational fissures between the hip-hop nation and an earlier generation of black activists. G-funk, in other words, emerged at the nexus of various affective investments associated with the mark of criminality. Whereas NWA primarily employed the mark of criminality through contested registers of violence and space, g-funk expressed criminality through the quotidian practices of black youth.

Killing Cops and Exorcising Willie Horton; or, G-Funk as the Love Child of Ice-T and Bill Clinton

The road that led to the g-funk era was littered with broken friendships and business deals, evolving artistic ambitions, and the aesthetic contours of a deeply changed post-riot Los Angeles. While the breakup of NWA and the business acumen of Dr. Dre and Suge Knight undeniably helped forge this path forward, it is unlikely g-funk would have been possible were it not for the twin forces of West Coast rapper Ice-T and the newly elected Democratic president William Jefferson "Bill" Clinton. Whereas the former altered the political economy of hip-hop cultural production, the latter helped solidify the status of law and order as a "bipartisan" issue. Their dual impacts forged the rhetorical situation of the g-funk era.

In 1990, Ice-T formed the heavy metal, or "thrash," band Body Count. This was not the first convergence of rap and hard rock. For example, in 1986, Run-DMC collaborated with Aerosmith to release a rap version of the latter's classic track "Walk This Way." In 1991, Public Enemy contributed to metal band Anthrax's cover of their single "Bring the Noise."[8] Indeed, the subsequent notoriety of Ice-T's crossover act had little to do with the pairing of traditionally "black" rap music and "white" heavy metal and everything to do with one of gangsta rap's most recognizable tropes: cop killing.

Released on their 1992 self-titled debut album, Body Count's "Cop Killer" contained the same general themes as 1988's "Fuck Tha Police," including violent fantasy ("I got my twelve gauge sawed off / I got my headlights turned off / I'm 'bout to bust some shots off / I'm 'bout to dust some cops off!"), vengeful ethos ("I'm 'bout to kill me somethin' / A pig stopped me for nuthin'!"), and cold-blooded cruelty ("I know your momma's grievin' / Fffuck her!"). However, whereas Ice Cube, MC Ren, and Eazy-E rapped their lyrics, Ice-T yelled them over frantic drums and electric guitars, harnessing the affective energies that usually mobilized primarily white bodies in mosh pits to express outrage toward white supremacist law enforcement.[9] Still, mainstream news coverage and the subsequent political backlash against the song almost universally fixated on Ice-T's status as a rap artist, and not Body Count's heavy metal credentials. We were, after all, talking about a black man fantasizing aloud about unleashing violent fury against police officers in the wake of the Los Angeles riots. Regardless of a song's tonality, the status of "Cop Killer" as gangsta rap was overdetermined given the ways political and cultural elites deployed the mark of criminality to condemn this emerging form of black cultural production.[10] The song generated such intense backlash from law enforcement and elected officials that Ice-T eventually halted production of the album in order to remove the song. To this day, it exists solely in the form of original recordings, YouTube videos, and illegal online mp3s. Writing for the *New York Times*, Jan Pareles lamented, "Now that 'Cop Killer' has been withdrawn, a new mechanism is in effect: if police groups don't like a song, they can make it disappear."[11]

The fallout surrounding Body Count's controversial song saturated the entire hip-hop nation—even though it was not a rap song.[12] Following Ice-T's decision to remove the song from his band's album, Pareles's concerns about a precedent for suppressing antipolice discourse in rap came to fruition. Eithne Quinn writes, "Violence against the authorities was expurgated from gangsta rhymes in the wake of the riots." Even established artists like Ice Cube began producing "funky beats and (in relative terms) less politicized themes" following "Cop Killer."[13] Christopher Sieving argues that the mainstream backlash and Ice-T's subsequent acquiescence "deracialized" the song, diluting its capacity for potent political critique. What might have represented a confluence of culture and politics that enabled critical reflection on the intersection between race and crime in America soon became a deluge of reactionary post-riot hysteria and election year politics that had a chilling effect on the production practices of rap artists and their record distributors. In other words, this heavy metal song helped solidify gangsta rap's status as a central bogeyman of mainstream deployments of the mark of criminality.[14]

While Ice-T's inflammatory recording provided politicians and law enforcement organizations with a scapegoat for rationalizing an ever-growing prison-industrial complex, the election of Arkansas governor Bill Clinton to the White House helped entrench a bipartisan consensus surrounding law-and-order politics. Although George Bush's policies and rhetoric associated with race and crime were unsurprising to most given the similar legacy of Republican politicians ranging from Goldwater to Reagan, Clinton pursued a remarkably similar course after unseating the incumbent Bush in the 1992 election. After three consecutive humiliating presidential electoral defeats, the Democratic Party began espousing a more conservative agenda. Prominent Democrats were particularly eager to recover from the devastation wrought by the Willie Horton ad, adopting a "tough on crime" rhetorical strategy that proved incredibly effective. For example, the Arkansas governor ceremoniously halted campaigning to preside over the execution of an intellectually disabled black man named Rickey Ray Rector who had been convicted of murdering a police officer. This public performance of vigilance helped dispute accusations that Clinton was "soft on crime." During his first term, Clinton signed the 1994 Omnibus Crime Control Act and the 1996 Anti-Terrorism and Effective Death Penalty Act. These twin legislative forces expanded the federal death penalty to sixty crimes, appropriated $10 billion for prison construction, allocated funds for hiring more police officers, and significantly curtailed death row appeals and habeas corpus claims. The early 1990s also saw the passage of "three-strikes" ordinances that mandated a life sentence for anyone convicted of three felonies.[15] Public opinion corresponded with such policies. For example, although national support for the death penalty steadily increased beginning in the late 1960s, it reached an all-time high of 80 percent during Clinton's first term in 1994.[16]

Rhetorical strategies similar to those of Reagan and Bush accompanied Clinton's "tough-on-crime" policies. In addition to emphasizing the importance of law and order, Clinton routinely blamed problems like poverty and crime on urban populations. He characterized these as matters of personal and community failure rather than consequences of neoliberal public policies. Clinton worked with a Republican Congress to enshrine such attitudes in domestic policy when he signed the 1996 Personal Responsibility and Work Opportunity Act, which placed significant limits on welfare eligibility. The bill's advocates predicated their support on the same caricatures of lazy, racialized welfare recipients that figured so significantly into deployments of the mark of criminality during the Reagan years.[17]

Adopting the conservative claim that the Los Angeles riots were largely a failure of "family values" rather than a collective response to institutional oppression, Clinton also joined the chorus of politicians attacking the hip-hop nation.[18] During a 1992 event hosted by Jesse Jackson's Rainbow Coalition, Clinton inaugurated what, in contemporary political argot, is now known as a "Sister Souljah moment," or an instance of public figures rhetorically distancing themselves from perceived extremists. Less than a month following the Los Angeles riots, the *Washington Post* profiled Souljah, a political rapper and activist. Describing the riots as a rebellion against white supremacy, the former Public Enemy member spoke in characteristically polemical terms: "I mean, if black people kill black people every day, why not have a week and kill white people? You understand what I'm saying? In other words, white people, this government and that mayor were well aware of the fact that black people were dying every day in Los Angeles under gang violence. So if you're a gang member and you would normally be killing somebody, why not kill a white person? Do you think that somebody thinks that white people are better, or above dying, when they would kill their own kind?"[19] While it should come as no surprise that the *Post* read Souljah's words as evidence that her solidarity with the rioters had "reached a chilling extreme," a close reading reveals she is attempting to make an argument about the value of black life in America.[20] In other words, when people of color kill each other, it is taken as the norm. If a white person, like trucker Reginald Denny, experiences violence at the hands of African Americans, it is cause for moral panic. The American public, in short, had stronger affective investments in white bodies than black ones.[21] Spying an opportunity to distance himself from the liberal legacies of Carter, Mondale, and Dukakis, Clinton read Souljah's words aloud at the Rainbow Coalition event. Noting she had spoken on a panel on that very stage the previous night, Clinton scolded the predominantly black crowd, stating that her remarks "were filled with the kind of hatred that you do not honor here tonight."[22] He added, "If you took the words 'white' and 'black' and reversed them, you might think [Louisiana politician and former Ku Klux Klan Grand Wizard] David Duke was giving that speech."[23] In Clinton's telling, Souljah was not only guilty of inciting violence but also embodied the worst excesses of "reverse racism," itself a popular trope among those who wished to dismantle affirmative action programs and other legacies of the civil rights movement.[24]

Clinton's words outraged many members of the African American community in general, and the hip-hop nation in particular. One contributor to the hip-hop magazine the *Source* said plainly that Clinton "fucked up royally when he dissed Sister Souljah."[25] For her part, Souljah demanded, but of course never received, a formal apology from the then governor. As James Bernard's opening epigraph reveals, many hip-hop journalists and other figures interpreted the candidate's speech as a naked attempt to court conservative white voters by appealing to their fears of black people in general and hip-hop in particular.[26] Journalist Kierna Mayo offered the following analysis: "To the white, liberal politician, the object of course, is to maintain the black vote without ruffling the feathers of too many white, conservative voters—nothing new."[27] Clinton, in other words, regarded his Sister Souljah moment as an opportunity to move his candidacy toward the political "center" by mobilizing the affective investments of primarily white voters who subscribed to the racialized logics of the war on crime, and simply take black votes for granted. After securing 83 percent of black votes on Election Day, such an assumption appeared to be validated. Even for black voters who were painfully aware of Clinton's similarities to Reagan and Bush, they regarded him as the lesser of two evils following twelve years of a Republican White House. Bernard opined as he began his sojourn with the Clinton campaign, "America may still be Amerikkka under the Democrats, but they will loosen the boot off our necks a bit. No matter who wins, I'm still going to be working toward a social revolution. But I'd rather do it under Clinton than Bush."[28]

"Wave the Muthafuckas Like You Just Don't Care": G-Funk and the Crimes of Black Leisure and Style

With Bill Clinton's 1993 inauguration, two key pieces were in place for the proliferation of the g-funk era. Following the backlash against and subsequent erasure of "Cop Killer," recording companies made violent lyrics directed toward symbols of state power a nonstarter for any ambitious rap artist. Rather, rappers increasingly revised the mark of criminality in ways that celebrated exclusively black-on-black violence, the objectification of black women's bodies, heavy drug and alcohol use, and materialism. The anger of "Fuck Tha Police" and "Cop Killer" was now directed inward toward other African Americans.[29] Simultaneously, the prison-industrial complex was as empowered as ever, as Clinton, other influential politicians, and numerous culture warriors deployed the mark of criminality in manners virtually identical to the strategies of Reagan and Bush before them. With the Los Angeles riots as their opening act, the 1990s were shrouded in ominous uncertainty for many black Americans.

This is not to suggest that the post-riot era was a dystopian disaster from its inception. Following the riots, California's largest gangs entered a short-lived truce. While South Central was still an impoverished urban sector, the gang peace movement helped create a palpable shift in the area's climate. However, while the truce sparked a dramatic and steady decline in gang-related deaths in Los Angeles and elsewhere, law enforcement persisted in targeting young people of color.[30] Police were suspicious of the truces, believing they were a ploy to collectively target officers. In a remarkable homology to the recording industry's capitulation to institutional panic following the release of "Cop Killer," law enforcement was deeply anxious about violence focused toward establishment targets, as opposed to other African Americans. In many cities, police began patrolling and breaking up intergang parties. Such gatherings, often enjoyed outdoors and over barbecued food, quickly became symbols of the fledgling peace movement. However, police departments viewed these assemblies of black, gang-affiliated bodies within the formal norms of the mark of criminality. They were ticking time bombs of violence and vice.[31]

Another part of the institutional response to the LA riots and the subsequent gang peace movement was significant changes in local criminal codes. Cities across the country passed racially lopsided curfew and "anticruising" (that is, driving around town in customized lowrider cars with no particular destination) ordinances that effectively criminalized the gathering of minority youth on city streets. Thus while the scapegoated youth of America's gangs began making gestures toward reconciliation outside the norms of mainstream American culture, law enforcement devised new mechanisms of containment. Chang writes, "During the 1980s there had been scattered anti-breakdancing ordinances and outbreaks of boom box citations. But what united the sweep laws of the '90s was a new logic of erasing youths—particularly youths of color—from public space. Not only were there to be no more boom boxes, sagging jeans, street dancing, or public displays of affection, there were to be *no more young people*. Youth itself was being criminalized."[32] Black communities have long reckoned with the infiltration of autonomous spaces by white power establishments. Leisure itself has served as a mode of transgression for African Americans on the plantation, under Jim Crow, and in other domains of white supremacy. Robin D. G. Kelley writes, "Hidden in homes, dance halls, and churches, embedded in expressive cultures, is where much of what is choked back at work or in white-dominated public space can find expression."[33] Such spaces of leisure allowed African Americans to temporarily step outside white supremacy's watchful eye and articulate their relationships to the social structures that governed their daily being and enact what Kelley calls "freedom dreams." Enactments of leisure, in other words, functioned as sites for the organization and expression of affect amid conditions that otherwise prohibited it.[34]

Law enforcement also, as Chang notes, targeted public expressions of black youth style during this period, including, as he noted, playing rap music on boom boxes, dancing, and wearing sagging jeans. Historically, deployments of style also figure significantly into expressions of black agency in the context of white supremacy. Barry Brummett argues that style is a system of signs and the grounds from which social and political life spring. While we draw on style to make claims about identity, style itself enables and constrains expressions of identity.[35] Dick Hebdige explains that the signs that compose style are often material objects that become symbolically rich expressions of culture.[36] For black Americans, style historically serves salient countercultural roles in the mobilization of affect. For example, Monica L. Miller reads black dandyism during and after slavery as an ambivalent site of black performance. She notes that while the high fashion attire of the dandy was initially a marker of enslavement, it also enabled what she calls "crimes of fashion," or acts of "racial and class cross-dressing" that functioned as critiques of contemporary race relations and enactments of black agency.[37] Similarly, Kelley argues that the emergence of the zoot suit among urban black youth during the 1940s was a stylized refusal of other modes of black performance, including crass caricatures of the ignorant southern migrant and the urban black bourgeoisie.[38] While such expressions of style were subject to appropriation and often served to entrench white supremacy and other modes of domination, they gesture toward the salient role of style in enabling the production of alternative black subjectivities. As I discuss subsequently, style factored significantly into the cultural politics of the g-funk era, as objects including car components, clothing, and name-brand liquor helped give form and expression to a post-riot South Central aesthetic that invited and commodified affective investments in the period's communal energies.[39] Furthermore, like other generations' expressions of style, g-funk's were subject to contestation and appropriation, figuring significantly into different and antagonistic deployments of the mark of criminality.

The lyrical and aesthetic components of g-funk gangsta rap embodied the leisure and style practices of many African American youths in South Central and other impoverished urban areas. In addition to portraying the social gatherings so feared by law enforcement in their music videos, artists like Dr. Dre and Snoop Dogg celebrated these practices in their lyrics and sonic arrangements.[40] G-funk was especially notable for its liberal sampling of the funk and neosoul recording catalogs, drawing heavily from the 1970s work of artists like Curtis Mayfield as well as George Clinton and his groups Parliament and Funkadelic. Clinton and his fellow travelers relied on keyboards and bass lines to produce what Nelson George calls a "raw black music aesthetic."[41] Coupled with the group's use of colorful, extravagant costumes and elaborate science-fiction-themed theatrics, 1970s funk was simultaneously playful, psychedelic, carnal, and utopian. In a decade dominated by vacuous disco and disco-inspired hits, funk moved bodies on the dance floor but also possessed a distinctly political underpinning of black joy. As he moved further from NWA, Dr. Dre began perfecting a production style that generated what Quinn describes as a hard/soft tension in gangsta rap. While a song's lyrics might contain themes ranging from leisurely abandon to misogynistic violence, its tonality was decidedly at ease with the world. G-funk was a sound to which one could dance in spite of the lyrics. If post-riot Los Angeles was the party, g-funk was the soundtrack.[42]

To be sure, violence was a major element of the g-funk equation. For example, on *The Chronic*'s ninth track, "Rat-Tat-Tat-Tat," Dr. Dre and Snoop Dogg boast, "Rat-tat-tat-tat like that, and I / Never hesitate to put a nigga on his back." Throughout

The Chronic and Snoop Dogg's solo debut, *Doggystyle*, both men adopt personas reminiscent of the most savage badmen like Stagger Lee and Dolomite. However, as Gussow reminds us in his reading of Mississippi Delta blues, espousing fantasies of black-on-black violence functions as a peculiar kind of agency. Similarly, we can regard the violence of g-funk as a displacement of communal anxieties about continued state violence, even if Dr. Dre, Snoop Dogg, and Death Row Records CEO Suge Knight were chiefly concerned with generating profits through the circulation of the mark of criminality. Embedded in these troubling and divisive narratives of black-on-black violence remained a founding impulse in the realities of white supremacy, if also music capital and masculinity.[43]

In addition to Dr. Dre and Snoop Dogg, influential g-funk artists included DJ Quik, Warren G, and Nate Dogg. However, Dr. Dre and Snoop Dogg were undeniably the most important artists in establishing g-funk's status as the most popular rap subgenre of the early 1990s. Whereas *The Chronic* perfected g-funk, *Doggystyle* became the best-selling debut album of the SoundScan era. Both albums, therefore, are exemplary of g-funk's circulation of the mark of criminality through the increasingly stigmatized leisure and style practices of black youth, as well as the shifting dynamics of musical commerce and the remarkably stable consensus surrounding law-and-order politics.[44]

The Chronic's Post-Riot Utopia

Obsessed as *Time* magazine is with chronicling human experience through lists, in 2010 *Time* identified the one hundred greatest albums since 1954. Sharing space with such classics as Miles Davis's *Kind of Blue*, the Beatles' *Sgt. Pepper's Lonely Hearts Club Band*, Aretha Franklin's *I Never Loved a Man the Way I Loved You*, Michael Jackson's *Thriller*, and Nirvana's *Nevermind* was *The Chronic*. Music critic Josh Tyrangiel writes, "Over grooves built from liberally sampled pieces of the Funkadelic catalog, Dre delivers his verses with hypnotically intimidating ease, so that 'Let Me Ride' and 'Nuthin' But a G Thang' feel like dusk on a wide-open L.A. boulevard, full of possibility and menace."[45] In addition to his near-perfect description of the g-funk aesthetic, Tyrangiel identifies two of *The Chronic*'s three singles: "Nuthin' But a G Thang," "Let Me Ride," and "Fuck wit' Dre Day." All three contain boastful lyrics about hip-hop virtuosity ("You never been on a ride like this befo' / With a producer who can rap and control the maestro / At the same time with the dope rhyme that I kick") and vitriol directed toward Eazy-E and Jerry Heller in the wake of Dr. Dre's departure from NWA ("Don't even respect your ass / That's why it's time for the Doctor to check your ass, nigga / Used to be my homey, used to be my ace / Now I wanna slap the taste out yo mouth / Nigga bow down to the Row").[46] Furthermore, as Dr.

Dre's insistence that Eazy-E "bow down to the Row" reveals, the album enacts his loyalty to Death Row Records. In "Nuthin' But a G Thang," for instance, he and Snoop Dogg declare, "Death Row is the label that paaaaays me."[47]

More than any other track on *The Chronic*, "Let Me Ride" embodies, in its lyrical, tonal, and visual components, the totality of g-funk's revision of the mark of criminality through the registers of leisure and style. The lyrics, penned by rapper RBX, chronicle a gangsta odyssey of a lone badman surviving in South Central's treacherous urban terrain. Dr. Dre, in this song's telling, is a prototypical "badman" or "crazy motherfucker" in the traditions of Stagger Lee, "Boyz-N-The-Hood," or "Straight Outta Compton." The liberal use of funk recording samples and the track's music video, on the other hand, function as celebratory enactments of post-riot leisure and style. Dr. Dre's violence is more restrained than that of his criminalized predecessors. It exists primarily as a potentiality, rather than an inevitability. The track opens with Dr. Dre rapping, "Creepin' down the street on D's / I got my Glock cocked, 'cause niggas want these." "D's" refer to designer tire rims popular on low-riding cars in the 1990s. While lowriders have their origin in East Los Angeles Latinx neighborhoods, such customized vehicles became symbols of status and leisure for people of color throughout Los Angeles County and other urban areas. They were also targets of proliferating "anticruising" ordinances.[48] Dr. Dre drives through South Central flaunting his material accumulation and stands ready to defend it with a cocked Glock against any and all who might envy his acquisition. He is at ease, but prepared to retaliate against "some nigga with a [semiautomatic] TEC-9, tryin' to take mine."[49]

But while violence is a possibility in Dr. Dre's Compton cityscape, he would prefer to remain "rollin' in my 6-4," or souped-up 1964 Chevy Impala. As he declares to his imagined female passengers, "Bitches relax, while I get my proper swerve on."[50] To those who might "Try to set me up for a 211," or felonious robbery, he asks, "Why don't you let me roll on?"[51] Dr. Dre is, therefore, willing to "put a nigga on his back," but is far more inclined toward the leisurely joys of post-riot Los Angeles.[52] In the track's second verse, he raps, "Gotta get the chronic / The Remy Martin and my soda pop," indicating that violence would only interrupt his desire to smoke some high quality marijuana and sip on cognac and soda while behind the wheel of his designer car. An evening of inebriated cruising through the streets of South Central is ideal because Dr. Dre "don't represent no gangbang."[53] Dr. Dre is, therefore, enacting the mark of criminality in two respects. First, the legacy of the black badman remains a distinct possibility in "Let Me Ride," as it does throughout *The Chronic*. This central theme of black criminality is less abandoned than it is subordinated to Dr. Dre's desire to roll through the streets of Compton in his lowrider while conspicuously consuming name-brand liquor. Such desires compose the second elements of criminality at play here: leisure and style. At the very moment *The Chronic* and its singles are

Figure 6: Dr. Dre rolling in his 6-4. "Let Me Ride" music video. Death Row Records, 1994.

selling in the millions, making Dr. Dre, Suge Knight, and Snoop Doggy Dogg millionaires, Los Angeles police and their counterparts across the country are making it increasingly difficult for always and already criminalized young people of color to enjoy and express themselves. Whereas mainstream discourses situated these leisure practices in affective registers of racialized fear, g-funk posited partying and cruising as expressions of bravado and joy.

The music video for "Let Me Ride" also functions as a celebration of South Central Los Angeles truce-era leisure. The vast majority of the video portrays Dr. Dre cruising through South Central in his "6-4." The former NWA member sits reclined behind the wheel, rarely steering with more than one hand. He is in complete control of his stylish machine and maintains that control effortlessly, even when riding the vehicle through empty parking lots on only its two driver-side wheels. Thus in addition to being a rap and DJ virtuoso who deploys "hyped ass lyrics and dope beats," Dr. Dre is a master of the lowrider. The camera also pays homage to the machinery itself, frequently zooming in on expensive tire rims and elaborate engines. It invites us to behold the lowrider in all its stylish glory.[54]

During the "Let Me Ride" video, when he is not "rollin' in my 6-4" in South Central and attracting the adoration of young women, Dr. Dre raps directly to the camera.[55] In the single most consistent characteristic of videos from Dr. Dre,

Snoop Dogg, and other g-funk artists of the early 1990s, such direct address occurs almost entirely amid other black bodies dancing at parties. Whether consuming copious amounts of alcohol and marijuana at indoor house parties or enjoying the open South Central air in a park or parking lot, the extras of "Let Me Ride" and other videos engage in the kinds of assemblies that the LAPD and other law enforcement entities disrupted with increasing regularity during the post-riot and truce era. Thus while Dr. Dre raps in the most individualistic terms about virtuosity, virility, and violence, this track's visual accompaniment suggests an investment in the communal hopefulness and joy of the gang peace movement. While he may be in charge of the party, Dr. Dre is nonetheless flanked by fellow black bodies whose desire to gather openly and, largely, peacefully was coded as criminal by the upper echelons of law and order. Images of assembled black bodies were, therefore, a key element of g-funk's revisions of the mark of criminality.[56]

When we account for the heavy use of funk and postsoul samples on the track, the communal desire on display in "Let Me Ride" becomes more complex. Four songs factor significantly in Dr. Dre's production: Bill Withers's "Kissing My Love," James Brown's "Funky Drummer," Parliament's "Mothership Connection," and a live recording of their "Swing Down, Sweet Chariot." The mixture of an earlier generation's soul, rhythm and blues, and funk standards creates a smooth aesthetic of drumbeats, bass lines, horns, and keyboards. Whereas it complements the boastful and celebratory content of the "Let Me Ride" music video, Dr. Dre's trademark tonality has a more ambivalent relationship to the song's lyrics. Whether Dr. Dre raps about his willingness to violently dispense with his foes or his desire to simply carry on riding through the streets of South Central, the assemblage of samples invokes an atmosphere of ease—likely induced by copious alcohol and marijuana consumption.

Dr. Dre's reliance on two classic Parliament recordings is particularly notable. George Clinton's germinal funk group was most active in the United States during the 1970s. In addition to having a penchant for psychedelic neosoul aesthetics and elaborate stage theatrics, Parliament structured much of their work around a "mothership" theme. Their live shows concluded with the landing of the intergalactic ark "designed to take all the party people to a better place."[57] Kelley situates the mothership in a broader Exodus narrative he argues is ubiquitous in black expressive traditions. Along with slave maroon societies, appropriations of Old Testament theology, and pan-African currents in antiracist struggle, Parliament's mothership expressed "the desire to leave the place of oppression for either a new land or some kind of peaceful coexistence."[58] This theme persisted across George Clinton's funk catalog, and it was especially pronounced in the two tracks Dr. Dre chose for "Let Me Ride." Both "Mothership Connection" and "Swing Down, Sweet Chariot" possess distinctly messianic characteristics.

Drawing from old slave spirituals that spoke expectantly of spiritual and corporeal deliverance from the horrors of the plantation, the combined samples provide the lyrical chorus of "Let Me Ride": "Swing down, sweet chariot, stop, and / Let me ride." For the slaves who uttered these words in the fields, they expressed a yearning for rescue. For Parliament, such Exodus-inspired imagery corresponded extremely well with the mothership narrative and their overarching theme of Afrocentric science fiction. For Dr. Dre, the request "let me ride" likely represented nothing more than a clever lyric for a song about customized cars. However, tethered as it was to the broader arc of black vernacular traditions of deliverance, as well as the quotidian practices of black youth in South Central and other urban areas, this sonic element of "Let Me Ride" imbues the track with a utopian undercurrent that lingers across the historical trajectory of black expressive and leisurely traditions.

"Let Me Ride" functions as an anthem of g-funk abandon and, more broadly, the politics of leisure, style, and criminality following the Los Angeles riots. At a time when police departments in several predominantly African American urban locales were doubling down on their surveillance of black youth, Dr. Dre and his g-funk contemporaries deployed celebratory rhymes describing those very practices. The gathering of black bodies at this time was, therefore, polysemic: provoking fear and suspicion from law enforcement and much of civil society while providing those very bodies with a joyful respite from the violence of the market, the state, and the gangs. Whereas the parties of South Central were largely earnest attempts at community resuscitation in the wake of the 1992 riots, the artists and staff of Death Row Records were chiefly interested in transforming such practices, as well as a continued appetite among black and white listeners for hyperviolence and misogyny, into exorbitant profits.[59] Nonetheless, g-funk's mixture of historical shifts in youth practices, a changing hip-hop market, and a distinct convergence of sonic, visual, and lyrical invention made for a highly complex regime of meaning. While certainly guilty of deploying the mark of criminality in ways that reinforced long-standing stereotypes of black men's relationships to violence, consumption, and misogyny, Dr. Dre's "Let Me Ride" and others in the g-funk catalog also adapted the genre in ways that situated black leisure and style in a broader sonic historical arc of yearning and community.

Doggystyle: Race, Space, and Violence in the Post-Riot Era

In addition to declaring Dr. Dre's independence from Eazy-E and Jerry Heller, *The Chronic* introduced the hip-hop nation to Snoop Doggy Dogg. The young Long Beach native's impeccable flow and lackadaisical drawl created an alluring badman aesthetic perfectly suited for g-funk. Snoop Dogg was, to be sure, a virtuoso capable of uttering "dope rhymes," but he did so in a way that made it sound entirely effortless. He, like Dr. Dre, was simultaneously in control and just didn't give a damn.

Doggystyle strayed little from the g-funk formula. Tracks like "Gin and Juice" and "Doggy Dogg World" espoused celebratory lyrics about South Central leisure and carnal practices. Snoop Dogg raps in the opening of "Gin and Juice": "With so much drama in the L-B-C [Long Beach, California] / It's kinda hard bein' Snoop D-O-double-G / But I, somehow, some way / Keep comin' up with funky ass shit like every single day / May I, kick a little something for the G's (yeah) / And, make a few ends as (yeah!) I breeze, through / Two in the mornin' and the party's still jumpin' / 'Cause my momma ain't home." In addition to asserting his leisurely independence from an older generation, Snoop Dogg proclaims his uncanny capacity to produce lyrical "funky ass shit." He makes a similar proclamation in the song's second verse, stating, "Everything is fine when you listenin' to the D-O-G / I got the cultivating music that be captivating he / Who listens / To the words that I speak." Snoop Dogg, in his own estimation, holds the capacity to bring tranquility with his every utterance. While there was no shortage of "drama" in 1993 Long Beach, Snoop Dogg simply desired to refine his lyrical form and enjoy the party. The track's sung chorus gleefully declares, "Rollin' down the street, smokin' indo, sippin' on gin and juice / Laaaaid back (with my mind on my money and my money on my mind)."[60] He is, as one of this chapter's epigraphs asserts, trying to help his people "party their way through their problems."[61]

Of course, Snoop Dogg also has his mind on his money and his money on his mind. Thus, like his collaborator Dr. Dre, the Long Beach rapper is prepared to retaliate against those who might threaten his supremacy on the streets of South Central. For example, in the album's first single, "Who Am I (What's My Name)?," he and Dr. Dre briefly reprise the incendiary *Chronic* track, "Rat-Tat-Tat-Tat," and remind listeners that they "never hesitate to put a nigga on his back."[62] Additionally, the track "Serial Killa" is a full-throttled boast of violent potential. Following verses from guest rappers RBX and Daz Dillinger, Snoop Dogg warns his anonymous adversary, "Now break yourself motherfucker, 'fore you make me / Take this 211 to another level." Recalling that a "211" signifies felonious robbery under the California penal code, "another level" would likely be a more violent offense, like a "187," or homicide.[63] Dre's use of a sustained, synthesizer-simulated flute note from the Ohio Players' funk track "Funky Worm" throughout the track adds credibility to Snoop Dogg's dire warnings by creating a haunting, ominous, almost occult aesthetic.

While it appeared tenth on the full *Doggystyle* album, Death Row records released "Who Am I (What's My Name)?" as Snoop Dogg's first single. To this day, it remains the artist's best-selling track.[64] As its title and chorus of women adoringly singing "Snoop Doggy Dooooog" to the tune of George Clinton's "Atomic

Figure 7: Waving the motherfuckers like they just don't care. "Who Am I (What's My Name)?" music video. Death Row Records, 1993.

Dog" demonstrates, the song functions as a post-*Chronic* unveiling for the talented rapper making his solo debut. Sampled over several intertwined funk classics, "Who Am I (What's My Name)?" is unabashedly joyful in its tonality. Its production is designed to move bodies on the dance floor, for its heavy break beats and funky synthesizers create a sonorous envelope of g-funk abandon. Lyrically, the track establishes Snoop Dogg's supremacy as the newest act on the hip-hop scene. He boasts, "Like I said, niggas can't FUCK with this / And niggas can't FUCK with that / Shit that I drop cuz ya know I don't stop," briefly elevating his pitch with each uttered "FUCK." Later in the song, he encourages listeners, "Now just throw your hands in the motherfuckin' air / And wave the motherfuckers like ya just don't care."[65] Delivered atop a Long Beach record store in the single's music video, Snoop Dogg compels the assembled black masses on the street to do precisely that. Indeed, waving one's hands in "the motherfuckin' air" and waving "the motherfuckers like ya just don't care" is the g-funk gesture par excellence. Delivering the line like a gangsta televangelist, he compels his flock to surrender their bodies to the leisurely excesses of post-riot South Central. While dangers still linger in the shadows, this new enactment of the mark of criminality occurs primarily at the party. Snoop Dogg partakes in g-funk's new version of black criminality by reveling in the very communal practices that were at this time a chief target of law enforcement. His is a largely affirmative and celebratory deployment of the mark of criminality.

However, in a remarkable, and possibly unintentional, sleight of hand, Snoop Dogg manages to refashion another generation of rappers' contempt for law enforcement within the constraints of the post-"Cop Killer" rap industry. The music video narrative of "Who Am I (What's My Name)?" contains a strong homology to an earlier and highly influential gangsta rap video. Much of the video portrays Snoop Dogg and his posse, the Dogg Pound, who morph back and forth from human to Doberman pinscher, being pursued by dog catchers. The dynamic is unmistakably similar to NWA's "Straight Outta Compton," in which LAPD officers pursue the young black men through the streets of Compton. However, in the g-funk era, explicit references to literal police are relatively absent in popular tracks and videos, replaced here by bumbling comedic men with nets attempting to quash the Dogg Pound's party (precisely as the LAPD and other law enforcement entities across the nation were attempting to do with black youth in the post-riot era). However, by the end of the video, even the dog catchers have joined the festivities, dancing along with a young black crowd embodying g-funk leisure. At least in this episode, Snoop Dogg has succeeded in helping his people party their way through their problems.

At a time when dominant deployments of the mark of criminality equated black leisure and style with violence or drug dealing, Snoop Dogg, like Dr. Dre, fashioned a new gangsta ethos around the commercial and political constraints of the early 1990s. NWA's deployment of the mark of criminality operated chiefly at the nexus of violence and space, but the g-funk era saw a heavier emphasis on the communal yearnings being enacted by post-riot black youth. However, while *The Chronic* and *Doggystyle* helped elevate the hip-hop nation to music industry dominance, not all observers were eager to attend the party. On the contrary, g-funk was the object of an intense generational conflict that noted important limitations of gangsta's deployments of the mark of criminality but also empowered those invested in expanding the prison-industrial complex to continue circulating equally intoxicating, if also more damaging, rhetorics of black criminality.

G-Funk and the Culture War

Hip-hop came of age in an era of neoliberalism that, in addition to empowering financiers and other capitalists, provided significant political space for cultural conservatism. Following the 1973 *Roe v. Wade* decision, in which the US Supreme Court struck down state bans on abortion, members of the religious right began organizing in earnest around so-called moral issues. Seeking new ways to prevent abortion and combating perceived encroachments on "traditional" family structures, many conservative groups in the 1980s and 1990s also fixated on music as a potential threat to public decency. Groups like the Parents Music Resource Center (PMRC) and American Family Association (AFA) represented a concerted bipartisan push against "obscene" lyrics primarily in heavy metal and rap music. In the judgement of antiobscenity-movement leaders such as Tipper Gore and Florida lawyer Jack Thompson, recording artists including the Dead Kennedys, Guns N' Roses, and Ice-T threatened the cultural foundations of society by trading in sexual degradation, racial invective, and hyperviolent fantasy. In one of its most important victories, the PMRC successfully pressured the recording industry to begin adorning potentially offensive albums with now-ubiquitous "Parental Advisory" stickers.[66]

In 1990, a Broward County judge deemed Florida rap group 2 Live Crew's album *As Nasty As They Wanna Be* obscene. While a federal court overruled the decision, it nonetheless made the hip-hop nation a key battleground in the culture wars. Given its liberal use of violent and sexual imagery, gangsta rap was a particularly popular target for the late twentieth century's purveyors of good taste. Artists like NWA and Ice-T, of course, sustained various attacks for their antipolice content, but g-funk represented a new phase in the hip-hop culture wars by attracting the elevated ire of other African Americans. While many elders of the black community (that is, members of the civil rights generation) had always had an ambivalent relationship to the genre, the work of Dr. Dre, Snoop Doggy Dogg, and their contemporaries inflamed new passions that coincided with and ultimately helped sustain the prevailing iterations of the mark of criminality in American public culture.[67]

By virtue of its use of sampling from the soul, funk, reggae, and other black vernacular music catalogs, as well as its emergence in postindustrial cityscapes like New York and Los Angeles, hip-hop has long had a complicated generational politics embedded in its DNA. Following the deindustrialization of urban spaces in the 1970s and 1980s, many members of the black middle class left cities for the suburbs, whereas poor and working-class blacks, with fewer opportunities for mobility, remained. Mark Anthony Neal argues that such intradiasporic shifts resulted in major cultural and generational divisions. Specifically, he claims that members of the black middle class interpreted narratives of urban black youth, often expressed through hip-hop, "as the products of individuals who lack the civility and determination that befit their middle class sensibilities."[68] An older and more economically privileged generation came to regard young black people in impoverished urban areas as an embarrassing archetype of blackness, similar to the "old Negro" of the agrarian South that the Harlem Renaissance of the early twentieth century sought to supplant. In other words, the group that Neal calls the black middle class possessed strong affective investments in a vision of blackness that was rooted in an ethics of upward mobility and respectability. The ghettocentric aesthetics of hip-hop, especially gangsta rap's deployments of the mark of criminality, offended such sensibilities. The affect that emerged from this generational encounter helped turn gangsta rap into a cultural site of struggle over the very meaning of blackness in the United States.[69]

Neal laments that such interpretations of black youth culture foreclosed on opportunities for critical engagement stemming from shared nostalgic investments in the soul aesthetics of the 1960s and 1970s.[70] G-funk was especially salient in this regard because it drew on an earlier generation's music of freedom dreams (that is, the work of Parliament/Funkadelic and others) while rapping lyrics that many older listeners found unacceptable. Rose describes this phenomenon as the "manipulation of the funk," given the convergence of aesthetically pleasing beats with offensive lyrics.[71] For their part, g-funk artists expressed an ambivalent relationship with their elders. In the video for the *Doggystyle* track "Doggy Dogg World," directors Dr. Dre and Ricky Harris construct a nostalgic homage to 1960s and 1970s black popular culture by casting figures like the soul group the Dramatics, blaxploitation stars Fred Williamson and Pam Grier, and Fred "Rerun" Berry of television's *What's Happening!!*. Snoop Dogg, Dr. Dre, and other contemporary stars of g-funk also donned period-specific attire, such as zoot suits. By incorporating earlier generations' deployments of the mark of criminality, particularly through its references to 1970s blaxploitation cinema, the video posits a historical continuity across vernacular rhetorics of criminality. The song's lyrics, however, are unmistakably g-funk, including boasting ("It's like everywhere I look, and everywhere I go / I'm hearin' motherfuckers tryin' to steal my flow") and misogyny ("Well if you give me ten bitches then I'll fuck all ten") built around the chorus "It's a crazy mixed up world, it's a Doggy Dogg World / It's a Doggy Dogg World, it's a Doggy Dogg World / The Dogg's World" sung by a female vocalist. Thus by placing himself within the commonplaces of an earlier cultural terrain of black sexuality, criminality, and artistry, Snoop Dogg performs the tensions inherent to the g-funk era and hip-hop in general: invoking the cultural artifacts of old to construct a new vernacular landscape. This dialectic of familiarity and sheer terror defined many of the tensions associated with the mainstream response to g-funk.[72]

The first prominent African American figure to wage a bold and public battle against all things gangsta was Rev. Calvin Butts of the Abyssinian Baptist Church in Harlem. In 1993, Butts threatened to drive a steamroller over piles of gangsta rap CDs to protest the genre he believed was denigrating the spiritual and political legacy of black culture. Drawing an unambiguous parallel between gangsta and institutional racism of old, Butts declared, "If you use money to justify what you're doing, you're just like the white man who sold you into slavery."[73] In other words, those who commodified and profited from the mark of criminality were complicit in a sinister cycle of exploitation and oppression dating back to the Middle Passage. Elsewhere, Butts opined, "Most of the rappers come out of the black community, and they are prostituting an art form. They're trying to pass off as culture something that is antithetical to what our culture represents."[74] Butts imagined himself as a legitimate representative of African American (that is, "our") culture—a veteran of the civil rights era and a patriarch of the black church—while denigrating the gangsta rapper as an unrepentant prodigal son who has departed the community just as he distorts and exploits its cultural heritage. Inherent to Butts's commentary is a fundamental antagonism regarding what it means to be black in the United States. He and others who shared his sentiments were committed to a legacy of black affective investments that emphasized respectability, the church, and middle-class aspirations. Gangsta rap, on the other hand, mobilized affect through its celebratory deployments of the mark of criminality. Dr. Dre undoubtedly helped validate this perceived antagonism when he rapped in "Let Me Ride," "No medallions, dreadlocks, or Black fists / It's just that / Gangster glare / With gangster raps / That gangster shit / Makes a gang of snaps." Not only was Dr. Dre too busy cruising through South Central to be bothered by violence, but also he had no interest in an earlier generation's lofty political projects.[75]

Following Butts's lead was the National Political Congress of Black Women, which was formed in 1984 to promote "the political and economic empowerment of African American women and their families."[76] The group's founder, C. Delores Tucker, was an activist from the civil rights era who marched with King in Selma and was an ally of Jesse Jackson. After a series of unsuccessful turns at mainstream politics, Tucker faded into obscurity until 1993 when the brewing controversy surrounding gangsta rap provided a new opportunity for intervention.[77] One of her early successes was persuading Time Warner to sell all of its gangsta rap interests.[78] Routinely invoking the popular memory of the civil rights movement, Tucker insisted, "Our nation cannot be whole if we permit the continuation of an art form that teaches children that rape, hate, and disrespect are OK, and threatens the safety of our communities."[79] Tucker was particularly committed to confronting gangsta's misogynistic tendencies, commenting before a special congressional hearing on music lyrics and interstate commerce,

> I come to you in the spirit of Dr. King, and on behalf of millions of African American women, women who should not be seen as objects of disdain but rather as grandmothers, mothers, sisters, aunts and daughters who demand respect. And who demand that the human decency and dignity that is defended and protected for other members of American society should not be so freely compromised in our case. Yes, images that degrade our dignity and insult our children and families concern us too, as any other self-respecting member of society. Even if it comes out of our own mouths, the gangsta rap and misogynist lyrics that glorify violence and denigrate women is nothing more than pornographic smut! And with the release of Snoop Doggy Dogg's debut album "Doggystyle," that includes the graphic artwork that is sold with it.[80]

The artwork Tucker described appears on *Doggystyle*'s CD cover and liner notes. The front cover portrays Snoop Dogg in his comic book canine persona, sitting atop a doghouse and wearing a flannel shirt and blue jeans. With a sparkle

Figure 8: *Doggystyle* album cover. Death Row Records, 1993.

in his eye, he reaches down for the "tail" of a female dog—or "bitch"—whose head is hidden inside the doghouse, but her bottom is in full sight. A more detailed story unfolds inside the CD booklet. Snoop orders his canine girlfriend to find him some potent marijuana, declaring "Beeitch, if you ain't got no kinda chronic, yo' punk ass gots to go." Outside of her capacity to provide the "goods," this woman is of no use to Snoop Dogg. After he and a fellow member of the Dogg Pound (also a literal dog in this visual narrative, who is assaulted by police officers on his way to the "doghouse") realize that the weed the woman has provided is mere "hocus pocus," which a footnote describes as "stress weed bullshit," they quite literally kick her out of the doghouse with the injunction, "Bitch, & take dis bag of bull shit wit' you! Bitch dis is da Dogg Pound ho!" Any woman that does not correspond with the leisurely ethos of *Doggystyle*, we learn before hearing a single note, is unwelcome. She is a mere "ho."[81]

Tracks like "Bitches Ain't Shit" from *The Chronic* and *Doggystyle*'s "Gin and Juice" also provide ample evidence for Tucker's concerns about the objectification of black women's bodies. Describing a party scene in "Gin and Juice," Snoop Dogg raps, "I got bitches in the living room getting' it on / And, they ain't leavin' til six in the mornin (six in the mornin') / So what you wanna do, sheeeit / I got a pocket full of rubbers and my homeboys do too / So turn off the lights and close the doors / But (but what) we don't love them hoes, yeah! / So we gonna smoke a ounce to this / G's up, hoes down, while you motherfuckers bounce to this."[82] The mantra "g's up, hoes down" captures the role of gender in the g-funk era. Women's bodies, like marijuana and gin, are objects of enjoyment. Furthermore, such exaltations of black masculinity continued the legacy of other deployments of the mark of criminality by tethering blackness to dominant male hypersexuality. The mythically insatiable sexual appetite of the black male inspired white fears through dominant iterations of the mark of criminality, and g-funk artists like Snoop Dogg refigured it as a resource for celebratory boasting. For Tucker and her allies, such imagery had downright dystopian ramifications: "Because this pornographic smut is in the hands of our children, it coerces, influences, encourages and motivates our youth to commit violent behavior—to use drugs and abuse women through demeaning sex acts. The reality of the 90's is that the greatest fear in the African American community does not come from earthquakes, floods or fires, but from violence. The kind of violence that has already transformed our communities and schools into war zones, where children are dodging bullets instead of balls and planning their own funerals."[83] Tucker's descriptions of black life stand in stark contrast to g-funk's portrait of a no doubt violent but ultimately joyful cityscape of parties, consumption, and sexuality. Just like Reverend Butts, Tucker invoked a pious fantasy of the civil rights era, assuming an emancipatory posture that demands the hard-won "human decency and dignity" that survived fire hoses, police dogs, and assassinations during the 1960s. As a writer for the *Atlanta Journal-Constitution* wrote in 1993, "After years of fighting for an accurate image of black people, it's hard for the civil rights generation to see a new generation proudly embracing the stereotypes—and making big money of it."[84] One generation fashioned the mark of criminality as a cultural burden and g-funk revised it into something to be embraced, packaged, and sold.

Tucker and Butts were not alone in their crusade to rescue black youth from all things gangsta. For example, Jesse Jackson commented in *Newsweek*'s cover story on gangsta's "culture of violence," "We're going to take away the market value of these attacks on our person. Anyone white or black who makes money calling our women bitches and our people niggers will have to face the wrath of our indignation."[85] In her testimony before a Senate committee on violence and popular music, African American senator Carol Moseley Braun offered her summary of the contestation over gangsta: "Obviously, the issue here today involves much more than just the right of the artists to create and perform music of violence and hate if they choose. What is also at issue is whether the music industry that makes so much money from these lyrics has any responsibility for the type of music it promotes and disseminates. Should the question of whether or not an album sells be the only issue that concerns the industry? Or, do those involved in the creation, performance, promotion, production and distribution of these lyrics have any responsibility to all of our children, to all of our families, and to all of our communities?"[86] Consistently, critics like Tucker, Jackson, and Braun invoked the rhetoric of civil rights while directing much of their contempt not toward the gangsta rap artists themselves, but at the record companies and distributors who profited from their cultural labor. Their efforts were, in some ways, quite successful. As g-funk evolved into a potent cultural commodity, many radio stations—several of them black-owned—refused to play Dr. Dre or Snoop Dogg's songs. The emergence of g-funk came to represent a generational battle over the mobilization of black affect toward middle-class sensibilities on one hand and criminalized leisure and style on the other.[87]

A campaign waged solely on challenging a predominantly white-owned profit-making entertainment machine invested in the commodification of the mark of criminality is, in many ways, a noble, even radical endeavor. Indeed, Butts's and Tucker's experiential affective relationships to the civil rights movement are often resonant and quite moving in their espoused investment in the fate of African American youth. However, this generational backlash against gangsta rap was not solely interested in sustaining the dream of Martin Luther King Jr. For example, a 1994 issue of *Newsweek* describes Jesse Jackson's political tone at the time: "Jackson sees no choice but to focus on the black community itself. . . . He rebuked Chicago blacks who are championing the release of a convicted—but supposedly 'reformed'—gang leader. Jackson won't object to spending more on prisons. He won't rule out a voluntary program to use the implantable contraceptive Norplant to prevent teen pregnancies. To stop the murder, he says, blacks must undergo a 'social-values revolution.' Students must report drug and gun users. Families must lay down rules. Cops must be on the beat in the schools."[88] The article also noted Jackson's then-recent admission that he feared being followed down the street at night by a black person. A man traditionally associated with speaking to power on behalf of the African American community now focused inward, advocating policies such as increased policing and drug law enforcement that would strengthen the prison-industrial complex. Testifying before the Senate, Tucker warned, "Being coaxed by gangster rap, [black youth] will trigger a crime wave of epidemic proportions that we have never seen the likes of. Regardless of the number of jails built, it will not be enough."[89] Tucker, in effect, appeals to the prevailing fears of ravenous black youth that structured dominant deployments of the mark of criminality at the time.

The ambivalences of Tucker's and Jackson's rhetoric become acutely apparent considering the strange bedfellows they attracted. For example, Tucker became a close ally of William Bennett, who, as drug czar for the Bush administration, was a chief architect of the very policies that placed so many black youths in prison at the time.[90] Jeff Chang comments, "As the [1996] presidential season rolled around, [Tucker] joined with Republican candidate Bob Dole. Together, Bennett, Dole, and Tucker made Suge Knight, Death Row Records and Snoop Dogg into clay pigeons for their culture war." He adds, "Tucker was enormously helpful to white cultural conservatives," because she "insulated white cult-cons from criticism" with her soaring references to Martin Luther King Jr. and Rosa Parks.[91] Furthermore, Rose notes that white conservative critiques of gangsta's misogynistic content are themselves structured within a problematic racialized fantasy of the nuclear family that sustains women's oppression and ignores misogyny in white cultural spaces. She adds, "the disrespect shown to black women by some black men is, for [cultural conservatives], a sign of insubordinate black masculinity and thus needs correction and containment."[92]

Indeed, the mark of criminality is highly gendered and, as we've discovered previously, black vernacular traditions have deployed masculinity in fraught ways well before the advent of gangsta rap. Difficult as such content may be to embrace, and I am advocating no such thing, a careful encounter with it reveals that a wholesale disavowal of such work is equally problematic. In other words, Tucker and her allies waged a battle against gangsta rap by refashioning the mark of criminality in ways that, while espousing an investment in saving young people of color from themselves, also construed black bodies and communities as pathological threats to the social order, or as the type of people one would fear encountering on a dark street. While g-funk certainly led young black listeners on a dangerous journey of criminalized leisure, Tucker et al.'s co-opted allusions to an earlier era had significant limitations of their own.

G-Funk and the Politics of Listening

At the same Senate hearing where C. Delores Tucker waged war on gangsta rap in the name of Martin Luther King Jr. and his civil rights legacy, black California congresswoman Maxine Waters struck a different tone: "These are my children. Indeed, they are your children, too. They have invented a new art form to describe their pains and fears and anger with us as adults. I do not intend to marginalize them or demean them. Rather, I take responsibility for trying to understand what they are saying. I want to embrace them and transform them."[93] Waters encouraged the Senate committee to assume a hospitable posture toward this strange new music. She wanted them to recognize that "they are your children, too." To the extent that she advocates, just as this book does, a measure of nuance when engaging the difficult terrain of gangsta rap, she is decidedly correct. However, the children of South Central and other urban areas whose minority residents languished under the forces of capital flight, austerity, and mass incarceration were not the concern of the US Senate in 1994 nor, it seemed, most other participants in federal, state, and local governance at the time. It was, rather, the piety of Tucker and her allies that corresponded best with the prevailing deployments of the mark of criminality in a political climate that thrived on cultivating fear among a predominantly white and middle-class constituency who would, in turn, entrust elected leaders with unprecedented powers to surveil, contain, and even end black life. These were not their children.

If g-funk was not going to awaken elected officials to the struggles of black inner-city life during the early 1990s, it stood a chance of exalting the criminalized joys of life in such neighborhoods for those who cruised down its streets. Whereas early gangsta rappers like NWA enacted the mark of criminality in fairly straightforward ways by assuming the hypermasculine posture of the "crazy motherfucker," g-funk artists performed criminality in a manner that was deeply faithful to the exigencies of American racial politics in the early 1990s. G-funk was uniquely suited to the increasingly criminalized leisure and style practices of poor and working-class African American youth. These young people, in effect, had been deemed illegal in numerous municipalities, especially in Los Angeles County. The very act of assembling in large groups to partake in leisure activities and enact modes of vernacular style was a cause for suspicion and frequent infiltration. Waters would have us view gangsta rap as a straightforward commentary on the horrors of racism, crime, and poverty at the close of the twentieth century, but a contextualization of g-funk in the post-riot 1990s suggests a more celebratory project. Just as marooning during slavery and juke joints under Jim Crow offered autonomous spaces for cultivating community where it was otherwise forbidden, g-funk expressed the affective bonds of criminalized black youth through a bricolage of lyrical bravado, visual representations of leisure and style, and sonic appropriations of earlier generations' utopian dreams.

G-funk's celebration however, was deeply fraught with the limitations of misogyny and violence, as well as the changing contours of hip-hop commerce. First, while Tucker and other crusaders against gangsta rap stand rightfully accused of forming alliances with those whose deployments of the mark of criminality were helping justify the mass incarceration of unprecedented numbers of black men, their critiques of g-funk's content had considerable merit. A mere glance at the album artwork for *Doggystyle* is enough for anyone remotely invested in the principles of feminism to take issue with its denigration of the female body. While numerous black feminist scholars have challenged critics of misogyny in hip-hop and other modes of African American expression for partaking in an attack on black masculinity that ultimately supports white supremacy, they have also refused to ignore what Tricia Rose calls the "gangsta-pimp-ho" trinity.[94] In other words, one can, indeed must, engage in vigorous critiques of lyrics and images that debase women. Doing so in a way that resists the circuitries of white supremacy and the logics of neoliberalism that underwrite hegemonic deployments of the mark of criminality requires an analysis that is thoroughly intersectional and contextual. Understanding the ambivalent era called g-funk as an expression of twentieth-century law-and-order politics is one valuable way to arrive at such a critique.[95]

In addition to its gender trouble, the g-funk era also signaled major changes in the hip-hop nation. With the release and staggering success of *Doggystyle*, Death Row Records became the most successful and influential hip-hop label in the country. Alongside pioneers like Russell Simmons and Andre Harrell, as well as contemporaries (and bitter rivals) like Sean "Puff Daddy" Combs, Death Row CEO Suge Knight embodied the growing role of black entrepreneurship in the hip-hop nation. While this was a welcome development in a music industry accustomed to extracting surplus value from black cultural labor to generate profits for white producers, it also came at important costs. Knight, in particular, had a reputation as a ruthless businessman with strong gang ties. His penchant for feuds and sensationalism helped push the criminalized content of gangsta rap far beyond the recording studio, and into the lived realities of the artists and their fans. Enactments of the mark of criminality came to encompass hip-hop commerce itself. Few rappers embodied these shifting industry dynamics more than Tupac Amaru Shakur.[96]

4

The Politics, Commerce, and Rage of "Thug Life"

It is a central moral contention of Christianity that God may be disguised in the clothing—maybe even the rap—of society's most despised members.

—Michael Eric Dyson

I ain't a killer, but don't push me.

—Tupac Shakur

I knew you was conflicted / Misusing your influence.

—Kendrick Lamar

Two months before Death Row Records released *Doggystyle*, the *Source* published cultural critic dream hampton's interview with Snoop Doggy Dogg. The article's first page features a large photograph of the ascendant rapper staring menacingly at the camera and gripping a silver pistol. He was, like his Death Row brethren, enacting the mark of criminality to bolster his credibility as a viable gangsta artist. However, the interview also imbues Snoop Dogg's relationship to the cultural and political economy of crime in the late 1990s with considerably more authenticity than many of his other popular gangsta counterparts. As hampton recounted her drive around South Central with Snoop Dogg, she wrote, "At a stop sign a young brotha waiting for a bus recognized Snoop, a Long Beach Crip, and tied his red bandanna over his face. He pulled out a .22 and pointed it at Snoop Doggy Dogg, one of the most anticipated rap artists in hip-hop history. [The car] swerved slightly. Snoop told the Cross Colours rep who was driving . . . to 'just keep on driving.' He sang it in his laid back, distinctive LA twang, *nuthin' but a G thang, baby*. He pulled out his two .380s uncocked both of them and stared at the Blood. The Blood kept his shit up until Snoop's car and his .380s were around the bend."[1] While many gangsta rap pioneers enacted the mark of criminality to establish street credentials and move records, hampton wanted readers to understand that this young Long Beach native represented a new version of the mark of criminality. Here was a hugely successful rapper whose actual gang background contributed to his cultural heft and impacted his daily life. Snoop Dogg did not simply rap within the generic contours of the mark of the criminality, but he fully embodied them. Moreover, he appeared as calm and collected in the face of a Blood's .22 as his musical persona was when confronting various existential threats. But on a different day, on a different corner, encountered by a different "brotha," Snoop Doggy Dogg may have left the hip-hop nation before his star had a chance to truly rise. And this, of course, was to say nothing of his impending murder trial.

During the early 1990s, many of the hip-hop nation's most prominent figures encountered serious legal problems. In addition to doing time as an eighteen-year-old Crip for selling crack to an undercover police officer, Snoop Dogg faced murder charges for the drive-by-shooting death of a former associate. Although the trial ended in the rapper's acquittal, it nonetheless provided C. Delores Tucker and her allies with ample rhetorical fodder for their war against gangsta rap. It also, however, added significantly to *Doggystyle*'s commercial appeal. Snoop Doggy Dogg was a "genuine" gangsta. Dr. Dre also faced legal trouble, most notably for the 1991 physical assault of female rapper and hip-hop journalist Dee Barnes. The British expatriate and hip-hop pioneer Slick Rick was sentenced to three-and-a-half to ten years in prison for a 1990 drive-by shooting, and Public Enemy trickster Flavor Flav faced numerous legal troubles for assault and attempted murder during the early 1990s.[2]

Many hip-hop journalists characterized these artists' legal problems as high-profile symptoms of a racist criminal justice system, yet mainstream media responded with characteristic commentary on the so-called gangsta lifestyle and noted its alleged encroachment on the lives of ordinary Americans.[3] For example, a writer for the *Washington Post* wrote that Snoop Dogg and his contemporaries were "blurring the lines between the supposed fiction of 'gangsta' rap and the reality of today's gun culture."[4] Elsewhere, the *Charleston Gazette* invoked an infestation metaphor with the headline "Rap Violence Moves out of Recording Studio, into Street," while the *Buffalo News* led with "Controversial Hard-Core Rappers Who Act Out Their Anti-Social Messages."[5] In its cover story on gangsta rap, *Newsweek* posed the following: "But for rap music—particularly for the school known as gangsta rap, which has found a pot of gold in selling images of black-on-black crime to mainstream America—the confluence of the arrests raises disturbing questions: what is the relationship between the violence on the records and the violence in the communities, between capital rhymes and capital crimes? In broader terms, how does art—particularly art often consumed by very young listeners—influence life?"[6] While Eazy-E, Ice Cube, Ice-T, and others provoked significant public outcry, none so starkly mirrored the fantasies they conjured in their music. And with incidents like the Ohio shooting death of three-year-old Aniva Johnson by her eleven-year-old brother, Michael, who claimed he was impersonating his idol Snoop Doggy Dogg, it appeared the fears of Tipper Gore, C. Delores Tucker, and the Fraternal Order of Police were coming to fruition. Gangsta was creating a culture of violence. Rappers' deployments of the mark of criminality were a genuine threat to the social order, as these Pied Pipers of black vernacular expression led youth into a dark cave of nihilism and erasure.[7]

The mark of criminality was now a public performance beyond the stage or recording studio for many rappers, as artists' legal troubles became topoi for heightened authenticity and reinvention, as well as intensified criticism from their detractors. No artist represented this kind of embodied criminality more thoroughly or complexly than Tupac Shakur. Under the stage names 2Pac and Makaveli, Shakur's short but profoundly influential hip-hop career was consistently accompanied by high-profile encounters with law enforcement. In addition to producing many perilous, if profitable, detours in his artistic trajectory, Shakur's legal troubles contributed significantly to his ethos in the hip-hop nation. Few rap artists placed their life stories at the center of their work more than Shakur. Michael Eric Dyson writes, "A considerable measure of Tupac's cultural heft was certainly extramusical," ranging from his frequent invocation of his troubled childhood and radical family lineage to the public's fascination with his confrontations with law enforcement and other rap artists.[8] Shakur came to posit his life as synecdoche for the experiences of poor and working-class African Americans. His life narrative, in other words, was as much a part of his deployments of the mark of criminality as his music.[9]

Whereas NWA and the germinal recordings of the g-funk era represented distinct versions of the mark of criminality that expressed discrete historical junctures in crime and public culture during the 1980s and 1990s, Shakur's body of work represented a wholesale embodiment of black criminality. His central performative theme, "Thug Life," was the most visible effort by a popular rapper to deploy the mark of criminality in ways that explicitly invited politically charged affective investments from listeners. Specifically, Shakur used the mark of criminality to mobilize black rage. Written in the context of the urban uprisings of the late 1960s, psychiatrists William Grier and Price Cobbs's *Black Rage* drew from years of clinical work with black patients to advance a theory of anger intrinsic to the African American community—one born of centuries of institutional racism. They wrote, "The black man of today is at one end of a psychological continuum which reaches back in time to his enslaved ancestors."[10] While bell hooks has argued that Grier and Cobbs's work relied too heavily on Eurocentric psychiatric models and risks reinforcing stereotypical associations of blackness with anger and violence, she nonetheless agrees that there resides within black Americans a seething anger stemming from shared origins of enslavement, segregation, and other modalities of dehumanization. She and other race scholars have claimed that such anger, when mobilized in a way fundamentally invested in a love for one's community, possesses emancipatory potential.[11] Black rage, in other words, is a distinctly racialized expression of affect whose genesis is the brutalizing histories of white supremacy. Furthermore, legal scholar Paul Harris advances black rage as a litigious resource for challenging jurisprudential norms that discipline black anger and violence without any consideration for the role of white supremacy in producing the acts our legal system designates as criminal. Describing what he calls the "black rage defense," Harris writes, "Most of all, it says this to the American legal system: You cannot convict me without hearing who I am and what shaped me."[12] For Harris, crime itself, under specific circumstances, can be understood as an expression of black rage—as an affectively charged violation of societal norms that emerges when alternative modes of expression are lacking. Within the contours of hegemonic deployments of the mark of criminality from figures like Richard Nixon, black rage figured as a threat to the social order. As I shall discuss, alternative versions of the mark of criminality situated black rage at the center of a potentially emancipatory cultural-political project.

I argue that Tupac Shakur's "Thug Life" represents a mobilization of black rage through the generic norms of the mark of criminality. For him, appropriating and refashioning the cultural logics of racialized criminality offered young, primarily male African Americans a resource for directing their anger toward the perilous racial inequities of the late twentieth century. The black criminal, in Shakur's hands, became a creators' nightmare that confronted interpretations of the mark of criminality from white civil society and the black middle class. However, because affect is fundamentally unstable, capable of escape and always subject to capture, Shakur's project was enabled and constrained by the forces of white supremacy, music capital, and other determinants associated with race and cultural production. Specifically, as Shakur became entrenched in the cutthroat world of gangsta rap commerce, the confrontational logics of "Thug Life" fixated less on embodiments of white supremacy and mass incarceration and more on other black artists he regarded as mortal enemies. Shakur's career, in other words, does not stand as a heroic testament to the bountiful possibilities of a politics of criminality but as a cautionary tale of the promise and limitations of such a project. In this chapter, I demonstrate how "Thug Life" was a malleable theme whose enactments of the mark of criminality shifted through encounters with black radical politics, musical commerce, and personal trauma.

"Thug Life" as Black Rage

Tupac Shakur was born in New York City on June 16, 1971, a mere month after his mother, Afeni Shakur, was released from jail. An active member of the Black Panther Party in New York, Afeni, along with twenty other Panthers, was arrested in 1969—at the height of FBI infiltration of the Panthers and other radical organizations—on charges of planning to bomb several public places.[13] As Tupac recalls in an interview, "I was cultivated in prison. My embryo was in prison."[14]

In other words, the rapper argues that his subjectivity was always and already conditioned by the deep historical connection between America's black communities and its criminal justice system. In 1971, Tupac Shakur entered an America increasingly saturated with Nixonian rhetorics of law and order that fashioned the mark of criminality to discipline escalating enactments of black rage.

After several years spent between jobs and houses, Afeni moved her family to Baltimore in 1986 before making a final pilgrimage to Marin City, California, three years later. It was at this time that Afeni, amid the pressures of poverty, became addicted to crack cocaine. For a brief period, Tupac joined the local drug trade. He later rationalized this in his popular 1995 track "Dear Mama," rapping, "I ain't guilty 'cause, even though I sell rocks / It feels good puttin' money in your mailbox."[15] Here, Shakur deploys the mark of criminality in largely pragmatic terms. Absent other resources for income—and this is, after all, at the height of Reagan-era neoliberalism—Shakur imagines drug commerce as an alternative means for black men to support their beloved, if deeply troubled, families. Shakur also began developing a political analysis of inner-city black life in America. In one wide-ranging interview he conducted at the age of seventeen, the Marin City teenager commented on poverty and the role of the American education system in supporting oppressive social structures. Shakur was, by many measures, wise beyond his years.[16]

Just as the Shakurs journeyed to the West Coast, NWA and other gangsta rappers were transforming American popular music and producing multiple provocative deployments of the mark of criminality. The epicenter of hip-hop was rapidly shifting from New York to California. Shakur became heavily involved in the underground hip-hop scene.[17] Archival video footage from the documentary *Tupac: Resurrection* shows him performing at the Marin City Fair in 1989, where he raps polemical lyrics like, "The American Dream wasn't meant for me / 'Cause Lady Liberty's a hypocrite / She lied to me."[18] Echoing Martin Luther King Jr.'s claim that America had written the black community a "bad check" vis-à-vis the lofty ideals of the Republic, Shakur posits a severe contradiction between those ideals and his experiences as a young black man.[19] His first major breakthrough followed a successful audition for the popular rap group Digital Underground. While touring with the group as a backup dancer and occasional rapper, Shakur began launching a solo career.[20]

In 1991, Shakur landed a record deal with Interscope Records and released *2Pacalypse Now*.[21] Danyel Smith, the editor in chief of *Vibe* magazine, described the album as "the words of a boy weary of doing the 'Humpty Dance' [Digital Underground's most popular single], and tired of standing on the corner in Marin City, selling weed."[22] Shakur described his inaugural recording effort as "the story of the young black male."[23] The album featured tracks such as "Trapped," "Young Black Male," "Brenda's Got a Baby," and "Rebel of the Underground," which interrogated numerous problems confronting urban black communities. For example, "Trapped" described the paralyzing fear of inner-city violence ("You know they got me trapped in this prison of seclusion / Happiness, living on the streets is a delusion / Even a smooth criminal one day must get caught / Shot up or shot down with the bullet that he bought") and constant surveillance by law enforcement ("They got me trapped / Can barely walk the city streets / Without a cop harassing me, searching me / Then asking for my identity") endemic to predominantly black urban areas at the time. Yet the track retained a trace of militant optimism in its chorus, "Naw, they can't keep a black man down."[24] The album was an expression of rage associated with a life largely conditioned by mainstream deployments of the mark of criminality. At a time when NWA and other early gangsta rappers fashioned the mark of criminality in the service of commerce and occasional social critique, Shakur reformulated hip-hop's relationship to the genre by offering meditations from within the constraints of dominant iterations of the mark of criminality.

Others chased fortune at the expense of substance, but Shakur fashioned himself as a militant radical who remained loyal to his struggling black fan base. In one press interview, Shakur strikes a confrontational tone: "I think that my music is revolutionary because it's for soldiers. It makes you want to fight back. It makes you want to think. It makes you want to ask questions. It makes you want to struggle, and if struggling means when he swings, you swing back, then hell yeah—it makes you swing back."[25] Shakur, in other words, hoped his music would inspire anger among listeners that they, in turn, would deploy against various forces of domination as black rage. He also adopted an aesthetic that contrasted significantly with the danceable tonality of the emerging g-funk of the early 1990s. Journalist Kevin Powell wrote in 1994, "I think of Tupac's music: It's a cross between Public Enemy and N.W.A., between Black Power ideology and 'Fuck tha Police!' realism. When he raps, Tupac is part screaming, part preaching, part talking shit. The music is dense and, at times, so loud it drowns out the lyrics. You cannot dance to it. Perhaps that is intentional."[26] Shakur's tracks typically employed sharp, abrasive beats (for example, "Trapped," "Young Black Male," "Holla If Ya Hear Me") or soulful melodies reminiscent of socially conscious icons like Marvin Gaye (for example, "Brenda's Got a Baby," "Dear Mama," "Keep Ya Head Up"). Shakur's deep, sometimes hoarse voice often sounded unhinged, remarkable in its flow while suggesting that it may, at any moment, stray wildly from the track's break beat. He seemed less interested in inducing pleasure than provoking the same kinds of rage and communal love he expressed in his lyrics.

It was at this early stage in his career that Shakur developed the theme of "Thug Life," which would remain a centerpiece of his work for the rest of his life. Shakur originally imagined "Thug Life" as "a new kind of Black Power."[27] Speaking at the Indiana Black Expo in 1993, Shakur polemically declared, "These white folks see us as thugs, I don't care what y'all think. I don't care if you think you're a lawyer, if you a man, if you an 'African American,' if you whatever the fuck you think you are. We thugs and niggers to these motherfuckers! You know? And until we own some shit, I'm gonna call it like it is. . . . We thugs and we niggers until we set this shit right!"[28] Donning a stocking cap and baggy overalls, attire widely associated with the very "thugs" to whom he spoke, Shakur stood in stark contrast with his fellow panelists, who wore either tailored suits or colorful Afrocentric garb. Much like an earlier generation of young black men's adoption of the zoot suit allowed them to resist the aesthetic norms of white supremacy and the black intelligentsia, Shakur's style constituted a refashioning of hegemonic deployments of the mark of criminality and intervened in the emerging generational tensions between black urban youth and the black middle class.[29] He also shouted angrily into the microphone and was barely able to stand still behind the podium. Much like his rapping style, Shakur's approach to oratory was of a man whose rage was only tenuously contained by the decorum of the platform. As his parodic, nasal delivery of the term "African American" implies, he had little patience for what he saw as the politically correct platitudes of the late twentieth century's civil rights mainstream.[30]

This frustration with contemporary black politics was also apparent in his 1992 speech at a Malcolm X Grassroots Movement (MXGM) dinner in Atlanta. Wearing a red hooded sweatshirt, matching backward baseball cap, and gold chains, Shakur again embodied the ascendant gangsta styles of the hip-hop nation in the early 1990s. Speaking to a largely black separatist audience, Shakur insisted, "Before we can be African, we have to be black first." He then meditated on the legacy of the organization's namesake, choosing to focus on Malcolm X's life before his incarceration and conversion to Islam, or what he calls the "real Malcolm." He argued, "You gotta remember, this was a pimp, you know what I'm sayin'? A pusher and all that." He then generalized the "street" Malcolm to the experiences of the modern young black male, claiming, "But we forgot about all of that. In our strive to be enlightened, we forgot all about our brothers in the street, about all our dope dealers, our pushers and our pimps."[31] Within this neglect of black youth most readily associated with dominant deployments of the mark of criminality, Shakur spied a fundamental hypocrisy in an earlier generation's attitude about contemporary problems in the black community. While black elders like Jesse Jackson and C. Delores Tucker espoused concern for the welfare of this younger generation, they were invested in an iteration of the mark of criminality that stigmatized the lived experiences of black youth in favor of idealized and, Shakur claimed, illusive fantasies about black life. Referring to the criminals of the inner city, the popular artist claimed, "And that's who's teaching the new generation, 'cause you're all not doing it. I'm sorry, but it's the pimps and the pushers who teachin' us. So, if you've got a problem with the way we was raised, it's because they was the only ones who could do it. They the only ones who did it. While everybody else wanted to go to college and, you know, yeah, everything has changed, they was the ones that was tellin' ya 'The White man ain't shit.' Here you go, check this out young blood." He adds that drug dealers were among the few members of the black community offering youth a seemingly viable way out of the ghetto: sell drugs, make money, and build a new life. Such promises, of course, were a sham, as a life of dealing was more likely to lead to incarceration or death than a lavish life of plenty. However, absent alternative modes of upward mobility, Shakur argued, the youth of black urban areas would embrace a life of crime.[32] He echoed this sentiment in "Dear Mama" when he claims, "I hung around with thugs / And even though they sold drugs / They showed a young brother love."[33] "Thug Life," for Shakur, was a politics of self-fashioned pragmatism angrily expressed through a politicized refashioning of the mark of criminality. In this version, the young black male appeared as an abandoned subject for whom the structural and symbolic resources of criminality offered avenues for survival and critique.

Shakur also devised an acrostic for "Thug Life"—"the hate you gave little infants fucks everyone"—to articulate the enactment of black criminal rage toward self-emancipation.[34] Just as he did in his jeremiad at the MXGM banquet, Shakur convicted an earlier generation of high-minded black liberals for failing to grasp the anger and desperation circulating through inner-city streets in the 1990s. These infants were now coming of age and the hatred they inherited was going to fuck everyone. Adopting what James Darsey calls a prophetic voice, Shakur projected the black criminal as a testament to the civil rights generation's failure to embody its own ideals.[35] In the absence of viable alternatives, Shakur encouraged his young, black audience to reckon with their criminalized status by viewing it as a source of agency and upward mobility. "Thug Life" was, Shakur evidently hoped, a mechanism for deploying the mark of criminality in emancipatory ways.

The concept of "Thug Life" was understandably controversial among rap music's already forceful critics. In response, Shakur argued, "I don't understand why America doesn't understand 'Thug Life.' America is 'Thug Life'! What makes me sayin' 'I don't give a fuck' different than Patrick Henry sayin' 'Give me liberty or give me death'? What makes my freedom less worth fighting for than Bosnians or whoever they want to fight for this year?"[36] The gesture of inverting the syntaxes of criminality and violence is consistent with NWA's reconfiguration of Compton as a colonized battleground and also reifies the much broader political economy of crime and punishment. "Thug Life" was invested in politicizing those subjects and behaviors designated for incarceration and supervision, arguing forcefully that they were entirely consistent with the regimes of power occupying the upper echelons of American society. "Thug Life," in other words, hoped to highlight the hypocrisy at the core of America's war on crime. As Shakur put it in on the television show *Live from LA with Tanya Hart*, "The message is that we comin'. All the people you threw away—the dope dealers, the criminals— they will be legit sitting next to you in first class thanks to your boy."[37] "Thug Life" sought to invert the hegemonic meanings of the mark of criminality, en-acting those racialized discourses toward black capital accumulation and em-powerment. While equating black wealth with resistance holds serious limita-tions for a broad and inclusive emancipatory politics, "Thug Life" nonetheless created new conditions of possibility for public deliberation regarding race and criminality. Shakur was the self-fashioned savior of the mark of criminality from its entrapment within dominant American discourses of law and order. "Thug Life" was his prophetic mission.

Shakur's second album, 1993's *Strictly 4 My N.I.G.G.A.Z.*, solidified the "Thug Life" thread that ran through his music. Frank Williams wrote that the album "injected a sensitivity to the gangsta rap genre that was rare at the time."[38] De-scribing the title in an interview, Shakur explained, "This album is my last at-tempt to say, *This is how we going to swing this*. And it's geared for my niggas— strictly for my niggas. Not for the people who say, 'I'm not a nigga, I'm an African American.' This is strictly for the people who don't cringe when I say 'my nig-gas' 'cause they know that's out of love."[39] Reiterating his angry mockery of self-righteousness at the Indiana Black Expo, Shakur demanded that those invested in the future of black youth engage life as it truly is for them, not as elites may wish it to be. The track most emblematic of "Thug Life" was "Holla if You Hear Me." Sampled over a funk beat and several Public Enemy tracks, the song high-lighted Shakur's deep identification with his criminalized status and commitment to the militant expression of black rage. He raps, "Will I quit, will I quit? / They claim that I'm violent, but still I keep / Representin', never give up, on a good thing / Wouldn't stop it if we could it's a hood thing / And now I'm like a major threat / Cause I remind you of the things you were made to forget."[40] Recog-nizing that mainstream critics of rap music marked him as a threat to the social order, Shakur espoused his investment in "reminding" his brethren of their loca-tion within the broader apparatuses of a racist society. He also jettisoned any il-lusions of passive resistance, declaring in the song's second verse, "Pump ya fists like this / Holla if ya hear me—PUMP PUMP if you're pissed / To the sell-outs, livin' it up / One way or another you'll be givin' it up, huh / I guess cause I'm black born / I'm supposed to say peace, sing songs, and get capped on / But it's time for a new plan, BAM! / I'll be swingin' like a one man, clan / Here we go, turn it up, don't stop / To my homies on the block getting' dropped by cops / I'm still around for ya / Keepin' my sound underground for ya."[41] By declaring "I'm still around for ya" and "Keepin' my sound underground for ya," Shakur functioned as a self-fashioned prophet. As a product of the devastating conditions present in African American communities during the 1980s and early 1990s, Shakur positioned himself as a hermeneutic warrior, angrily unearthing the grim truths of black urbanity and outlining a new political program enacted with and within the mark of criminality. Coupling the analysis of his radical political lineage with the racialized discourses of criminality associated with contemporary rap music, Shakur created "Thug Life" as a mechanism for reimagining black political practice through the affective register of black rage.

To be clear, Shakur's early work was not uniform in its political character. For instance, his 1993 track "I Get Around" declared "All respect to those who break they neck / To keep they hoes in check," revealing that the perfectly lucid political musician is more a fantasy than an empirical reality.[42] Furthermore, for all of its polemical appeal, it remained difficult to determine precisely what a politics of "Thug Life" might entail outside of the recording studio or Shakur's musings. If this was a movement, what kind would it be? Still, Shakur's earliest, most notable work mobilized the mark of criminality in a way that found expression in the historical racial realities of the late 1980s and early 1990s, as well as the conditioning influences of Shakur's biography. It invited affective investments from young black listeners who rejected hegemonic versions of the mark of criminality and more conservative black visions of citizenship. By many measures, his work represented the conscious ideal of hip-hop exalted by so many scholars and some artists.[43] However, while recording his third studio album, *Me against the World*, Shakur encountered an explosive combination of personal trauma and changing dynamics in the hip-hop nation that illuminated affect's capacity for escape, capture, and redeployment.

Doing Time on Death Row

While Tupac Shakur was by no means the only rap artist of the early and mid-1990s to have high-profile encounters with law enforcement, the sheer volume of the young rapper's legal troubles distinguished him from his peers. In one interview, Shakur commented, "I had no record all my life, no police record, until I made a record."[44] The artist, in other words, believed his affectively charged deployments of the mark of criminality made him a threat in the eyes of institutional forces—just as the radical activism enacted by his mother and other relatives during the 1960s and 1970s made them targets. To be sure, his work attracted the ire of culture warriors and law enforcement figures. For example, when a young black man claimed the music on *2Pacalypse Now* inspired him to fatally shoot a Texas state trooper, the officer's widow filed suit against Shakur. The incident also prompted Vice President Dan Quayle, ever the family values crusader, to call for record stores to boycott the album. Furthermore, one of Shakur's first public legal entanglements emerged from a 1993 confrontation with two off-duty Atlanta police officers. He was charged with aggravated assault for nonfatally shooting the two officers, who he claimed first fired at his car after it nearly struck the two men and their wives. The state eventually dropped all charges in the case. Two years earlier, Shakur filed a brutality case against the Oakland police department following a jaywalking arrest. Because such incidents pitted Shakur against the very forces he critiqued in his music, they corresponded with his "Thug Life" ethos as an angry, even heroic critic of the prison-industrial complex.[45]

However, many of Shakur's encounters with law enforcement lacked the political undertones of his clashes with culture warriors and law enforcement. In 1992, while attending the very community festival in Marin City where he used to perform as a younger man, Shakur drew his gun during a confrontation, only to have it discharge and kill a six-year-old boy playing in an adjacent schoolyard. The rapper would often say the incident still haunted him. Furthermore, Shakur served a fifteen-day jail term for assaulting acclaimed director Allen Hughes after hearing rumors that Shakur was to be dropped from an upcoming film. Such incidents reflected the masculine bravado of many of Shakur's gangsta contemporaries that, while also central to "Thug Life," appeared to lack the political substance of the theme's espoused black rage.[46]

In 1994, Shakur was convicted of a crime that dramatically changed the trajectory of his career and the meaning of "Thug Life." According to a nineteen-year-old woman named Ayanna Jackson, Shakur held Jackson down while his friends sodomized her in a New York City hotel room following a 1993 concert. Shakur claimed he was asleep during the incident. On November 31, 1994, a jury found Shakur guilty and sentenced him to one and a half to four and a half years in prison for sexual assault.[47] After spending several years carving a place for himself in the hip-hop nation, Shakur entered prison for the first time in his life for a crime profoundly consistent with prevailing deployments of the mark of criminality: a black man convicted of sexual assault.[48] Indeed, Shakur expressed precisely this sentiment in some of his postconviction work, rapping on the track "Ambitionz Az a Ridah," "Fuck doin' jail time / Better day / Sacrifice / Won't get a chance to do me / Like they did my nigga Tys."[49] Referring to the world champion boxer Mike Tyson, who in 1992 was convicted of the rape of Desiree Washington, Shakur expressed a sentiment shared by many members of the African American community. Loyal supporters cast the boxer who "embodied the authentic street brother whose athletic glory never undermined his identification with the ghetto from which he sprang" as a victim of white supremacy, whereas Washington was a race traitor responsible for sending yet another young black man to prison.[50] At least one Shakur fan saw a strong homology between the two men's cases. In a letter to the editor published in *Vibe*, Stella Williams of Norfolk, Virginia, wrote about Jackson, "maybe one day she can write a movie script to go along with that Academy Award–winning performance, and she can get Desiree Washington . . . to play her in the role. They're both great actresses."[51] Such conflation of black female victims of sexual assault reified the gendered dimensions of the mark of criminality already present in gangsta rap, as well as older tales of badmen like Stagger Lee. The female body figured as an empty signifier for expressing masculine prowess or, in iterations following the rape convictions of prominent black men like Tyson and Shakur, defending the integrity of criminalized black males.[52]

In addition to his incarceration, Shakur's entanglement in the escalating feud between East Coast and West Coast rap artists further complicated the trajectory of his career and profoundly transformed the substance of "Thug Life." Arguably inaugurated with New York rapper Tim Dog's 1991 single "Fuck Compton," this feud circulated around the explosion of West Coast gangsta rap in the late 1980s and early 1990s. Until this time, New York City, where hip-hop originated, dominated the scene.[53] However, with the release of *Straight Outta Compton*, the geography of hip-hop changed.[54] Many West Coast rappers felt slighted by their East Coast counterparts. During the early days of hip-hop ascension, New York–based hip-hop media like MTV, the *Source*, and *Billboard* largely ignored Los Angeles–based rap artists. Furthermore, the entrenched public associations of Los Angeles County with gang violence prompted some East Coast artists to avoid touring in the area for safety reasons.[55] The feeling of being ignored, even amid soaring success, soured West Coast artists' and fans' attitudes toward the East. Many New York artists and critics dismissed West Coast rap as more sensationalistic than artistic, insisting that the East, with or without commercial success, remained the "true" home of hip-hop.[56]

Two closely intertwined forces helped intensify the affective intensity of the coastal feud and revise the mark of criminality in ways that encompassed the commercial business practices of black artists and producers. The first was an emerging profit war between the respective coasts' flagship record companies. Suge Knight's Death Row Records was the face of West Coast gangsta rap. Knight was already notorious for his aggressive business practices, and this reputation played a significant role in the rivalry. The other label was Sean "Puff Daddy" Combs's Bad Boy Entertainment. Bad Boy rose to prominence in 1994 with the release of Notorious B.I.G.'s (a.k.a. Biggie Smalls) first album *Ready to Die*. In addition to competing fiercely within the same market, Death Row and Bad Boy had drastically different styles. While Knight continued to deploy the gangsta ethos of Dr. Dre, Snoop Dogg, and, after signing him, Shakur, Bad Boy deployed the mark of criminality with a more lavish, club-based, and mafioso style.[57] While many West Coast artists released "dis" tracks aimed at the East (for example, Tha

Dogg Pound's "New York, New York" and Ice Cube's "Bow Down"), figures like Puff Daddy and Biggie Smalls often plead ignorance on the feud, dismissing it as "trivial and meaningless."[58]

Prior to his incarceration, Shakur claimed allegiance to neither coast of the hip-hop nation. However, his loyalty began a distinct westward shift in 1994. On November 30, the night before the verdict in his sexual assault case, Shakur went to Quad Recording Studio in Times Square to record a track for Uptown Records. While he waited for the lobby elevator, two men wearing camouflage fatigues approached Shakur. They shot him repeatedly and fled with several thousand dollars' worth of rings and gold chains. Police believed the shooting, which required Shakur to undergo surgery, was part of a random robbery, but in a jailhouse interview with *Vibe*, Shakur implicated Puff Daddy, Biggie Smalls, and Uptown Entertainment CEO Andre Harrell in planning the attack in order to remove him from the hip-hop scene. The three men forcefully denied any involvement in the shooting. However, with the poorly timed release of Biggie Smalls's single "Who Shot Ya?," which Shakur believed was about the Quad shooting, as well as the shooting death of one of Knight's close associates at an Atlanta party, members and affiliates of Death Row Records increasingly implicated Bad Boy Entertainment and their allies for escalating the coastal feud.[59]

In the wake of a conviction for a crime he claimed he did not commit, and a shooting for which he blamed supposed friends, Shakur adopted a more vitriolic and paranoid enactment of the mark of criminality. After his shooting, the imprisoned rapper commented, "If anything, my mentality is like, 'Trust nobody! Trusty no-body!' It's not like I'm untouchable; I can be killed as soon as I get out of here." From prison, he lamented, "My closest friends did me in." In light of his claims of betrayal, Shakur sought a means of retribution. He explained, "So I just thought about, how can I make them sorry they ever did this to me? You know what I mean? How can I come back, like, fifty-times stronger and better?"[60] While the rage that fueled the politically infused "Thug Life" of Shakur's earlier work remained, it found new expression amid changing conditions. His increasingly criminalized body and accompanying work seemed less invested in community uplift and systemic critique than in settling personal scores. If Shakur was Stagger Lee, Bad Boy Entertainment was a collectively constituted Billy Lyons.

This opportunity to "come back" and redefine "Thug Life" arrived less than one year into Shakur's sentence. In October 1995, Suge Knight presented the still-popular artist with $1.4 million bail and a handwritten recording contract committing the artist to three albums under the Death Row label. Shakur relocated to Los Angeles while awaiting appeal and completed two albums before he was shot to death in 1996. Knight, along with producer and Death Row cofounder Dr. Dre, began fitting Shakur's talent, and "Thug Life," into the Death Row mold, characterized by hedonistic, violent, and misogynistic deployments of the mark of criminality, as well as Dr. Dre's danceable, funk-inspired aesthetic. This was a significant departure from the aggressive tonality of Shakur's earlier work. His first single under Death Row, "California Love," was a brass-filled, celebratory duet with Dr. Dre, pledging his allegiance to his new home. By claiming loyalty to California, and particularly Los Angeles, Shakur was tethering "Thug Life" to the most contested space amid myriad deployments and revisions of the mark of criminality near the end of the twentieth century. In the opening verse, Dre declares, "We in that Sunshine State where that bomb ass hemp be / The state where ya never find a dance floor empty." This new stage in Shakur's career, it seemed, was invested in registers of pleasure, even abandon, rather than the black rage of "Thug Life."[61]

In addition to adapting to the g-funk norms of Death Row, Shakur directed the rage he had previously reserved for the structures of white supremacy and an out-of-touch black middle class toward his new East Coast enemies. For example, at the 1996 Soul Train Music Awards, Shakur and his posse aggressively approached Biggie Smalls and his crew. Some witnesses claimed that Shakur pointed a pistol at the New York artist and his entourage.[62] In a posthumously published interview, Shakur speaks antagonistically of Biggie Smalls: "I have no mercy in war. I said in the beginning I was gonna take these niggas out the game, and sure enough I will. Already people can't look at Biggie and not laugh. I took every piece of his power. Anybody who tries to help him, I will destroy. Anyone who wanna side with them or do a record with them, whatever, try to unify with them, I'ma destroy. I swear to God. Can't nobody touch me right now. Maybe next month all of this will be over, but this month I'm takin' every moving target out."[63] Shakur's words and behaviors reinforced the popular view that the coastal feud was getting out of hand. The increasingly vocal and visceral expressions of coastal tensions refashioned the mark of criminality in ways that framed hip-hop commerce itself as criminal.[64] "Thug Life" proved tragically malleable in the face of Shakur's personal vendettas and the commercial demands of Death Row Records.

The most potent outlet for Shakur's rage toward his enemies was his music. Both *All Eyez on Me* and *The Don Killuminati: The 7 Day Theory* contained tracks that posited Shakur and his allies as a thug army committed to market dominance and violent confrontation. As Dr. Dre boasted in "California Love," he and the Death Row crew were "lean mean money-making machines."[65] What would later be revealed as a litany of exploitative relationships between Suge Knight and his signed artists were at this time badges of honor.[66] In the most notorious track of the feud era, "Hit 'Em Up," Shakur declares, "Our shit goes triple and 4-quadruple," whereas he speculates earlier in the song, "I don't know why I'm even on this track / You all niggas ain't even on my level." While Shakur and other Death Row artists produced "triple and 4-quadruple" platinum records, he dismissed the work of Biggie Smalls and other Bad Boy artists as amateurish. This represented a pronounced break with the politics of his earlier work, even as it continued to function within the formal contours of the mark of criminality. Shakur makes this much clearer in "Hit 'Em Up" when he boasts, "We ain't no motherfuckin' joke / Thug Life, niggas better be known / Be approaching in the wide open, gun smoking / No need for hoping, it's a battle lost." As the track progresses and Shakur literally yells vitriolic verbiage toward Biggie Smalls, Puff Daddy, and their associates, one is tempted to take him at his word that, "This ain't no freestyle battle / All you niggas getting killed with your mouths open." By the track's conclusion, the artist has abandoned the perfectly pleasant, danceable tonality of its production. The sampled melody from former Temptation Dennis Edwards's 1980s soul hit "Don't Look Any Further" functions as a brittle container for Shakur's outrage. His spiteful lyrics represent not only a departure from the decorum of the dozens, itself a long-standing black vernacular practice of mockery and name-calling, but from the communal bonds of black cultural production so many feared were under threat, not only from the raging coastal battle but also from the ascent of gangsta rap in general. Rather than a militant prophet, Shakur fashions himself as an unhinged and violent man with a vendetta—the kind of man who might shoot Billy Lyons for stealing his Stetson hat. Such a reformulation of the mark of criminality fashions the angry black man as a destructive force in ways similar to NWA's "crazy motherfucker" or the archetypical racialized violence that inspired so much white fear through more hegemonic deployments of the genre. A new brand of "Thug Life" had arrived with a mission of vengeance and profit.[67]

The cover photograph of Shakur's first Death Row release, the best-selling double album *All Eyez on Me*, also reveals Shakur's newfound investment in the West Coast–East Coast rivalry. Sitting on a backward chair and staring into the camera, Shakur flashes the "West Side" hand signal and displays a gold chain featuring the Death Row Records coat of arms (an electric chair). Before the first beat or lyric, the vengeful Shakur and his employer posit the album as a line in the sand between East and West. The artist's photographed body, after sustaining bullets and incarceration, stood as a testament to his solidarity with the West Coast, and, by employing hand signals and gold jewelry widely associated with the Los Angeles gang scene, did so in ways that corresponded with Death Row's market-driven deployments of the mark of criminality.[68] The first track, "Ambitionz Az a Ridah," begins with several soft piano chords and Shakur lightly singing, "I won't deny it, I'm a straight ridah / You don't wanna fuck with me / Got the po-lice bustin' at me / But they can't do nuttin' to a G." This soft incantation is proceeded by a sample of the famous "Let's get ready to ruuumbllle!" cry of boxing announcer Michael Buffer. While the track begins as a relatively straightforward exercise in boasting ("This niggaz is jealous 'cause deep in they

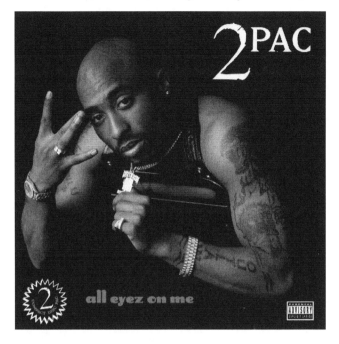

Figure 9: *All Eyez on Me* album cover. Death Row Records, 1996.

heart they wanna be me"), the second verse launches into far more direct terri-
tory, "Peep it—it was my only wish to rise / Above these jealous coward muther-
fuckers I despise / When it's time to ride, I was the first off this side, give me
the nine / I'm ready to die right here tonight, and motherfuck they life (yeah
nigga!) / That's what they screamin' as they drill me, but I'm hard to kill / So
open fire, I see you kill me (that's all you niggaz got?) witness my steel / Spittin'
at adversaries envious and after me / I'd rather die before they catchin' me, watch
me bleed."[69] Shakur raps over a slow, ominous tempo. It is the sound of gathering
storm of vengeance waiting to unleash righteous fury—or the rebirth of "Thug
Life" as a less politicized expression of black rage. Making a none-too-subtle reference to his 1994 shooting, Shakur proclaims his resilience in the face of literal bullets. He and his ravaged, criminalized body are poised for further battle,
even "ready to die here tonight" if need be. The enemies in this battle, however,
are not police or politicians, but other black artists.

The album's second single, "2 of Amerikaz Most Wanted," is especially laden
with imagery and language connecting black masculinity and rap virtuosity to
discourses of criminality. Indeed, the very title invokes two salient texts relevant
to the hip-hop nation and the politics of late twentieth-century law and order.
Debuting in 1988, the same year the Willie Horton ad and NWA's *Straight Outta*

Compton haunted the psyches of white civil society with potent, if divergent, images of the black masculine predator, the Fox series *America's Most Wanted* and its host, John Walsh, circulated the mark of criminality in ways that rationalized the tough-on-crime politics of the period. Framed as a direct response to the crime reenactment series's perceived race-baiting, Ice Cube's solo debut, *Amerikkka's Most Wanted*, featured numerous samples of Walsh's voice along with lyrics that boastfully deployed the mark of criminality with the same violent rage Ice Cube displayed in *Straight Outta Compton*.[70] By dropping two of three "k's" in its title and enacting the common tropes of violent hypermasculinity and unapologetic materialism, Death Row presented yet another version of the mark of criminality and, for Shakur, a refashioning of "Thug Life." White supremacy in "Amerikkka" was no longer the primary target of Shakur's rage. Death Row was on a new warpath, and the destination was an apocalyptic confrontation with the East Coast.

Before we hear a single beat of "2 of Amerikaz Most Wanted," its connection to gangsta's increasingly public embodiments of the mark of criminality is fairly obvious to anyone familiar with the dynamics of the hip-hop nation at the time. Fellow Death Row artist Snoop Doggy Dogg joins Shakur, composing the second half of "Amerika's Most Wanted." Snoop Dogg had recently been acquitted of murder, and Shakur was "Out on bail, fresh out of jail, California dreamin'."[71] The track thus contained the two most popularly criminalized rappers in the United States at the time. Shakur recognizes precisely this as he opens the track, stating, "Ahh shit, you done fucked up now! You done put two of America's most wanted in the same motherfuckin' place, at the same motherfuckin' time, hahahahaha!" Various modalities of public culture had come to regard Shakur and Snoop Dogg as the most dangerous figures in hip-hop, for they had forcefully injected gangsta's criminal fantasies into real life. However, in the artists' hands, the mark of criminality becomes a source of power as they invoke gangsta commonplaces and their own legal troubles to fashion themselves as aggressive virtuosos who dominate the rap scene. Both survived the apparatuses of the American criminal justice system and were now poised to enlist their criminality toward cultural production, profit accumulation, and vengeance. While deploying the mark of criminality was part and parcel of Shakur's "Thug Life" ethos, the ensuing lyrics demonstrated a new and less politically radical calculus of battle.

The artists rap over a smooth, g-funk-styled beat consisting of a synthesizer melody one might hear in a popular 1980s rhythm and blues hit and a pulsating break beat. In the first verse, Snoop Dogg asserts his and Shakur's return to gangsta dominance: "Sho nuff, I keep my hand on my gun, cuz they got me on the run / Now I'm back in the courtroom waitin' on the outcome / Free 2Pac, is all that's on a niggaz mind / But at the same time it seem they tryin' to take mine / So I'ma get smart, and get defensive and shit / And put together a million march, for some gangsta shit." Invoking the collective memory of Farrakhan's

Million Man March, Snoop Dogg articulates the Nation of Islam's culturally conservative message of collective self-care to the gangsta life, insisting on the need to "get defensive and shit." Near the end of the track, "Free 2Pac" raps, "Now give me fifty feet / Defeat is not my destiny, release me to the streets / And keep whatever's left of me / Jealousy is misery, suffering is grief / Better be prepared when you cowards fuck wit' me." In other words, now that he is out of jail, he asks that the carceral state "give me fifty feet" so that he may settle his personal scores with the "cowards" at Bad Boy. Later, he declares, "They wonder how I live, with five shots / Niggaz is hard to kill, on my block." Drawing explicitly from his experience in the prison system and at the hands of his assailants, and continuing to express spatial loyalty to his criminalized "block," Shakur sounds like a man prepared to do damage to his rivals. While this might easily be read within the confines of virtuosity and the recording studio, such taunts are also inseparable from the corporeal violence unfolding at the time of this single's release (for example, the shooting death of Knight's friend and associate in Atlanta and a drive-by shooting allegedly targeting Death Row artists during a New York video shoot).[72]

The song's popular video importantly adds to its criminal element, as well as its articulation of "Thug Life" to the East Coast–West Coast feud. It portrays Snoop Dogg and Shakur donning mafia-style suits while dining on a whole roasted pig, sipping champagne, smoking cigars, and enjoying the company of their posse and beautiful women. A large portion of the video also includes a dramatic courtroom scene where the two men dispense verses as if they were oral arguments to the judge and jury. Dyson suggests that the use of a classical *gangster* motif is intended to highlight the hypocrisy of mainstream criticisms of *gangsta*'s supposed excesses. By embodying the likes of *The Godfather*'s Corleone family, James Cagney, and other celebrated pop culture icons, the video functions as a parodic testament to the double standards associated with race, profit, and criminality in America.[73] In this light, "2 of Amerikaz Most Wanted" retains some of "Thug Life's" earlier political critique.

However, the video also makes unmistakable reference to Shakur's belief that Bad Boy Entertainment was responsible for his shooting. The video's opening scene portrays an office conversation between "Piggie" and "Buff," two clear parodies of Biggie Smalls and Sean "Puff Daddy" Combs. They enthusiastically discuss their ability to dominate the hip-hop scene now that "he's gone, baby!," further enforcing Shakur and his allies' belief that Bad Boy played a role in his shooting. A bloodied and bandaged Shakur enters the room flanked by two bodyguards to confront the dumbfounded East Coast stars. Shakur assures them that he is not going to kill them, explaining, "We was homeboys once, Pig. Once we homeboys, we always homeboys." However, given this prelude's reference to Biggie Smalls and Sean Combs, the presence of a roasted pig on Shakur and

Snoop Dogg's table throughout the video takes on a new meaning. It is as if the two key struggles in Shakur's life—that with the legal system and with Bad Boy Entertainment—converge within the sign of the roasted pig. The swine simultaneously represents its traditional referent, police officers and the prison-industrial complex writ large (given the video's setting in a courtroom and a closing police chase), and the 300-plus-pound Notorious B.I.G., characterized in the video as "Piggie." With this visual gesture, Shakur redraws the battle lines of the hiphop nation, placing the despised police and the East Coast in the same camp and making it perfectly clear that he intends to devour both. Bad Boy's supposed violence against Shakur's body is indistinguishable from the institutional violence of American law enforcement. "Thug Life" becomes an expression of rage directed toward all of Shakur's enemies, as opposed to a prophetic critique of the social structures associated with racism and mass incarceration that do violence to the African American community as a whole and inspire black rage.[74]

It would be misleading to suggest that the totality of Shakur's postincarceration and shooting work dealt myopically with his contempt for East Coast rappers. A significant portion of his postincarceration work provides thoughtful existential meditations on his own mortality and that of other racialized bodies. Tracks including "I Ain't Mad Atcha" and "Life Goes On" portray a contemplative Shakur rapping lyrics like "How many brothas fell victim to the streets? / Rest in peace young nigga, there's a Heaven for a 'G'" that express the kinship that comes with shared relationships to the structural and bodily violence associated with dominant expressions of the mark of criminality.[75] In addition to exploring more deliberately communal themes than the coastal feud, some of Shakur's work at this time connects his contempt for Biggie Smalls and others to an ongoing investment in those he still regards as part of his "Thug Life" community. The 1996 recording "To Live and Die in L.A." begins with a television reporter interrogating a young black man about his affinity for "Hit 'Em Up," asking, "Don't you feel like that creates tension between East and West?" The track then transitions to a soulful sample of Prince's "Do Me Baby"—the kind of music one would enlist for a romantic evening, as opposed to a heated coastal battle. Shakur raps, "I love Cali like I love women / 'cause every nigga in L.A. got a little bit of Thug in him / We might fight against each other, but I promise you this / We'll burn this bitch down, get us pissed."[76] Taken in its own right, but also contextualized within Shakur's more vitriolic work, "To Live and Die in L.A." reveals an affective dialectic of political activism, communal love, and rage. If all identification implies a degree of division, then the coastal feud functions as a struggle over black authenticity.[77] If Shakur conveys love for his criminalized black brethren in songs like "To Live and Die in L.A.," then the Bad Boy crew lies outside this communal equation—they are not authentically black. This stark division, while problematic, also convinces me that there resides in this sec-

Figure 10: Feasting on "Piggie." "2 of Amerikaz Most Wanted" music video. Death Row
Records, 1996.

ond act of Shakur's work a reminder that even the most degraded expressions of
criminality retain a latent yearning for community.[78] One might rightfully raise
concerns about the targets of Shakur's rage, but even these artifacts of the rapper's final days reveal a love for blackness.

Public Memory and the "Lessons" of "Thug Life"

Almost immediately after he was critically wounded in a Las Vegas drive-by shooting on the evening of September 7, 1996, legions of journalists and supporters
rushed to University Medical Center to observe Shakur's condition and begin
the long process of inscribing meaning, once again, upon his bullet-ridden body.[79]
In an otherwise spiteful and dismissive article in the conservative magazine the
American Spectator, author Mark Steyn makes the astute, if polemical, observa-
tion, "[As] surgeons cut open [Shakur's] 'Thug Life' tattoo to get at the three bullets inside him, Jesse Jackson and the Nation of Islam were both in attendance at
the hospital, laying claim to his legacy."[80] A wealth of print media published in
the year following Shakur's death reveals a complex struggle over his legacy and,
ultimately, the destiny of a criminalized generation. The result, I argue, was a do-
mestication of "Thug Life" within public memory that subordinated the emancipatory potential residing therein. In other words, it articulated "Thug Life"
through the era's familiar, sensationalistic deployments of the mark of criminality.

The most prevalent accounts of Shakur's demise asked whether young African Americans would "learn the lesson" implicit in the rapper's death. In an article announcing Shakur's passing, a reporter for the *Chicago Sun-Times* wrote, "Tupac Shakur, the rapper whose raw lyrics seemed a blueprint of his own violent life, died Friday from wounds suffered in a drive-by shooting."[81] His death, in effect, was the logical conclusion of his "Thug Life." As one fan commented following his death, "He had a big mouth. He was always running off his mouth." Such unabashed expressions of rage, politically charged and otherwise, seemed to foreshadow his untimely death. Another fan noted, "He pumped 'Thug Life' to its fullest."[82] Indeed, his demise came from one of the chief tropes of racialized criminality: the drive-by shooting.[83] Shakur, in these tellings, paid the ultimate price for revising the mark of criminality in ways that traversed the hyperbolic narratives of the gangsta track or music video, and came to encompass real life.

The belief that Shakur's music and lifestyle foreshadowed his violent death led many journalists and commentators to, like Shakur himself, posit the slain rapper's body as synecdoche for young African Americans in general. For example, Shakur's attorney, Shawn S. Chapman, lamented the violent and sensationalistic character of his client's death, telling the *New York Times* that "there was this wonderful, charming, bright, talented, funny person that no one is going to get to know; they are just going to know this other side. Hopefully, this will have some positive effect on people—the gang members—who are shooting each other."[84] Brad Krevoy, who produced the Shakur film *Gang Related*, asked, "Is there anything positive that can be learned from a tragedy like this? Hopefully, kids can learn from it."[85] The *Washington Post* commented in its obituary that Shakur and other gangsta rappers were "selling many young people a lifestyle leading only to an early grave, life behind bars or a place in the growing urban armies of young people disabled by gunfire." The article also commented that "[Shakur's 'Thug Life'] movement had nothing to offer his would-be followers except an eventual return ticket to jail." The piece's author, Esther Iverem, ponders the implications of Shakur's problematic message, noting, "Well-to-do kids, white and black, could flirt with these images, then head off to college. But for kids without this option, the images were powerfully seductive. Tupac's death showed that 'realness' is not invincible—but will the message get through?"[86] By situating Shakur's death in a version of the mark of criminality that privileges the tragedy of black criminality over other potential deployments, the political content of "Thug Life" becomes an injunction to abandon any affective investments therein. One young rapper's demise became a resounding endorsement of previous warnings from C. Delores Tucker and other members of what Neal calls the black middle class, as well as white culture warriors like Tipper Gore and William Bennett, that gangsta rap was a cultural recipe for disaster.[87]

Writing for the Cleveland *Plain Dealer*, high school student Robin Moppins espoused precisely the lesson others hoped young black teenagers would learn from Shakur's violent death. Moppins wrote, "The death of Tupac Shakur made me see that living in the fast lane can lead to a fast and senseless death." The article continued, "Shakur's death was a wake-up call for teens everywhere, because so many are very loyal fans."[88] Writing for the magazine *Essence*, Darrell Dawsey expressed doubt that black young people would "wake up" after Shakur's death. He argued, "On the airwaves, however, the hip-hop community expressed hope that Pac's death would be a 'wake-up call.' I don't see that happening. Not because I don't think we can stop the violence. We can. But alarms for my generation have been going off for more than a decade. If seeing our closest childhood friends with their chests opened by Mac-10 fire hasn't shaken us out of a gangsta stupor, what can we glean from the brutal murder of a superstar we knew only in CD format?" He continued, "What we need is the courage to wake up. But waking up will require sacrifice from a generation too hell-bent on accumulating," and asked, "Who's going to take the weekends off to organize food and clothing drives, the free-Mumia [Abu-Jamal] campaigns, the African-centered independent schools?"[89] For Dawsey, there was a definitive line between genuine community work and the "gangsta stupor" of "Thug Life." Shortly following Shakur's death, the Nation of Islam held a "peace meeting" designed to "give some clarity to his life so [his admirers] won't immortalize the worst of him and try to imitate that."[90] The following year, the organization sponsored a rap concert as "an effort to end violence among rap artists and their fans" following Biggie Smalls's 1997 shooting death in Los Angeles.[91]

It was, of course, reasonable to hope that youth might use Shakur's death as an opportunity to launch a soberer assessment of "Thug Life." However, it is problematic to suggest that in the wake of the rapper's demise it was now up to black youth to emerge triumphantly from the abyss of "Thug Life." Such rhetorics of personal responsibility can obscure the role of social structures in producing crime and poverty by personalizing social issues. Furthermore, the rage central to the theme of "Thug Life," no matter how Shakur deployed it, provided an affective avenue for young black youth to express learned hostilities associated with white supremacy.[92]

Shakur's death nonetheless functioned as an opportunity to deconstruct the sensationalism of "Thug Life," recognizing its many contradictions and, perhaps most importantly, its status as a commodity marketed to working-class and poor youth of color. Poet Kenneth Carroll wrote of Shakur's death, "It says clearly that we cannot afford to be minstrels for dollars or our own dreams of stardom. His death was a lamentable loss of a gifted, misguided, young poet who spoke with insight and energy to his hip-hop world, but who committed the unpardonable sin of using his immense poetic talents to degrade and debase the very people who needed his positive words most—his fans."[93] Tupac Shakur's death *did* serve as an object lesson for the "Thug Life." The question is precisely how one chose to interpret "Thug Life" and the nature of that lesson. If one resituated the death of this black artist within prevailing discourses of degraded black criminality, then the lesson was one that fashioned the mark of criminality in the most cautionary and conservative terms, privileging personal responsibility as the primary modality for reckoning with the previous decade's structural violence. Shakur's death offered an injunction to abandon the foolishness of "Thug Life" and pursue a largely elusive American dream characterized by the norms of white civil society. If, however, this 1996 shooting enabled a contextualization of Shakur's body within the social structures that produce criminality and the commodity relations that market it, then his death and "Thug Life" might have spoken volumes about the potential for reflection and political practice in their wake. Such a gesture would undoubtedly be prophetic.

Acts of Crime, Acts of Love

In 1997, mere months after Shakur's violent death in Las Vegas, the beloved feminist poet and Black Power veteran Nikki Giovanni published *Love Poems*. She dedicated the book, which she called "a valentine from me to the world" to the recently slain rapper. She described Shakur as "a lover whose love was often deliberately misunderstood but who will live in the sun and the rains and whose name will echo through all the winds whose spirit will flower and who like Emmett Till and Malcolm X will be remembered by his people for the great man he could have become and most especially for the beautiful boy that he was."[94] The small-framed Giovanni, who was then in her late 50s, also had the words "Thug Life" tattooed on her left arm in homage to Shakur—who himself had the career-defining phrase tattooed across his muscular stomach. She described Shakur as "the first martyr" of a young generation of African Americans.[95]

Whereas other figures who laid claim to the legacy of the civil rights movement vilified Shakur and other gangsta rappers, Giovanni compared him to fallen figures like Emmett Till and Malcolm X, whose legacies had profound impacts on American antiracist politics. Shakur certainly came from a family with deep roots in the Black Power movement. In addition to his mother's time with the Black Panther Party, his aunt Assata Shakur and stepfather Mutulu Shakur remain salient figures of that era. His lineage was firmly rooted in politicized expressions of black rage. Mutulu Shakur argued in a 2011 prison interview that "Thug Life" represented the rapper's attempt to reformulate Panther radicalism for a new generation of black youth. However, given Tupac Shakur's detour into the perilous excesses of hip-hop commerce during the last years of his life, as well as the contested nature of his legacy immediately following his death, Giovanni's tribute is provocative.[96]

At the heart of Giovanni's words, and the legacy of Tupac Shakur in general, is, I believe, the complex intersection of the mark of criminality and communal love. Some, but certainly not all, rhetorics of criminality denote affective investments in collective welfare. While official versions of history tell a different story, figures like "Pretty Boy" Floyd stood as loyal representatives of marginalized peoples. They waged righteous warfare against forces of exploitation and oppression. Even unabashedly vicious black badmen like Stagger Lee offered post-Emancipation blacks equipment for living amid their shifting relationships to the carceral state. Later, blaxploitation cinema conjured violent and hypermasculine black heroes on both sides of the law who, nonetheless, retained firm investments in their racialized identity. More broadly, the historical arc of crime in an age of capitalist production reveals that transgressions against the law, particularly crimes against property and commerce, function as acts of refusal against the demands of those who would exploit or, later, abandon and confine living labor. Even the most conservative and repressive versions of the mark of criminality are themselves premised on a desire to protect an imagined community of potential, and primarily white, victims.[97]

A love for community explicitly motivated Shakur's earliest expressions of "Thug Life." While obviously ambivalent given some of his more troubling lyrics from this period and legal problems that reflected narcissistic bravado and misogyny more than civic engagement, "Thug Life" functioned as a militant political strategy dispersed through the cultural landscape of the hip-hop nation. However, Shakur's project changed dramatically after he joined the ranks of Death Row Records. The handwritten contract the young rapper signed with Suge Knight was, according to many in the industry, profoundly abusive and opportunistic given Shakur's desperate circumstances.[98] Aside from signing his artistic and financial autonomy away, however, Shakur also signed away much of the emancipatory potential of "Thug Life." He had, it seemed, made a deal with the devil.

Prior to his affiliation with Knight and Death Row, Shakur indicated that he intended to abandon "Thug Life" altogether, commenting from prison, "I'm going to start an organization called Us First. I'm going to save these young niggas, because nobody else want to save them. Nobody ever came to save me. They just watch what happen to you. That's why Thug Life to me is dead. If it's real, then let somebody else represent it, because I'm tired of it. I represented it too much. I was Thug Life. I was the only nigga out there putting my life on the line."[99] Suspecting that "Thug Life" was colliding with the limitations of the music industry and his own relationship with the law, Shakur allegedly sought alternative mechanisms for addressing black youth operating within and through the mark of criminality. While we can only speculate about Shakur's motivations following his release, it seems the desperation accompanying his incarceration and the opportunity presented by Knight prompted a reappraisal of the rapper's relationship to the hip-hop nation. His reinvention of "Thug Life" fit nicely within the broader gangsta ethos of Death Row Records and the emerging coastal feud. It is telling that Knight chose to pursue a contract with Shakur only after he was convicted of sexual assault and involved in a high-profile feud with the East Coast rap artists he believed had shot him. Shakur's potential to fashion the mark of criminality as a conduit for black rage in ways that critiqued the brutal logics of the carceral state and mainstream musical commerce was only as strong as its capacity to circumvent those very logics.

Sociologist Paul Hirst cautions against valorizing society's criminals as heroic or revolutionary figures. He writes, "The criminal career and the 'delinquent solution,' however much enforced by the harsh necessities of capitalism, are not in effect forms of political rebellion against the existing order but a more or less reactionary accommodation to them."[100] In other words, criminality is always subject to capture, whether it be by the communal yearnings of society's underclasses or the demands of its most powerful institutions. The circulation and numerous reinventions of the mark of criminality across the political terrain of the late twentieth century reveals nothing less, for while this genre has functioned as a resource for critiquing the cultural norms of American law-and-order politics, its origins are with the interests of those who surveil and confine racialized bodies, or who stand to gain from the sensationalism associated with such practices.

For "Thug Life," the forces of musical commerce, coupled with the haze of personal vendetta, proved too strong for the young Shakur's assurances that he would never sell-out. The result was a vitriolic criminal project that targeted other black artists rather than the social structures that had criminalized a generation. As Kevin Powell pondered at the height of Death Row's notoriety and success, "When a people feel like social, political, or economic outcasts, it gets easier to consider taking one another out—even over the pettiest beefs—in the name of survival."[101] Absent a more coherent analysis of criminality and political organizing outside of the recording studio, a cultural politics grounded in deployments of the mark of criminality was, perhaps, doomed to failure.

However, we have come too far to end in failure. Let us now turn to possibilities.

Conclusion

A Politics of Criminality?

Niggas been dyin' for years, so how could they blame us?

—Tupac Shakur

His hoodie killed Trayvon Martin as surely as George Zimmerman did.

—Geraldo Rivera

The mark of criminality is an affectively charged generic regime of discourses about blackness that possesses formal consistencies and strongly malleable characteristics. During the late 1980s and 1990s, an emerging form of music called gangsta rap appropriated the mark of criminality in the successful pursuit of staggering monetary gain. In the process, gangsta artists and producers also, and often unwittingly, participated in a discursive battle over the meanings of race, gender, and criminality during the war-on-crime era that closed the twentieth century. Reading gangsta rap in such terms enables not only a more nuanced approach to a long-maligned form of black vernacular expression but also reveals the war on crime was a far more complex period in American public culture than many scholarly accounts suggest.

This has been the central argument of my book. If I have convinced readers of this, one could conclude that I have done my job. However, over two million adults remain behind bars in the United States and disproportionate amounts of them are people of color. What, then, are we to do with these insights? To what extent do they enable new visions of antiprison activism that can resist the warehousing of black and brown bodies in America's jails and prisons? More broadly, what is the proper political role of scholarship, rhetorical or otherwise? How do we determine if scholarship is sufficiently engaged? Is it enough to publish work that produces and refines critical vocabularies? Is the scholarly monograph itself a salient site of critical reflexivity often unavailable amid the tumult of political activism? Or should we long to make our work speak directly to social problems and translate into concrete political practice?[1]

While I do not presume to offer unequivocal positions on the political efficacy of my work, I subsequently describe where my reading of gangsta rap in particular, and the mark of criminality in general, may lead us. Specifically, I outline what I believe a politics of criminality might do. To this end, I advance three topoi: criminal imaginaries, hip-hop activism, and repoliticizing crime. By attending to the ways communities of struggle reckon with the meanings of criminality, how hip-hop and other domains of cultural production can deploy the mark of criminality to more explicitly political ends, and the perils and promises of finding emancipatory potential in the criminal act as such, it becomes clearer how complicating the cultural history of criminality can inform critical praxis.

Criminal Imaginaries

In 1989, Charles Stuart (a white businessman from the affluent Boston suburb of Reading) told police that a black man with a raspy voice carjacked him and his wife in Boston. Stuart sustained a gunshot wound to the abdomen and his pregnant wife died from a bullet to the head. Several months later, police concluded Stuart had murdered his wife, and he committed suicide before they could make an arrest.[2] Five years later, white South Carolina resident and married mother of two Susan Smith told police an armed black man wearing a wool cap forced her from her car and drove off with her two young sons, Michael and Alex. For over a week, law enforcement, friends and family, and local and national media searched earnestly for the boys and the anonymous black man who abducted them. Smith eventually confessed to murdering her own sons.[3] During the 2008 US presidential election, Ashley Todd, a white campaign worker for Republican nominee John McCain, carved a reverse letter B onto her right cheek and told police a black male supporter of African American Democratic candidate Barack Obama was responsible. The story collapsed two days later as Todd confessed to mutilating herself and contriving the story in hopes that it would hurt Obama's campaign.[4]

While these events differ in important respects, all share a common, fictitious suspect: a black man. Furthermore, if for only a fleeting moment, the true culprit's families and friends, law enforcement, and, crucially, local and national media sought this "black man" who existed only in their collective imaginaries of criminality. By imaginaries, I am referring to what Dilip Gaonkar describes as symbolic matrices "within which people imagine and act as world-making collective agents."[5] As I have argued throughout this book, rhetorics of criminality in general, and the mark of criminality in particular, operate in such a way. We come to understand and act upon our world partially through the ways we talk about crime.

These three schemers, whether consciously or unconsciously, anticipated that Americans would instinctively believe that a black man was capable of such deeds. They had, after all, absorbed seemingly infinite hours of public address, news coverage, and popular culture that told them precisely that. While the fallout surrounding these cases inspired varying degrees of public discourse about race, crime, and suspicion, dominant iterations of the mark of criminality remained— the notion that blackness is fundamentally masculine, violent, and hypersexual lingered as common sense.[6] However, my preceding historicization of gangsta rap and the war on crime reveals that the mark of criminality, while formally consistent across its history, is also subject to reinvention and alternative deployments. Specifically, the black body is capable of appropriating and refashioning the genre to various ends. Interrogating the rhetorical dynamics of criminalization opens space for situating criminality within a broader critical project.

Something was different on February 26, 2012, when George Zimmerman, a neighborhood watch captain, shot and killed Trayvon Martin, an unarmed seventeen-year-old in a Sanford, Florida, townhome complex. If past were prelude to Martin's death, few would have questioned Zimmerman's justification for fatally shooting the young man he considered suspicious and who, Zimmerman claimed, had physically attacked him. While pockets of public outrage emerged following the fatal shootings of unarmed black men like Amadou Diallo in 1999 or Sean Bell in 2006, such incidents quickly faded from mainstream public discourse, remaining only as bitter memories for the communities most accustomed to racial profiling and police brutality.[7] But the death of Trayvon Martin inspired national mobilizations that fixated on challenging the presumption that a black teenager wearing a hoodie was inherently suspicious. Indeed, Trayvon Martin's legacy as a martyr to white supremacy persists amid mobilizations surrounding the deaths of black people like Mike Brown, Eric Garner, Walter Scott, Freddie Gray, Sandra Bland, Laquan McDonald, Alton Sterling, Philando Castile, Terence Crutcher, and Keith Lamont Scott at the hands of law enforcement (a list of names that I have had to update repeatedly during the process of completing this book).[8]

For their part, conservative media sympathetic to Zimmerman circulated pictures of Martin wearing grills (jewelry worn over one's teeth) and sagging pants, a Twitter account belonging to the teenager containing vulgar, gangsta-themed language, reports of disciplinary troubles at school, and a postmortem toxicology report revealing Martin had marijuana in his system at the time of the shooting.[9] They also believed a photograph of Zimmerman's injuries the night of the shooting (that is, bloody scrapes on the back of his head and a broken nose) provided definitive proof that he acted in self-defense.[10] All this material, for those who projected it onto the public screen, was prima facie evidence that Martin was a dangerous criminal. For them, he seemed to be as threatening as the imaginary black criminals who so many Americans believed murdered Charles Stuart's pregnant wife, kidnapped Susan Smith's children, and mutilated Ashley Todd. He was associated in their minds with Willie Horton, the convict who brutalized a white Massachusetts couple, "stabbing the man and repeatedly raping his girlfriend" and who was made nationally notorious through a George H. W. Bush campaign advertisement.[11] Joining the ranks of Horton and so many other violent and suspicious black men who haunt the public imaginary, Trayvon Martin embodied all the formal characteristics of the mark of criminality the night of his death and the months following. Indeed, after a jury acquitted Zimmerman of second-degree murder charges—which only materialized after massive public pressure—it was clear that the public affective investments in the overdetermined association of black masculinity with criminality remained strong, even in the face of public scrutiny.

The campaign to secure Zimmerman's conviction was primarily invested in dissociating the young Martin from the mark of criminality. The messaging sought to reclaim the hoodie from those, like Geraldo Rivera, who regarded it as a signifier of black masculine aggression. Campaigners also privileged the voices of Martin's parents to emphasize his status as a child rather than a criminal.[12] Opinions on the controversial case came to hinge on how we regarded Trayvon Martin. Was he the same kind of black man even Jesse Jackson feared while walking down the street at night or a kid simply heading home to enjoy the iced tea and Skittles he just purchased at the local 7-Eleven?[13]

It is tempting to argue that if the legacy of gangsta rap played any role in the shooting death of Trayvon Martin, it made George Zimmerman more likely to fear him. After all, much media revealed a teenage Martin who partook in many of the cultural performances of masculine bravado and violent fantasizing associated with the gangsta genre. If C. Delores Tucker, who died in 2005, had been alive to comment on the case, she likely would have claimed that the likes of Snoop Doggy Dogg and Tupac Shakur, as well as contemporary rappers like Lil Wayne, Kevin Gates, and A$AP Rocky, helped cultivate a cultural climate in which young black men emulated their gangsta heroes and white Americans grew to fear them even more. Indeed, Zimmerman's lawyers hoped associating Martin with "gangsta culture" would make jurors less likely to view him as a victim, and instead situate the events surrounding his death within the formal contours of dominant interpretations of the mark of criminality. Gangsta again provided a window into the alterity of black life in America. White civil society should be afraid—very afraid.[14]

While there can be no denying that long-entrenched assumptions about gangsta and its reflection of black criminality and masculinity feed pervasive stereotypes about black life in America, we should not be so quick to accept the prevailing logics associated with mainstream deployments of the mark of criminality by privileging its opposites. Trayvon Martin the son, teenager, and athlete was antithetical to the savage thug Zimmerman's supporters asked us to fear. While the Martin case produced more mobilization and public discourse on matters of race and the criminal justice system than any in recent memory, George Zimmerman was nonetheless acquitted of murder. While he was a villain to those who sought to challenge permissive gun laws and racial profiling, he was a hero, or at least worthy of sympathy, to those who identified with Zimmerman's predicament that fateful night.[15] In their estimations, all sensible people would fear for their lives when confronted with a young, tall, black body donning a hoodie. The mark of criminality clearly remains a centerpiece of American imaginations of race, gender, and violence. Unless we are prepared to recuperate this critical work from those reactionary forces that defend Zimmerman, the mark of criminality will continue to support regimes of domination when it could be informing critique and political practice.[16]

Gangsta rap does not provide a clear schematic for producing new readings of black masculinity or criminality. Rather, its history is instructive of how malleable the mark of criminality is. While combating stereotypes of young black men like Trayvon Martin is crucial cultural work, so is offering alternative explanations of the cultural norms that remain meaningful to them. How do grills, sagging pants, gangsta vernaculars, violent fantasizing, and drug use help members of the single most criminalized demographic in the United States make sense of their location therein? What kinds of criminal imaginaries do they produce? What, in other words, does gangsta do? This book has attempted to offer some explanations. To wish away these cultural practices that are so capable of capturing and mobilizing affect cedes important rhetorical ground to supporters of mass incarceration, police surveillance, and austerity as well as those who use gangsta rap to justify their own hateful rhetorics of race.[17] To do so is to demonstrate an utter lack of imagination and allow prevailing iterations of the mark of criminality that circulate in public culture to persist. Rather, we should be guided by Maxine Waters's decades-old injunction to listen by contextualizing and historicizing the mark of criminality.[18] If our current incarceration rates and the collateral consequences thereof have anything to teach us, it is that the mark of criminality has profoundly tangible consequences for black bodies and communities. When Trayvon Martin met George Zimmerman in Florida, his body also collided, as it likely had before, with prevailing versions of the genre. However, he also clearly found resources for affective investment and agency within those very gangsta discourses that have long valorized the status of the criminal. Attending to the malleable generic character of the mark of criminality provides indispensable resources for discovering and mobilizing alternative meanings for criminality capable of destabilizing the powerful formal logics that help sustain our incarceration nation.[19]

Hip-Hop Activism, Hip-Hop Memory

I have spent much of this book challenging the long-standing dichotomy between "conscious" or "message" rap and gangsta rap. A strong majority of hip-hop intellectuals and many culture producers regard conscious rap as a fulfillment of the genre's promise, whereas gangsta rap commits rhetorical violence and rationalizes stereotypes about black criminality.[20] In addition to the scholars and activists who write extensively on the emancipatory promise of hip-hop, artists including Common, Lauryn Hill, and the Roots have dedicated significant record space to critiquing their gangsta counterparts. Addressing rap as an estranged lover on his 1994 track "I Used to Love H.E.R.," Common lamented that what was once "Original, pure, untampered" and "on that tip about stopping violence" began "Talking about popping Glocks, serving rocks, and hitting switches."[21] On her 1998 debut solo album, Lauryn Hill asks male gangsta rappers, "Now, now, how come your talk turn cold?" claiming they "gain the whole world for the price of your soul."[22] These and other artists are partaking in an important conversation about the fate of an art form. How, they ask, shall hip-hop live? Will it provide the same kind of radical energy as Billie Holiday, Marvin Gaye, Nina Simone, Stevie Wonder, and countless other politically salient black musicians, or will it succumb to the commands of the market, patriarchy, and street violence?[23]

Such conversations should and do continue. However, harnessing hip-hop's cultural heft to challenge the logics of white supremacy and mass incarceration also benefits from resisting the temptation to, even lovingly, simply admonish its gangsta components. My own interest in gangsta rap and its relevance for understanding the rhetorical dynamics of law and order in the United States did not begin with performers like NWA or Snoop Doggy Dogg. While I was casually familiar with them, I generally accepted the thesis that conscious rap offered a more promising mode of emancipatory cultural practice. As an anti-death-penalty activist and graduate student, I came to enjoy the likes of the Coup, Lupe Fiasco, Yasiin Bey (Mos Def), and Talib Kweli. Eithne Quinn claims that such artists derive "energy and definition from their opposition to the dominant gangsta ethic."[24] For the vast majority of conscious rappers, Quinn is correct; they resist the gangsta sensationalism that they believe taints their beloved art form. However, the Florida-based duo dead prez suggests another avenue for reckoning with the long-standing tensions between conscious rap and gangsta rap.

Formed in 1996, dead prez remains one of the most visible activist hip-hop groups in the United States. With a deep investment in Black Nationalism, they routinely use their music to comment on broad issues like poverty, racial profiling, mass incarceration, and war, as well as specific controversies like the killing of Trayvon Martin.[25] It was their second studio album, *RBG: Revolutionary but Gangsta* that inspired this book. "Revolutionary but Gangsta," or RBG, expresses a radical political program through the criminality inherent to the signifier "gangsta." The acronym also corresponds with the red, black, and green colors of the traditional Black Nationalist flag. Thus they revise the mark of criminality by infusing it with nationalist politics. The album's most popular single, "Hell Yeah (Pimp the System)" engages in a playful reconfiguration of racialized criminal activity. Encouraging the young black listener to "pimp" the system, the group's MC, M-1, raps gleefully about mugging a white pizza delivery driver ("By the look on his face he probably shitted in his clothes"), committing credit card and welfare fraud ("Fuck welfare, we say reparations"), and insubordination at work ("Don't put me on dishes / I'm droppin' them bitches / And takin' all day long to mop the kitchen").[26]

By conventional measures, these acts of violence, abuse of welfare programs, and workplace laziness are long-standing stereotypes associated with poor and working-class African Americans. Hegemonic renderings of the mark of criminality, especially during the late 1980s and 1990s, relied on such narratives to persuade a primarily white voting public to support the mass imprisonment of black men and other marginalized populations, as well as the dramatic dismantling of the welfare state. However, these celebratory tales of criminality, rapped over a rapid-fire drum machine beat, are sources of intense excitement and political agency for dead prez. Committing crime, in this track's diegesis, is an affectively charged endeavor that allows the black criminal to aggressively reject the demands of white civil society—or, to pimp the system. In addition to delivering the lyrics with gangsta bravado, M-1 offers justification for these deeds. In the track's closing verse, he raps, "We ain't getting paid commission, minimum wage, modern day slave conditions / Got me flippin' burgers with no power / Can't even buy one off what I make in an hour / I'm not the one to kiss ass for the top position / I take mine off the top like a politician / Where I'm from doing dirt is a part of living / I got mouths to feed I gots to get it."[27] M-1 views crime as an economic necessity and, in the same spirit as Woody Guthrie's tribute to "Pretty Boy" Floyd, an opportunity to rhetorically reconfigure the norms that rationalize hegemonic definitions of criminality. Just as Guthrie portrayed Floyd as no worse than the greedy bankers of the Depression era, M-1 challenges listeners to distinguish his violent, fraudulent deeds from those performed at the upper echelons of American political and economic power. Crime becomes a mode of political and rhetorical practice.[28]

In addition to dead prez's militant work, public memory of 1980s and 1990s gangsta rap provides another modality for exploring the mark of criminality's capacity to enable critiques of white supremacy and the carceral state. As I noted earlier, the financial and critical success of the 2015 film *Straight Outta Compton* revealed the continuing cultural traction of NWA's story and music, while also providing a modality for public discourse regarding the emergence of the Black Lives Matter movement. The film, directed by F. Gary Gray and produced by Ice Cube and Dr. Dre, chronicles NWA's emergence in Compton's nascent rap scene, their commercial success and the accompanying public controversies, and the group's demise and Eazy-E's death. Gray and the film's writers explicitly contextualize the group's formation and early work in the racialized politics of law and order by featuring scenes of LAPD drug busts, blatant racial profiling, and law enforcement backlash against NWA for the release of "Fuck Tha Police." For example, a scene immediately preceding the writing and recording of the group's most controversial track portrays an encounter between NWA's original members and a group of Los Angeles police officers outside the studio where the group is recording its first album. The patrolmen, the most aggressive of whom is a black man ("Black police showing out for the white cop"), force the group to "kiss the sidewalk" and submit to a search.[29] The film posits the production of "Fuck Tha Police" as a direct response to this humiliating incident. Furthermore, critical reaction to the film explicitly tethered its release to concurrent and widespread national protests against police violence. *Rolling Stone* film critic Peter Travers described it as "an electrifying piece of hip-hop history that speaks urgently to right now."[30] During an interview with a writer for the *Source*, Gray also commented on his film's relevance to contemporary racial politics, explaining, "I think it's pretty sad that it's still relevant in its relationship to law enforcement, but I'm optimistic that a lot of the headlines we're experiencing will put pressure on the leaders and law enforcement to really change."[31]

In many respects, the film *Straight Outta Compton* does for NWA what the group itself was never explicitly interested in doing during the late 1980s and early 1990s: positing its deployments of the mark of criminality as a form of political activism. Ice Cube and Dr. Dre also participated in this (re)telling of the group's role in public culture during a promotional commercial for the film that featured the two rap pioneers driving through Compton and visiting with old friends and fellow rappers. Early in the advertisement, Ice Cube describes NWA's work as "nonviolent protest."[32] Thus the film itself, as well as much public discourse surrounding its release, sought to capture contemporary public affect regarding racist police violence and mass incarceration within the memory of NWA's enactments of the mark of criminality. The group, just as it certainly was by many during their most popular years, is to be remembered as a transformative cultural and political force that gave expression to the seething anger of black residents in municipalities like Compton near the end of the twentieth century. The film's resonance relied on its ability to produce a clear and compelling affective linkage between an earlier generation's outrage and those mobilizing black bodies in the streets today.

Like gangsta rap itself, the political character of work by artists such as dead prez or a film like *Straight Outta Compton* are deeply ambivalent. dead prez's nationalist political project is problematic in its own capacity to foment racial division (what did that pizza delivery driver do to them, anyway?) and forge incongruent lines of solidarity. Furthermore, while the film *Straight Outta Compton* makes crucial historical connections between the era chronicled in this book and the cultural politics of race and criminality today, its attempts to privilege the activist character of NWA's work resulted in the omission of the group's misogynistic excesses.[33] The work of dead prez and the film *Straight Outta Compton* constitute iterations of the mark of criminality, one as nationalist politics and the other as public memory, that are as fraught as their predecessors in black folklore, cinema, and, of course, gangsta rap. Nonetheless, they reflect the continuing ability of hip-hop to mobilize the mark of criminality in ways that resonate with lived experiences of subjugation and offer alternative modes for affective investment.[34] While the rappers chronicled in this volume may not have provided a form of cultural expression capable of using the mark of criminality in ways that galvanized powerful critical practice, they produced a vocabulary that remains useful to some artists in the hip-hop nation, as well as for rhetorics of public memory, that draw on that vocabulary for making sense of contemporary politics of race and state violence. They also, crucially, revealed ruptures in the syntax of American law and order.

Repoliticizing Crime

Crime is not reducible to its rhetorical representations. While the decision to regard certain acts as criminal is rhetorical, the deeds we choose to punish—and in many cases excuse—have real impacts on real bodies and communities. The vast majority of criminality, in fact, impacts members of the culprit's communities far more than the elites targeted in tall tales like Robin Hood.[35] Thus, to call for a retelling of the war on crime and a broader reconfiguring of the rhetorical norms of criminality in public culture is not to advocate for a recuperative project that imagines crime as simply a mode of political resistance. For example, the fact that black masculine bodies are disproportionately marked as sexually aggressive toward white and black women does not excuse the corporeal and rhetorical violence against women of color like Desiree Washington or Ayanna Jackson. The damage of sexual assault and other forms of violence against women are not things we should be seeking to frame as insurrectionary acts against the prison-industrial complex and white supremacy any more than a drive-by shooting or devastating drug epidemic.[36] As much as we rightfully critique the institutional responses to crime in communities of color and elsewhere, to allow our critical postures to excuse the deeds of men like Mike Tyson, Tupac Shakur, or countless other, less prominent black men—as well as their more privileged white counterparts who often act in identical ways with relative impunity—would constitute intellectual, political, and ethical failures.[37] The misogynistic musings of gangsta rap reveal weaknesses in the normative structures of American criminality. They are not satisfying substitutes.

But real crime has real meanings, and for every Trayvon Martin, there are numerous figures who are quite guilty of awful acts. Their deeds also require a politics of criminality underwritten by an attention to the mark of criminality's status as a malleable rhetorical genre. Such malleability is particularly salient when we consider criminal deeds that, while generating disgust and horror from most mainstream sectors of public discourse, inspire admiration from others. For example, in 2013, former Los Angeles police and naval officer Christopher Dorner went on a killing spree that left three police officers and one officer's daughter dead, and injured three other members of law enforcement. Dorner, a black man, described his acts as retaliation against a culture of institutional racism and brutality at the LAPD. He claimed he was dismissed from the department solely for his role in attempting to reveal these grim truths about one of the nation's most infamous law enforcement agencies. The Dorner saga ended at a cabin in the mountains of Southern California. During a shoot-out with his former law enforcement comrades, Dorner died from a self-inflicted gunshot wound in a fire caused by a tear gas canister.[38]

While mainstream coverage of the nine-day manhunt employed traditional interpretations of the mark of criminality by characterizing Dorner as a hypermasculine mortal threat to anyone who crossed his path, some users of social media praised him as a hero.[39] Using Twitter hashtags like #TeamDorner and #DornerGang, several users cheered the former police officer on as he murdered four people and injured three. On the day of Dorner's death, Twitter user "So Afficial" posted a photograph of Dorner's likeness being tattooed on an anonymous figure's flesh. The text "Shyt getn Real lol the homie said Happy Blacc History Month" accompanies the image.[40] The same day, user "Lawson" declared, "BRUH HE'S LEGENDARY," referring to conflicting early reports about Dorner's fate inside the charred California cabin.[41] Further commenting on her hero's "legendary" status, another user boasted, "He killed at least 5 pigs in a week, that's it. I bow down to him. Nobody would EVER be down to or pull that off."[42] User "Ro" claimed, "This is retribution for whoopin Rodney King's ass," tethering Dorner's acts to one of the foundational incidents of late twentieth century law-and-order politics in Los Angeles County.[43] While not mentioning Dorner by name, user "SKiZM" posted the headline, "California Man Dies after Female Cop Hits Him with Baton 10 Times!" followed by a link to a newscast describing the event and the hashtag #TeamDorner. Posting almost exactly three months after Dorner's death, this user expresses solidarity with his deeds in the wake of more alleged police brutality.[44]

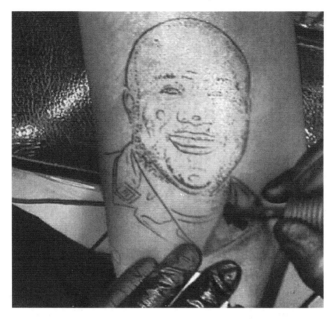

Figure 11: Christopher Dorner tattoo. Twitter, 2013.

To read these tweets, drafted exclusively by black men and women, is to see the violent fantasies of "Fuck Tha Police" or "Cop Killer" come to life. For them, Dorner is exacting rightful retribution on a loathed criminal justice apparatus that they believe exercises unjust violence on black bodies and communities. They refashioned the mark of criminality to cast Dorner's aggression as heroism. His story gave expression to the affective intensities emerging from their own lived encounters with white supremacy.[45] By using familiar gangsta terminology like "Shyt gettn Real" and "homie," speculating that Dorner was listening to Public Enemy's "Fight the Power" as if he were a more militant version of Spike Lee's Radio Raheem, and adorning their own account pages with background images of male figures donning backward baseball caps and other markers of gangsta aesthetics, the logics of gangsta are palpable in these heroic tributes to a black man the twenty-four-hour news cycle was casting as a vicious psychopath.[46] Dorner, for these and other "fans," was a "crazy motherfucker" for the twenty-first century. He was also, crucially, opening fire during the post–Trayvon Martin era when critiques of racial profiling and law enforcement were gaining new traction in mainstream circles.[47]

Were these young people experiencing the kind of catharsis black youth of the 1980s and 1990s surely sensed when enjoying tracks like "Fuck Tha Police"? The available evidence suggests they were. For them, Dorner's rampage became an affectively charged allegory of black resentment toward a racist criminal justice system. To take pleasure in the former police officer's acts was to feel, if only for a fleeting moment, a sense of retribution for generations of racist violence. However, while celebrating Dorner's rampage as a righteous expression of black rage undeniably reconfigures the mark of criminality to express long-standing frustrations with the carceral state, it does so in ways that simply cannot sustain a credible critique of law enforcement or the prison-industrial complex. To be clear, I do not believe it is my prerogative, especially as a white author, to sanctimoniously dismiss the felt intensities Dorner's acts inspired. These responses are born of shared histories of encounters with the vast machinery of surveillance and incarceration that disproportionately impacts young black lives. Thus I tread carefully as I attempt to recognize the exigencies that mobilized support for Dorner, while also asking how such energies might translate to more concrete political practice.

Our goal when engaging the Dorner tragedy should not be to excuse his decision to end four lives. The task at hand is producing better articulations of the mark of criminality, not ones that potentially justify its hegemonic iterations with fleeting, celebratory declarations about vengeance and masculinity. This entails the difficult, often publicly maligned, work of understanding that Dorner's acts are, in many important respects, the culmination of a horrible history of institutional racism at the LAPD and other arteries of law enforcement. In his lengthy manifesto, posted online before he fired his first shots, Dorner claimed, "The department has not changed from the Daryl Gates and Mark Fuhrman [the investigator in the O. J. Simpson murder case whose well-documented use of racial epithets helped derail the prosecution's case] days."[48] He also distanced himself from the violent legacies of gangsta, and, more broadly, most iterations of the mark of criminality, while claiming this is not a battle of his choosing: "I'm not an aspiring rapper, I'm not a gang member, I'm not a dope dealer, I don't have multiple babies momma's. I am an American by choice, I am a son, I am a brother, I am a military service member, I am a man who has lost complete faith in the system, when the system betrayed, slandered, and libeled me."[49] Furthermore, Dorner characterizes himself as a creator's nightmare for the LAPD, bragging that the very skills he learned in the navy and law enforcement enabled him to anticipate every police move. He framed his acts as macabre instances of chickens coming home to roost and invited readers to question the legitimacy of state violence against him. Dorner was not himself partaking in a reinvention of the mark of criminality. That was the work of his online following. Rather, Dorner fashioned himself as a warrior who represented the ideals of law and order, whereas those he targeted perverted such principles.[50] The former police officer's manifesto also revealed troubling misogynistic and homophobic tendencies when he promised to target "those lesbian officers in supervising positions who go to work, day in day out, with the sole intent of attempting to prove your misandrist authority (not feminism) to degrade male officers" and cold-hearted condescension to the families of those he planned to kill when he wrote, "to those children of the officers who are eradicated, your parent was not the individual you thought they were. As you get older, you will see the evidence that your parent was a tyrant who loss [sic] their ethos and instead followed the path of moral corruptness."[51]

The Dorner affair, in short, was a dark and disturbing tragedy that nonetheless requires nuanced critical attention. We dismiss his political salience at our own peril, but we must also avoid the temptation to uncritically sanctify him. Such a task requires contextualizing Dorner's acts and the public responses they inspired in order to develop critical insights about the mark of criminality. For example, we can recognize in his cold words directed toward his victims' survivors a potential for the critique of public silence regarding the collateral consequences of carceral violence toward communities of color, for the cruelty of public indifference toward black life is far more pervasive than the maligned taunts of a man like Dorner. Recuperating his story from those who would demonize or sanctify him is essential for detecting the kinds of lessons about race, masculinity, violence, and law enforcement we may stand to learn from such a bloody chapter in twenty-first-century history.

Dorner's deeds enabled a group of young people of color to harness the tools of social media to deploy the mark of criminality in ways that expressed their frustrations with a law enforcement apparatus that, as I write, is increasingly subject to black-led political mobilizations invested in the demand that black lives matter. For these young people, Dorner provided a rare example of a black masculine body inflicting violence on members of a police department whose violence against communities of color took many forms. The same affective investments that led them to view Dorner as a hero are also present in the streets of cities like Ferguson, Missouri, and Baltimore, Maryland, where traditional protests and violent insurrections coalesced to bring attention not only to the entrenched white supremacy of the US criminal justice system but also to the necessity of reexamining popular assumptions about the relationship between violence and black bodies in public culture.[52] Dorner's supporters, however few they may have been, viewed his killings as part of a large historical arc in which the mark of criminality, on balance, functions to rationalize the disproportionate surveillance and imprisonment of black men. Our task should be to do the same, but in ways that also seek to learn from the more politically explicit activist energies that continue to reshape public discourses on crime and public culture. This is not to call for brittle taxonomies that distinguish efficacious political rhetoric from more problematic vernacular expression, but to identify affective linkages between some deployments of the mark of criminality and modes of political practice that, I believe, are ultimately better suited to motivate social change.

If affect is a mobile reservoir of felt intensities that are the condition of possibility for political resistance, then we might imagine today's movements against white supremacy and state violence as crystallizations of the affective energies that found expression in Dorner's rampage, just as surely as the incendiary cultural productions of gangsta rap.[53] Deploying the mark of criminality to critique the very logics that produced it may not be an end in itself, but the mark of criminality remains a potent rhetorical genre that mobilizes affect and enables critique in ways that might find more fruitful expression in other modalities of discourse. If gangsta rap exposed limits to hegemonic uses of the mark of criminality, what we make of those limits will be best decided in the streets. Indeed, if the growing chorus of black voices in cities across the United States is any indication, such a project is already in the making.

Notes

Preface

I adopted the preface's title, "The White Boy Listens to Gangsta Rap," from James Baldwin, "The Black Boy Looks at the White Boy," in his *Nobody Knows My Name: More Notes of a Native Son* (New York: Dell Publishing, 1961), 171–90. Regarding the term the "mark of criminality," I used this term in a 2014 TEDxLSU presentation.

1. Introduced in 1991, Nielsen SoundScan was the first technology to track record sales electronically. Jeff Chang, *Can't Stop Won't Stop: A History of the Hip-Hop Generation* (New York: Picador, 2005).

2. Kheven Lee LaGrone, "From Minstrelsy to Gangsta Rap: The 'Nigger' as Commodity for Popular American Entertainment," *Journal of African American Men* 5 (2000): 117–31; S. Craig Watkins, *Hip Hop Matters: Politics, Pop Culture, and the Struggle for the Soul of a Movement* (Boston: Beacon Press, 2005). For an alternative perspective, see Kimberly Chabot Davis, *Beyond the White Negro: Empathy and Anti-Racist Reading* (Urbana: University of Illinois Press, 2014).

3. *Office Space*, directed by Mike Judge (Los Angeles: Twentieth-Century Fox Film Corporation, 1999).

4. See Eric King Watts, "Border Patrolling and 'Passing' in Eminem's *8 Mile*," *Critical Studies in Media Communication* 22 (2005): 187–206.

5. See Dustin Bradley Goltz, "Frustrating the 'I': Critical Dialogic Reflexivity with Personal Voice," *Text and Performance Quarterly* 31 (2011): 386–405; Charles E. Morris III, "Context's Critic, Invisible Traditions, and Queering Rhetorical History," *Quarterly Journal of Speech* 101 (2015): 225–43.

6. See David P. Terry, "Once Blind, Now Seeing: Problematics of Confessional Performance," *Text and Performance Quarterly* 26 (2006): 209–28.

7. See Tipper Gore, "Hate, Rape, and Rap," *Washington Post*, January 8, 1990, LexisNexis Academic.

8. For narrative and analysis on the Foster case, see Jennifer Asenas, et al., "Saving Kenneth Foster: Speaking with Others in the Belly of the Beast of Capital Punishment," in *Communication Activism*, vol. 3, *Struggling for Social Justice Amidst Difference*, ed. Lawrence R. Frey and Kevin M. Carragee (New York: Hampton Press, 2012), 264–90.

9. Ibid. Also see Erik Nielson and Michael Render (a.k.a. Killer Mike), "Rap's Poetic (In)justice: Column," *USA Today*, December 1, 2014, http://www.usatoday.com/story/opinion/2014/11/28/poetic-injustice-rap-supreme-court-lyrics-violence-trial-column/19537391/.

10. See Jav'lin, "Walk with Me," *YouTube*, February 8, 2007, https://www.youtube.com/watch?v=UaJdrxT8hiY.

11. See Mumia Abu-Jamal, *Live from Death Row* (New York: HarperCollins, 1996).

12. Asenas, et al., "Saving Kenneth Foster."

Introduction

1. On moral panic, see Stuart Hall, et al., *Policing the Crisis: Mugging, the State, and Law and Order* (Hampshire, UK: Palgrave Macmillan, 1978).

2. On mass incarceration at the close of the twentieth century, see Christian Parenti, *Lockdown America: Police and Prisons in the Age of Crisis* (London: Verso, 1999); Robert Perkinson, *Texas Tough: The Rise of America's Prison Empire* (New York: Metropolitan Books, 2010); Jonathan Simon, *Governing through Crime: How the War on Crime Transformed American Democracy and Created a Culture of Fear* (Oxford: Oxford University Press, 2007). On the prison-industrial complex, see Stephen John Hartnett, "The Annihilating Public Policies of the Prison-Industrial Complex; or, Crime, Violence, and Punishment in an Age of Neoliberalism," *Rhetoric and Public Affairs* 11 (2008): 491–515; Eric Schlosser, "The Prison-Industrial Complex," *Atlantic Monthly*, December 1998, http://www.theatlantic.com/issues/98dec/pris2.htm; "What Is the PIC? What Is Abolition?" *Critical Resistance*, 2015, http://criticalresistance.org/about/not-so-common-language/. On the racialized dimensions thereof, see Michelle Alexander, *The New Jim Crow: Mass Incarceration in the Age of Colorblindness* (New York: New Press, 2010). On current incarceration rates, see Jennifer Warren, *One in 100: Behind Bars in America* (Washington, DC: Pew Charitable Trusts, 2008).

3. Gabriel J. Chin, "The New Civil Death: Rethinking Punishment in the Era of Mass Conviction," *University of Pennsylvania Law Review* 160 (2012): 1789–833. Also see Alexander, *New Jim Crow*; Alexia D. Cooper, Matthew R. Durose, and Howard N. Snyder, "Recidivism of Prisoners Released in 30 States in 2005: Patterns from 2005 to 2010," *Bureau of Justice Statistics*, April 22, 2014, http://www.bjs.gov/index.cfm?ty=pbdetail&iid=4987; Hartnett, "Annihilating Public Policies of the Prison-Industrial Complex"; Marc Mauer, *Race to Incarcerate* (New York: New Press, 2006); Jennifer Medina, "California Sheds Prisoners but Grapples with Courts," *New York Times*, January 21, 2013, http://www.nytimes.com/2013/01/22/us/22prisons.html?_r=0; Anthony Romero and Mark V. Holden, "A New Beginning for Criminal Justice Reform," *Politico*, July 7, 2015, http://www.politico.com/magazine/story/2015/07/a-new-beginning-for-criminal-justice-reform-119822; Warren, *One in 100*.

4. Warren, *One in 100*. While, as of the Pew study, the United States incarcerates one in 355 adult women, they are the country's fastest-growing prisoner population. According to the advocacy organization the Sentencing Project, "The number of women in prison increased by 646% between 1980 and 2010." The Sentencing Project, *Incarcer-*

ated Women, September 2012, http://www.sentencingproject.org/doc/publications/cc
_Incarcerated_Women_Factsheet_Sep24sp.pdf.

5. Scott Phillips, "Racial Disparities in the Capital of Capital Punishment," *Houston Law Review* 45 (2008), LexisNexis Academic Universe. Also see Phillip Atiba Goff, Jennifer L. Eberhardt, Melissa J. Williams, and Matthew Christian Jackson, "Not Yet Human: Implicit Knowledge, Historical Dehumanization, and Contemporary Consequences," *Journal of Personality and Social Psychology* 94 (2008): 292–306.

6. Alexander, *New Jim Crow*. Also see Marc Mauer and Medea Chesney-Lind, eds., *Invisible Punishment: The Collateral Consequences of Mass Imprisonment* (New York: New Press, 2002).

7. Carol A. Stabile, *White Victims, Black Villains: Gender, Race, and Crime News in US Culture* (New York: Routledge, 2006), 8.

8. Michael Quinn, "'Never Shoulda Been Let out the Penitentiary': Gangsta Rap and the Struggle over Racial Identity," *Cultural Critique* 34 (1996), 69.

9. Imani Perry, *Prophets of the Hood: Politics and Poetics in Hip Hop* (Durham, NC: Duke University Press, 2004), 108–9.

10. Eric King Watts, "An Exploration of Spectacular Consumption: Gangsta Rap as Cultural Commodity," *Communication Studies* 48 (1997), 56.

11. Kenneth Burke, *Language as Symbolic Action* (Berkeley: University of California Press, 1966).

12. Greg Goodale, *Sonic Persuasion: Reading Sound in the Recorded Age* (Urbana: University of Illinois Press, 2011). Also see Joshua Gunn, et al., "Auscultating Again: Rhetoric and Sound Studies," *Rhetoric Society Quarterly* 43 (2013): 475–89. For exemplars of these tendencies, see Barry Brummett, *A Rhetoric of Style* (Carbondale: Southern Illinois University Press, 2008); David A. Carter, "The Industrial Workers of the World and the Rhetoric of Song," *Quarterly Journal of Speech* 66 (1980): 365–74; Lawrence Grossberg, "Rock, Territoriality, and Power," in *Dancing in Spite of Myself: Essays on Popular Culture* (Durham, NC: Duke University Press, 1997), 89–101; Joshua Gunn, "Gothic Music and the Inevitability of Genre," *Popular Music and Society* 23 (1999): 31–50; Jennifer C. Lena, "Voyeurism and Resistance in Rap Music Videos," *Communication and Critical/Cultural Studies* 5 (2008): 264–79.

13. Roland Barthes, *Image, Music, Text* (New York: Hill and Wang, 1977), 179. Also see Thomas J. Rickert, *Ambient Rhetoric: The Attunements of Rhetorical Being* (Pittsburgh: University of Pittsburgh Press, 2013).

14. George Lipsitz, "Turning Hegemony on Its Head: The Insurgent Knowledge of Américo Paredes," *Journal of American Folklore* 125 (2012): 112. Also see George Lipsitz, *Dangerous Crossroads: Popular Music, Postmodernism, and the Poetics of Place* (London: Verso, 1994), 39.

15. Tony Kirschner, "Studying Rock: Toward a Materialist Ethnography," in *Mapping the Beat: Popular Music and Contemporary Theory*, ed. Thomas Swiss, John M. Sloop, and Andrew Herman (Malden, MA: Blackwell, 1998), 249.

16. John Street, *Music and Politics* (Malden, MA: Polity Press, 2012), 1. Also see Brummett, *Rhetoric of Style*.

17. Greil Marcus, *Mystery Train: Images of America in Rock 'n' Roll Music*, 5th ed. (New York: Plume, 2008), 7. Also see Jacques Attali, *Noise: The Political Economy of Music*, trans. Brian Massumi (Minneapolis: University of Minnesota Press, 1985); Robert Francesconi, "Free Jazz and Black Nationalism: A Rhetoric of Musical Style," *Critical Studies in Mass Communication* 3 (1986): 36–49; Theodore Matula, "Contextualizing Mu-

sical Rhetoric: A Critical Reading of the Pixies' 'Rock Music,'" *Communication Studies* 51 (2000): 218–37; Deanna Sellnow and Timothy Sellnow, "The 'Illusion of Life' Rhetorical Perspective: An Integrated Approach to the Study of Music as Communication," *Critical Studies in Media Communication* 18 (2001): 395–415.

18. Kirschner, "Studying Rock: Toward a Materialist Ethnography," 263.

19. Lawrence Grossberg writes, "A conjuncture is always a social formation understood as more than a mere context—but as an articulation, accumulation, or condensation of contradictions." Lawrence Grossberg, "Does Cultural Studies Have Futures? Should It? (Or What's the Matter with New York?): Cultural Studies, Contexts, and Conjunctures," *Cultural Studies* 20 (2006): 5. On linkages and identification, see Paul Gilroy, "It Ain't Where You're From, It's Where You're At . . . The Dialectics of Diasporic Identification," *Third Text* 5 (1991): 3–16.

20. Joshua Gunn and Mirko M. Hall, "Stick It in Your Ear: The Psychodynamics of iPod Enjoyment," *Communication and Critical/Cultural Studies* 5 (2008): 144.

21. While high-profile criminal cases had long captured the national imagination and functioned as conduits for articulating broader social issues, the elevation of criminal justice to such prominence in the postwar era was largely unprecedented. See Marie Gottschalk, *The Prison and the Gallows: The Politics of Mass Incarceration in America* (Cambridge: Cambridge University Press, 2006).

22. Chang, *Can't Stop Won't Stop*; Quinn, "Never Shoulda Been Let out the Penitentiary."

Chapter 1

1. NWA, "Gangsta, Gangsta," *Straight Outta Compton*.

2. On definitional ruptures, see Edward Schiappa, *Defining Reality: Definitions and the Politics of Meaning* (Carbondale: Southern Illinois University Press, 2003).

3. Kenneth Burke, *Counter-Statement* (Berkeley: University of California Press, 1968), 31.

4. See Kenneth Burke, *Language as Symbolic Action* (Berkeley: University of California Press, 1966).

5. Joshua Gunn, "*Maranantha*," *Quarterly Journal of Speech* 98 (2012), 368.

6. See Karlyn Kohrs Campbell and Kathleen Hall Jamieson, "Form and Genre in Rhetorical Criticism: An Introduction," in *Form and Genre: Shaping Rhetorical Action*, ed. Karlyn Kohrs Campbell and Kathleen Hall Jamieson (Falls Church, VA: Speech Communication Association, 1978), 9–32; Gunn, "*Maranantha*."

7. Gunn, "*Maranantha*," 373.

8. Robert Seyfert, "Beyond Personal Feelings and Collective Emotion: Toward a Theory of Social Affect," *Theory, Culture, and Society* 29 (2012): 29.

9. Brian Massumi, *Parables for the Virtual: Movement, Affect, Sensation* (Durham, NC: Duke University Press, 2002), 71. Also see Lawrence Grossberg, *Cultural Studies in the Future Tense* (Durham, NC: Duke University Press, 2010).

10. Gilles Deleuze, "Lecture Transcripts on Spinoza's Concept of *Affect*," January 24, 1978, http://www.webdeleuze.com/php/texte.php?cle=14&groupe=Spinoza&langue=2.

11. See Sara Ahmed, *The Cultural Politics of Emotion*, 2nd ed. (New York: Routledge, 2015); Deleuze, "Lecture Transcripts on Spinoza's Concept of *Affect*"; Deborah Gould, "On Affect and Protest," in *Political Emotions: New Agendas in Communication*, ed. Ann Cvetkovich, Ann Reynolds, and Janet Staiger (New York: Routledge, 2010), 18–44;

Christian Lundberg, "Enjoying God's Death: *The Passion of the Christ* and the Practices of an Evangelical Public," *Quarterly Journal of Speech* 95 (2009): 387–411; Massumi, *Parables for the Virtual*; Erin J. Rand, *Reclaiming Queer: Activist and Academic Rhetorics of Resistance* (Tuscaloosa: University of Alabama Press, 2014); Jenny Edbauer Rice, "The New 'New': Making a Case for Critical Affect Studies," *Quarterly Journal of Speech* 94 (2008): 200–212; Gregory J. Seigworth and Melissa Gregg, "An Inventory of Shimmers," in *The Affect Theory Reader*, ed. Gregory J. Seigworth and Melissa Gregg (Durham, NC: Duke University Press, 2012), 1–25.

12. Charles Bazerman, "Speech Acts, Genres, and Activity Systems: How Texts Organize Activity and People," in *What Writing Does and How It Does It*, ed. Charles Bazerman and Paul Prior (Mahwah, NJ: Lawrence Erlbaum Associates, 2004), 311. Also see Carolyn R. Miller, "Genre as Social Action," *Quarterly Journal of Speech* 70 (1984): 151–67.

13. Miller, "Genre as Social Action," 163.

14. Gunn, "*Maranantha*," 364.

15. Debra Hawhee, *Moving Bodies: Kenneth Burke at the Edges of Language* (Columbia: University of South Carolina Press, 2009).

16. Colette Guillaumin, *Racism, Sexism, Power and Ideology* (London: Routledge, 1995).

17. Saidiya V. Hartman, *Scenes of Subjection: Terror, Slavery, and Self-Making in Nineteenth-Century America* (New York: Oxford University Press, 1997), 206.

18. Ibid., 57.

19. See E. Patrick Johnson, *Appropriating Blackness: Performance and the Politics of Authenticity* (Durham, NC: Duke University Press, 2003); Fred Moten, *In the Break: The Aesthetics of the Black Radical Tradition* (Minneapolis: University of Minnesota Press, 2003).

20. Hartman, *Scenes of Subjection*, 206.

21. PCARE, "Fighting the Prison-Industrial Complex: A Call to Communication and Cultural Studies Scholars to Change the World," *Communication and Critical/Cultural Studies* 4 (2007): 407.

22. Michel Foucault, *Discipline and Punish: The Birth of the Prison*, trans. Alan Sheridan (New York: Vintage Books, 1977); Hall, et al., *Policing the Crisis*.

23. See Marouf Hasian Jr. and Lisa A. Flores, "Mass Mediated Representations of the Susan Smith Trial," *Howard Journal of Communication* 11 (2000): 163–78; Casey Kelly, "Neocolonialism and the Global Prison in National Geographic's Locked Up Abroad," *Critical Studies in Media Communication* 29 (2012): 331–47; Caroline Joan S. Picart, "Rhetorically Reconfiguring Victimhood and Agency: The Violence against Women Act's Civil Rights Clause," *Rhetoric and Public Affairs* 6 (2003): 97–125; Carol A. Stabile, *White Victims, Black Villains: Gender, Race, and Crime News in US Culture* (New York: Routledge, 2006); John M. Sloop, *The Cultural Prison: Discourse, Prisoners, and Punishment* (Tuscaloosa: University of Alabama Press, 1996); Jennifer K. Wood, "Justice as Therapy: The Victim Rights Clarification Act," *Communication Quarterly* 51 (2003): 296–311; Bill Yousman, *Prime Time Prisons on U.S. TV: Representation of Incarceration* (New York: Peter Lang, 2009).

24. Stephen John Hartnett, *Executing Democracy*, vol. 1, *Capital Punishment and the Making of America, 1683–1807* (East Lansing: Michigan State University Press, 2010); Stephen John Hartnett and Daniel Larson, "'Tonight Another Man Will Die': Crime, Violence, and the Master Tropes of Contemporary Arguments about the Death Penalty," *Communication and Critical/Cultural Studies* 3 (2006): 263–87; Bryan J. McCann,

"Genocide as Representative Anecdote: Crack Cocaine, the CIA, and the Nation of Islam in Gary Webb's 'Dark Alliance,'" *Western Journal of Communication* 74 (2010): 396–416; "Redemption in the Neoliberal and Radical Imaginations: The Saga of Stanley 'Tookie' Williams," *Communication, Culture, and Critique* 7 (2014): 92–111; Bryan J. McCann, "Therapeutic and Material <Victim>hood: Ideology and the Struggle for Meaning in the Illinois Death Penalty Controversy," *Communication and Critical/Cultural Studies* 4 (2007): 382–401.

25. Dan Berger, *Captive Nation: Black Prison Organizing in the Civil Rights Era* (Chapel Hill: University of North Carolina Press, 2014); Lisa M. Corrigan, "Writing Resistance and Heroism: Guerilla Strategies from Castro's Gulag," *Communication Quarterly* 59 (2011): 61–81; Stephen John Hartnett, "Lincoln and Douglas Meet the Abolitionist David Walker as Prisoners Debate Slavery: Empowering Education, Applied Communication, and Social Justice," *Journal of Applied Communication Research* 26 (1998): 232–53; Stephen John Hartnett, Jennifer K. Wood, and Bryan J. McCann, "Turning Silence into Speech and Action: Prison Activism and the Pedagogy of Empowered Citizenship," *Communication and Critical/Cultural Studies* 8 (2011): 331–52; Gerard A. Hauser, *Prisoners of Conscience: Moral Vernaculars of Political Agency* (Columbia: University of South Carolina Press, 2012); Bryan J. McCann, "Redemption in the Neoliberal and Radical Imaginations: The Saga of Stanley 'Tookie' Williams"; PCARE, "Fighting the Prison-Industrial Complex"; Jonathan Shailor, *Performing New Lives: Prison Theatre* (London: Jessica Kingsley Publishers, 2011).

26. Jennifer Asenas, et al., "Saving Kenneth Foster: Speaking with Others in the Belly of the Beast of Capital Punishment," in *Communication Activism*, vol. 3, *Struggling for Social Justice Amidst Difference*, ed. Lawrence R. Frey and Kevin M. Carragee (New York: Hampton Press, 2012), 264–90; Stephen John Hartnett, ed., *Challenging the Prison-Industrial Complex: Activism, Arts, and Educational Alternatives* (Urbana: University of Illinois Press, 2011); Stephen John Hartnett, Eleanor Novek, and Jennifer K. Wood, eds., *Working for Justice: A Handbook of Prison Education and Advocacy* (Urbana: University of Illinois Press, 2013); John P. McHale, "Unreasonable Doubt: Using Video Documentary to Promote Justice," in *Communication Activism*, vol. 2, *Media and Performance Activism*, ed. Lawrence R. Frey and Kevin M. Carragee (New York: Hampton Press, 2007), 195–222; PCARE, "Fighting the Prison-Industrial Complex."

27. See Jeremy Engels, *Enemyship: Democracy and Counter-Revolution in the Early Republic* (East Lansing: Michigan State University Press, 2010); Rachel Hall, *Wanted: The Outlaw in American Visual Culture* (Charlottesville: University of Virginia Press, 2009); Stephen John Hartnett, *Executing Democracy*, vol. 1, *Capital Punishment and the Making of America, 1683–1807*; Hartnett, *Executing Democracy*, vol. 2, *Capital Punishment and the Making of America, 1835–1843* (Lansing: Michigan State University Press, 2012); Peter Linebaugh and Marcus Rediker, *The Many-Headed Hydra: Sailors, Slaves, Commoners, and the Hidden History of the Revolutionary Atlantic* (Boston: Beacon Press, 2000).

28. Eric Hobsbawm, *Bandits* (New York: New Press, 2000).

29. Also see Fred W. Allsopp, *Folklore of Romantic Arkansas*, vol. 1 (New York: Grolier Society, 1931); Paul Buhle, *Robin Hood: The People's Outlaw and Forest Hero; A Graphic Guide* (Oakland, CA: Oakland Press, 2011); Richard E. Meyer, "The Outlaw: A Distinctive American Folktype," *Journal of the Folklore Institute* 17 (1980): 94–124.

30. On women and banditry, see Hobsbawm, *Bandits*, 146–49. On the fraught dimensions of rhetoric and feminine criminality, see Kyra Pearson, "The Trouble with Aileen

Wuornos, Feminism's 'First Serial Killer,'" *Communication and Critical/Cultural Studies* 4 (2007): 256–75.

31. Allsopp, *Folklore of Romantic Arkansas*; Meyer, "Outlaw."

32. Hobsbawm, *Bandits*, 20.

33. US Const, amend. XIII, § 2. Also see Angela Y. Davis, *Are Prisons Obsolete?* (New York: Seven Stories Press, 2003); W. E. B. Du Bois, "The Spawn of Slavery: The Convict-Lease System in the South," in *Race, Crime, and Justice: A Reader*, ed. Shaun L. Gabbidon and Helen Taylor Greene (New York: Routledge, 2005), 3–8; Daniel A. Novak, *The Wheel of Servitude: Black Forced Labor after Slavery* (Lexington: University Press of Kentucky, 1978).

34. Cyril D. Robinson, "The Production of Black Violence in Chicago," in *Crime and Capitalism: Readings in Marxist Criminology*, ed. David F. Greenberg (Philadelphia: Temple University Press, 1993), 279–333.

35. W. E. B. Du Bois, *The Philadelphia Negro* (Philadelphia: University of Pennsylvania Press, 1899); Thorstein Sellin, "The Negro Criminal: A Statistical Note," *Annals of the American Academy of Political and Social Science* 140 (1928): 52–64.

36. W. E. B. Du Bois, *Black Reconstruction in America, 1860–1880* (New York: Free Press, 1998), 721.

37. Khalil Gibran Muhammad, *The Condemnation of Blackness: Race, Crime, and the Making of Modern Urban America* (Cambridge, MA: Harvard University Press, 2010), 272, 274.

38. Kobena Mercer, "Reading Racial Fetishism," in *Representation: Cultural Representations and Signifying Practices*, ed. Stuart Hall (London: Sage Publications, 1997), 290. Also see A. Susan Owen and Peter Ehrenhaus, "Looking at Lynching: Spectacle, Resistance, and Contemporary Transformations," *Quarterly Journal of Speech* 97 (2011): 100–113.

39. *The Birth of a Nation*, directed by D. W. Griffith (1915; Chatsworth, CA: Image Entertainment, 1998), DVD; Harper Lee, *To Kill a Mockingbird* (New York: HarperCollins, 2006); Richard Wright, *Native Son* (New York: Signet, 1961). For more on the gendered politics of lynching, see Dora Apel, *Imagery of Lynching: Black Men, White Women, and the Mob* (New Brunswick, NJ: Rutgers University Press, 2004).

Throughout this book, I use the term "masculine" (rather than "male") to emphasize the performative character of black masculinity. While the practices and characteristics associated with black masculinity are usually associated with the biological traits we identify as "male," masculinity is not reducible to these traits. See Bryant Keith Alexander, *Performing Black Masculinity: Race, Culture, and Queer Identity* (Lanham, MD: AltaMira, 2006); Ronald L. Jackson III, *Scripting the Black Masculine Body: Identity, Discourse, and Racial Politics in Popular Media* (Albany: State University of New York Press, 2006).

40. Patricia Hill Collins, *Black Sexual Politics: African Americans, Gender, and the New Racism* (New York: Routledge, 2005), 166.

41. Adam Gussow, *Seems Like Murder Here: Southern Violence and the Blues Tradition* (Chicago: University of Chicago Press, 2002); Hartman, *Scenes of Subjection*.

42. John W. Roberts, *From Trickster to Badman: The Black Folk Hero in Slavery and Freedom* (Philadelphia: University of Pennsylvania Press, 1990), 37–38. Also see Henry Louis Gates Jr., *The Signifying Monkey: A Theory of African-American Literary Criticism* (Oxford: Oxford University Press, 1988).

43. Raymond A. Bauer and Alice H. Bauer, "Day to Day Resistance to Slavery," *Journal of Negro History* 27 (1942): 388–419; Roberts, *From Trickster to Badman*; James C.

Scott, *Domination and the Arts of Resistance: Hidden Transcripts* (New Haven, CT: Yale University Press, 1990).

44. Roberts, *From Trickster to Badman.*

45. Nick Cave and the Bad Seeds, "Stagger Lee," *Murder Ballads*, CD, Mute Records, 1996.

46. On the folklore of Stagger Lee, see Cecil Brown, *Stagolee Shot Billy* (Cambridge, MA: Harvard University Press, 2004); Olive Woolley Burt, *American Murder Ballads and Their Stories* (New York: Oxford University Press, 1958); Bruce Jackson, "*Get Your Ass in the Water and Swim Like Me*": *Narrative Poetry from Black Oral Tradition* (Cambridge, MA: Harvard University Press, 1974); Derek McCulloch and Shepherd Hendrix, "Stackalee," in *A Treasury of American Folklore: Stories, Ballads, and Traditions of the People*, ed. B. A. Botkin (New York: Crown Publishers, 1944), 122–30.

47. See Kheven Lee LaGrone, "From Minstrelsy to Gangsta Rap: The 'Nigger' as Commodity for Popular American Entertainment," *Journal of African American Men* 5 (2000): 117–31.

48. Pat Boone, "Stagger Lee," *Moody River/Great! Great! Great!*, CD, Sepia Records, 2012; The Grateful Dead, "Stagger Lee," *Shakedown Street*, LP, Grateful Dead Productions, 1978; Woody Guthrie, "Stagger Lee," *The Asch Recordings*, vol. 2, CD, Smithsonian Folkways, 1999; Wilson Pickett, "Stagger Lee," *Pick It Wilson*, CD, Rhino Entertainment Company, 2007; Lloyd Price, "Stagger Lee," *Lloyd Price Greatest Hits: The Original ABC-Paramount Recordings*, CD, UMG Recordings, 1994.

49. Black crime novelists in the postwar era wove tales of sex and violence that resonated deeply with badman folklore. See Ronin Ro, "Pulp Fiction," *Source*, March 1995, 46–48, 82.

50. Jeff Chang, *Can't Stop Won't Stop: A History of the Hip-Hop Generation* (New York: Picador, 2005).

51. Jackson, "*Get Your Ass in the Water and Swim Like Me*," 47.

52. Ibid., 107.

53. Ibid., 60. On later iterations of Dolomite, see *Dolemite*, directed by D'Urville Martin (Los Angeles: Dimension Pictures, 1975); Dr. Dre, "Nuthin' But a 'G' Thang," *The Chronic*, CD, Death Row Records, 1992. As the title of Martin's film reflects, multiple spellings of Dolomite/Dolemite exist.

54. bell hooks, *We Real Cool: Black Men and Masculinity* (New York: Routledge, 2004), xii. Also see Stacy De Coster and Karen Heimer, "Crime at the Intersections: Race, Class, Gender, and Violent Offending," in *The Many Colors of Crime: Inequalities of Race, Ethnicity, and Crime in America*, ed. Lauren J. Krivo, Ruth D. Peterson, and John Hagan (New York: New York University Press, 2006), 138–56; Ronald L. Jackson III, *Scripting the Black Masculine Body: Identity, Discourse, and Racial Politics in Popular Media* (Albany: State University of New York Press, 2006); D. Marvin Jones, *Race, Sex, and Suspicion: The Myth of the Black Male* (Westport, CT: Praeger, 2005).

55. Angela Y. Davis, *Blues Legacies and Black Feminism: Gertrude "Ma" Rainey, Bessie Smith, and Billie Holiday* (New York: Pantheon Books, 1998), 4. Also see Gussow, *Seems Like Murder Here.*

56. There are, of course, myriad gendered stereotypes associated with black feminine sexuality. See Hill Collins, *Black Sexual Politics.*

57. Earlier, I noted that 2.3 million American adults are behind bars. This higher figure includes individuals confined in jails. Michelle Alexander, *The New Jim Crow: Mass Incarceration in the Age of Colorblindness* (New York: New Press, 2010); E. Ann Carson and

William J. Sabol, *Prisoners in 2011* (Washington, DC: US Department of Justice, 2012), http://www.bjs.gov/content/pub/pdf/p11.pdf; PCARE, "Fighting the Prison-Industrial Complex"; Jennifer Warren, *One in 100: Behind Bars in America* (Washington, DC: Pew Charitable Trusts, 2008), http://www.pewtrusts.org/uploadedFiles/wwwpewtrustsorg/Reports/sentencing_and_corrections/one_in_100.pdf.

58. On national politics of law and order in earlier periods, see Marie Gottschalk, *The Prison and the Gallows: The Politics of Mass Incarceration in America* (Cambridge: Cambridge University Press, 2006); Hartnett, *Executing Democracy*, vol. 1, *Capital Punishment and the Making of America, 1683–1807;* Hartnett, *Executing Democracy*, vol. 2, *Capital Punishment and the Making of America, 1835–1843.*

59. Heather Ann Thompson, "Why Mass Incarceration Matters: Rethinking Crisis, Decline, and Transformation in Postwar American History," *Journal of American History* 98 (2010): 703–34.

60. Lyndon B. Johnson, "Special Message to the Congress on Crime and Law Enforcement, March 9, 1966," *American Presidency Project*, http://www.presidency.ucsb.edu/ws/?pid=27478.

61. Devah Pager, *Marked: Race, Crime, and Finding Work in an Era of Mass Incarceration* (Chicago: University of Chicago Press, 2007). Also see Gottschalk, *The Prison and the Gallows.*

62. Barry Goldwater, "Goldwater's 1964 Acceptance Speech," *WashingtonPost.com*, May 1998, http://www.washingtonpost.com/wp-srv/politics/daily/may98/goldwaterspeech.htm, para. 36.

63. Thompson, "Why Mass Incarceration Matters."

64. Goldwater, "Goldwater's 1964 Acceptance Speech," para. 10.

65. Ibid.

66. Christian Parenti, *Lockdown America: Police and Prisons in the Age of Crisis* (London: Verso, 1999); Jonathan Simon, *Governing through Crime: How the War on Crime Transformed American Democracy and Created a Culture of Fear* (Oxford: Oxford University Press, 2007).

67. Gottschalk, *The Prison and the Gallows*; Dylan Rodríguez, *Forced Passages: Imprisoned Radical Intellectuals and the U.S. Prison Regime* (Minneapolis: University of Minnesota Press, 2006); Thompson, "Why Mass Incarceration Matters."

68. For many activists during the late 1960s and 1970s, imperialism was the primary lens through which they critiqued state violence abroad and in the United States. See Cynthia A. Young, *Soul Power: Culture, Radicalism, and the Making of a U.S. Third World Left* (Durham, NC: Duke University Press 2006).

69. Celeste Michelle Condit and John Louis Lucaites, *Crafting Equality: America's Anglo-African Word* (Chicago: University of Chicago Press, 1993).

70. Michael Eric Dyson, *I May Not Get There with You: The True Martin Luther King, Jr.* (New York: Touchstone, 2000).

71. Jeffrey O. G. Ogbar, *Black Power: Radical Politics and African American Identity* (Baltimore: Johns Hopkins University Press, 2004).

72. Huey P. Newton, "Patrolling," in *The Huey P. Newton Reader*, ed. David Hilliard and Donald Weise (New York: Seven Stories Press, 2002), 58. For more on the Panthers, see Joshua Bloom and Waldo E. Martin Jr., *Black against Empire: The History and Politics of the Black Panther Party* (Berkeley: University of California Press, 2014).

73. While Shakur and Davis were politically active prior to incarceration, Jackson radicalized behind bars. On the role of prisoners in the Black Power and other move-

ments, see Berger, *Captive Nation*; Lee Bernstein, *America Is the Prison: Arts and Politics in Prison in the 1970s* (Chapel Hill: University of North Carolina Press, 2010); Eric Cummins, *The Rise and Fall of California's Radical Prison Movement* (Stanford, CA: Stanford University Press, 1994); George Jackson, *Soledad Brother: The Prison Letters of George Jackson* (Chicago: Lawrence Hill Books, 1994); Joy James, *Imprisoned Intellectuals: America's Political Prisoners Write on Life, Liberation, and Rebellion* (Lanham, MD: Rowman and Littlefield, 2003); Rodríguez, *Forced Passages*.

74. On the gendered politics of Black Nationalism and Black Power, see Patricia Hill Collins, *From Black Power to Hip Hop: Racism, Nationalism, and Feminism* (Philadelphia: Temple University Press, 2006). For an exemplar of the central role of masculinity in the articulation of Black Power politics, see Eldridge Cleaver, *Soul on Ice* (New York: Delta, 1992).

75. James, *Imprisoned Intellectuals*.

76. Ed Guerrero, *Framing Blackness: The African American Image in Film* (Philadelphia: Temple University Press, 1993), 86.

77. Ibid. Also see Mark Anthony Neal, *Soul Babies: Black Popular Culture and the Post-Soul Aesthetic* (New York: Routledge, 2002).

78. Guerrero, *Framing Blackness*, 110.

79. On federal infiltration into the Panthers and other radical organizations during the 1960s, see Ward Churchill and Jim Vander Wall, *The COINTELPRO Papers: Documents from the FBI's Secret Wars against Dissent in the United States* (Cambridge, MA: South End Press, 1990); Jeffrey Haas, *The Assassination of Fred Hampton: How the FBI and the Chicago Police Murdered a Black Panther* (Chicago: Lawrence Hill Books, 2010); Carl Jorgenson, "Black in the 60s: A Centennial Reprise," *Social Text* (Spring–Summer 1984): 313–17; Seth Rosenfeld, *Subversives: The FBI's War on Student Radicals, and Reagan's Rise to Power* (New York: Farrar, Straus and Giroux, 2012). This is not to suggest that the Panthers were without fault. Their preoccupation with violence was often fetishistic and, in its final days, profoundly paranoid. See Curtis J. Austin, *Up against the Wall: Violence in the Making and Unmaking of the Black Panther Party* (Fayetteville: University of Arkansas Press, 2006). On more recent controversies surrounding federal surveillance practices, see Ewan MacAskill, Julian Borger, and Glenn Greenwald, "The National Security Agency: Surveillance Giant with Eyes on America," *Guardian*, June 6, 2013, http://www.guardian.co.uk/world/2013/jun/06/national-security-agency-surveillance.

80. Hannah Arendt, "On Violence," In *Crises of the Republic* (New York: Harcourt Brace Jovanovich, 1972), 103–84.

81. Rick Perlstein, *Nixonland: The Rise of a President and the Fracturing of America* (New York: Scribner, 2008).

82. Richard M. Nixon, "Nixon's Acceptance of the Republican Party Nomination for President," in *Republican National Convention*, Miami Beach, August 8, 1968.

83. Goldwater, "Goldwater's 1964 Acceptance Speech," para. 5.

84. On Nixon's political strategies during the 1968 campaign and the rest of his electoral career, see Perlstein, *Nixonland*.

85. Nixon, "9—Annual Message to the Congress on the State of the Union," January 22, 1970, *The American Presidency Project*, http://www.presidency.ucsb.edu/ws/?pid=2921, para. 64.

86. See Markus Dirk Dubber, "Criminal Justice Process and War on Crime," in *The Blackwell Companion to Criminology*, ed. Colin Sumner (Malden, MA: Blackwell), 49–67; Thompson, "Why Mass Incarceration Matters."

87. Although such commentary from a national figure was not unprecedented, Deeva Pager explains that Nixon's rise was a climactic moment in national crime politics. She writes, "Nixon's 'war on crime' rhetorically elevated crime policy to the level of national concern, calling for a coordinated effort to combat the problems of crime and social decay." Pager, *Marked*, 9.

88. Perlstein, *Nixonland*.

89. Dubber, "Criminal Justice Process and War on Crime," 50. Also see Rodríguez, *Forced Passages*.

90. On Nixon's political rhetoric in the 1972 campaign, see Walter R. Fisher, "Reaffirmation and Subversion of the American Dream," *Quarterly Journal of Speech* 59 (1973): 131–39; Perlstein, *Nixonland*.

91. For an important and consequential exception, see *Report on the National Advisory Commission on Civil Disorders* (New York: Bantam Books, 1968).

92. David Harvey, *A Brief History of Neoliberalism* (Oxford: Oxford University Press, 2005).

93. On Nixon's wage and health care stances, see "Nixon's Plan For Health Reform, in His Own Words," *Kaiser Health News*, September 3, 2009, http://www.kaiserhealthnews .org/stories/2009/september/03/nixon-proposal.aspx; Perlstein, *Nixonland*.

94. Milton Friedman, *Capitalism and Freedom*, 40th anniversary ed. (Chicago: University of Chicago Press, 2002); Harvey, *Brief History of Neoliberalism*; Naomi Klein, *The Shock Doctrine: The Rise of Disaster Capitalism* (New York: Picador, 2007); F. A. Hayek, *The Road to Serfdom* (Abingdon, UK: Routledge, 2001).

95. Harvey, *Brief History of Neoliberalism*, 2.

96. Friedman, *Capitalism and Freedom*; Hayek, *Road to Serfdom*. Also see Lisa Duggan, *The Twilight of Equality?: Neoliberalism, Cultural Politics, and the Attack on Democracy* (Boston: Beacon Press, 2003).

97. "News Conference," August 12, 1986, *The Ronald Reagan Presidential Foundation and Library*, 2010, http://www.reaganfoundation.org/reagan-quotes-detail.aspx?tx= 2079. See also https://www.youtube.com/watch?v=xhYJS80MgYA.

98. Harvey, *Brief History of Neoliberalism*, 19.

99. Harvey, *Brief History of Neoliberalism*; Klein, *Shock Doctrine*.

100. Stephen John Hartnett, "The Annihilating Public Policies of the Prison-Industrial Complex; or, Crime, Violence, and Punishment in an Age of Neoliberalism," *Rhetoric and Public Affairs* 11 (2008): 491–515.

101. Chang, *Can't Stop Won't Stop*.

102. Mike Davis, *City of Quartz: Excavating the Future in Los Angeles* (London: Verso, 2006); Howard Zinn, *A People's History of the United States: 1492–Present* (New York: HarperCollins, 1999).

103. Robinson, "Production of Black Violence in Chicago."

104. Jimmie L. Reeves and Richard Campbell, *Cracked Coverage: Television News, the Anti-Cocaine Crusade, and the Reagan Legacy* (Durham, NC: Duke University Press, 1994). On the nuances of crack cocaine addiction, see John Tierney, "The Rational Choices of Crack Addicts," *New York Times*, September 16, 2013, http://www.nytimes.com/2013/ 09/17/science/the-rational-choices-of-crack-addicts.html?pagewanted=all&_r=1.

105. Davis, *City of Quartz*, 309.

106. Alejandro A. Alonso, "Racialized Identities and the Formation of Black Gangs in Los Angeles," *Urban Geography* 25 (2004): 658–72; Felix M. Padilla, *The Street Gang as an American Enterprise* (New Brunswick, NJ: Rutgers University Press, 1992).

107. Peter Linebaugh, *The London Hanged: Crime and Civil Society in the Eighteenth Century* (Cambridge: Cambridge University Press, 1992).

108. Mike Davis, *Planet of Slums* (London: Verso, 2006).

109. Ronald Reagan, "Address before a Joint Session of Congress on the State of the Union," February 6, 1985. On Reagan's support of Goldwater, see Reagan, *An American Life: The Autobiography* (New York: Simon and Schuster, 1990).

110. Julia Jordan-Zacherys, "The Female Bogeyman: Political Implications of Criminalizing Black Women," in *Racializing Justice, Disenfranchising Lives: The Racism, Criminal Justice, and Law Reader*, ed. Ian Seinberg, Manning Marable, and Keesha Middlemass (New York: Palgrave Macmillan, 2007), 105.

111. See Robert Asen, *Visions of Poverty: Welfare Policy and the Political Imagination* (East Lansing: Michigan State University Press, 2002); Michael K. Brown, et al., *White-Washing Race: The Myth of a Color-Blind Society* (Berkeley: University of California Press, 2013).

112. Alexander, *New Jim Crow*; Daniel Mark Larson, "Killing Democracy; or, How the Drug War Drives the Prison-Industrial Complex," in *Challenging the Prison Industrial Complex: Activism, Arts, and Educational Alternatives*, ed. Stephen John Hartnett (Urbana: University of Illinois Press, 2011), 73–104.

113. Larson, "Killing Democracy"; Steve Macek, *Urban Nightmares: The Media, the Right, and the Moral Panic over the City* (Minneapolis: University of Minnesota Press, 2006); Doris Marie Provine, "Creating Racial Disadvantage: The Case of Crack Cocaine," in *The Many Colors of Crime: Inequalities of Race, Ethnicity, and Crime in America*, ed. Ruth D. Peterson, Lauren J. Krivo, and John Hagan (New York: New York University Press, 2006), 277–94; Reeves and Campbell, *Cracked Coverage*.

114. Provine, "Creating Racial Disadvantage," 280–81.

115. Marc Mauer, *Race to Incarcerate* (New York: New Press, 2006).

116. See Gil Troy, *Morning in America: How Ronald Reagan Invented the 1980s* (Princeton, NJ: Princeton University Press, 2005).

Chapter 2

1. Steve Early, "An Old Lesson Still Holds for Unions," *Boston Globe*, July 31, 2006, http://www.boston.com/news/globe/editorial_opinion/oped/articles/2006/07/31/an_old_lesson_still_holds_for_unions/; Joseph A. McCartin, "The Strike That Busted Unions," *New York Times*, August 2, 2011, http://www.nytimes.com/2011/08/03/opinion/reagan-vs-patco-the-strike-that-busted-unions.html.

2. David Harvey, *A Brief History of Neoliberalism* (Oxford: Oxford University Press, 2005).

3. Mario Matthew Cuomo, "1984 Democratic National Convention Keynote Address," *American Rhetoric*," July 16, 1984, http://www.americanrhetoric.com/speeches/mariocuomo1984dnc.htm, para. 4; Howell Raines, "Reagan Wins by a Landslide, Sweeping at Least 48 States; G.O.P. Gains Strength in House," *New York Times*, November 7, 1984, http://www.nytimes.com/1984/11/07/politics/07REAG.html?pagewanted=1.

4. Walter R. Fisher, "Reaffirmation and Subversion of the American Dream," *Quarterly Journal of Speech* 59 (1973): 131–39; Raines, "Reagan Wins by a Landslide."

5. On Reagan's political style, see William F. Lewis, "Telling America's Story: Narrative Form and the Reagan Presidency," *Quarterly Journal of Speech* 73 (1987): 280–302; Gil Troy, *Morning in America: How Ronald Reagan Invented the 1980s* (Princeton, NJ:

Princeton University Press, 2005). On the connections between Reagan's economic policies and today's crisis, see Larry M. Bartels, *Unequal Democracy: The Political Economy of the Gilded Age* (Princeton, NJ: Princeton University Press, 2010); Paul Krugman, *The Conscience of a Liberal* (New York: W. W. Norton, 2007).

6. Roger Simon, "How a Murderer and Rapist Became the Bush Campaign's Most Valuable Player," *Baltimore Sun*, November 11, 1990, http://articles.baltimoresun.com/1990–11–11/features/1990315149_1_willie-horton-fournier-michael-dukakis.

7. "Willie Horton (National Security PAC, 1988)," *The Living Room Candidate*, 2012, http://www.livingroomcandidate.org/commercials/1988/willie-horton.

8. Simon, "How a Murderer and Rapist Became the Bush Campaign's Most Valuable Player," para. 1. For excellent analysis of the Horton ad's role in the 1988 election, see Kathleen Hall Jamieson, *Dirty Politics: Deception, Distraction, and Democracy* (New York: Oxford University Press, 1993).

9. Kobena Mercer, "Reading Racial Fetishism," in *Representation: Cultural Representations and Signifying Practices*, ed. Stuart Hall (London: Sage Publications, 1997), 290.

10. Simon, "How a Murderer and Rapist Became the Bush Campaign's Most Valuable Player."

11. Naomi Klein, *The Shock Doctrine: The Rise of Disaster Capitalism* (New York: Picador, 2007); Daniel Mark Larson, "Killing Democracy; or, How the Drug War Drives the Prison-Industrial Complex," in *Challenging the Prison Industrial Complex: Activism, Arts, and Educational Alternatives*, ed. Stephen John Hartnett (Urbana: University of Illinois Press, 2011), 73–104.

12. Recording Industry of America, *Gold and Platinum Searchable Database*, n.d., http://www.riaa.com/goldandplatinumdata.php.

13. Terry McDermott, "Parental Advisory: Explicit Lyrics," in *Da Capo Best Music Writing 2003: The Year's Finest Writing on Rock, Pop, Jazz, Country & More*, vol. 4, ed. Matt Groenig and Paul Bresnick (Cambridge, MA: Da Capo Press), 12.

14. Ibid. Brent Lang, "'Straight Outta Compton' Final Box Office Soars to $60.2 Million," *Variety*, August 17, 2015, http://variety.com/2015/film/news/straight-outta-compton-box-office-opening-final-1201571387/.

15. On parody as a mode of resistance, see M. Lane Bruner, "Carnivalesque Protest and the Humorless State," *Text and Performance Quarterly* 25 (2005): 136–55; Judith Butler, *Gender Trouble: Feminism and the Subversion of Identity* (New York: Routledge Classics); Robert Hariman, "Political Parody and Public Culture," *Quarterly Journal of Speech* 94 (2008): 247–72. On parody in rap and other black vernacular practices, see Henry Louis Gates Jr., *The Signifying Monkey: A Theory of African-American Literary Criticism* (New York: Oxford University Press, 1988); Quinn, "Never Shoulda Been Let out the Penitentiary."

16. Edward W. Soja, "Taking Los Angeles Apart: Towards a Postmodern Geography," in his *Postmodern Geographies: The Reassertion of Space in Critical Social Theory* (London: Verso, 1989), 222.

17. Mike Davis, *City of Quartz: Excavating the Future in Los Angeles* (London: Verso, 2006).

18. Darnell Hunt, "Dreaming of Black Los Angeles," in *Black Los Angeles: American Dreams and Racial Realities*, ed. Darnell Hunt and Ana-Christina Ramón (New York: New York University Press, 2010), 1–17.

19. Katherine McKittrick and Clyde Woods, "No One Knows the Mysteries at the Bottom of the Ocean," in *Black Geographies and the Politics of Place*, ed. Katherine McKit-

trick and Clyde Woods (Toronto: Between the Lines; Cambridge, MA: South End Press, 2007), 4.

20. Paul Robinson, "Race, Space, and the Evolution of Black Los Angeles," in Hunt and Ramón, *Black Los Angeles*, 21–59.

21. Ibid., 43. For information on similar discriminatory housing policies across the United States, see Kenneth T. Jackson, *Crabgrass Frontier: The Suburbanization of the United States* (Oxford: Oxford University Press, 1985).

22. For example, in 1964, white voters in California overwhelmingly voted for Proposition 14, which codified housing discrimination into state law. While the victorious referendum did not survive judicial review, its impact on race relations was devastating. See Mark Anthony Neal, *What the Music Said: Black Popular Music and Black Public Culture* (New York: Routledge, 1999); Robinson, "Race, Space, and the Evolution of Black Los Angeles."

23. Martin J. Schiesl, "Behind the Badge: The Police and Social Discontent in Los Angeles since 1950," in *20th Century Los Angeles: Power, Promotion, and Social Conflict*, ed. Norman M. Klein and Martin J. Schiesl (Claremont, CA: Regina Books), 155.

24. Brian Cross, *It's Not about a Salary . . . Rap, Race, and Resistance in Los Angeles* (London: Verso, 1993), 8; Schiesl, "Behind the Badge."

25. Jeff Chang, *Can't Stop Won't Stop: A History of the Hip-Hop Generation* (New York: Picador, 2005); Davis, *City of Quartz*; Schiesl, "Behind the Badge."

26. Davis, *City of Quartz*, 268.

27. Carol Baker, "L.A. Cops Drop 'Hammer' on Gangs," *United Press International*, July 10, 1989, LexisNexis Academic; Chang, *Can't Stop Won't Stop*; Davis, *City of Quartz*; "Police Arrest Hundreds in L.A. Gangland Areas," *Washington Post*, August 21, 1989, LexisNexis Academic; Schiesl, "Behind the Badge."

28. Murray Forman, *The 'Hood Comes First: Race, Space, and Place in Rap and Hip-Hop* (Middletown, CT: Wesleyan University Press, 2002), xviii.

29. Ibid., 200.

30. On the use of "Latinx" as an alternative to the gendered "Latina/o," see Josh Logue, "Latina/o/x," *Inside Higher Ed*, December 8, 2015, https://www.insidehighered.com/news/2015/12/08/students-adopt-gender-nonspecific-term-latinx-be-more-inclusive.

31. Chang, *Can't Stop Won't Stop*; Tricia Rose, *Black Noise: Rap Music and Black Culture in Contemporary America* (Middletown, CT: Wesleyan University Press, 1994).

32. On Jamaica's political tumult during this period and the role of music therein, see Robin Denselow, *When the Music's Over: The Story of Political Pop* (London: Faber and Faber, 1989).

33. Chang, *Can't Stop Won't Stop*.

34. Ibid., 79. For a marvelous description of this practice from Herc himself, see "Kool DJ Herc, Merry Go Round," YouTube, October 26, 2009, http://www.youtube.com/watch?v=Hw4H2FZjfpo.

35. Greg Goodale, "The Sonorous Envelope and Political Deliberation," *Quarterly Journal of Speech* 99 (2013): 218–24; Joshua Gunn and Mirko M. Hall, "Stick It in Your Ear: The Psychodynamics of iPod Enjoyment," *Communication and Critical/Cultural Studies* 5 (2008): 135–57.

36. Rose, *Black Noise*. Also see Eithne Quinn, *Nuthin' But a "G" Thang: The Culture and Commerce of Gangsta Rap* (New York: Columbia University Press, 2005).

37. Quinn, *Nuthin' But a "G" Thang*, 119.

38. Cheryl L. Keyes, *Rap Music and Street Consciousness* (Urbana: University of Illinois Press, 2002), 26.

39. Paul Gilroy, *The Black Atlantic: Modernity and Double Consciousness* (Cambridge, MA: Harvard University Press, 1993).

40. Imani Perry, *Prophets of the Hood: Politics and Poetics in Hip Hop* (Durham, NC: Duke University Press, 2004), 19.

41. Chang, *Can't Stop Won't Stop*; Grandmaster Flash and The Furious Five, "The Message," *The Message*, CD, Sugar Hill Records, 1982.

42. Chang, *Can't Stop Won't Stop*; Rose, *Black Noise*; S. Craig Watkins, *Hip Hop Matters: Politics, Pop Culture, and the Struggle for the Soul of a Movement* (Boston: Beacon Press, 2005).

43. Cross, *It's Not about a Salary*; Ward Churchill and Jim Vander Wall, *The COINTELPRO Papers: Documents from the FBI's Secret Wars against Dissent in the United States* (Cambridge, MA: South End Press, 1990); Keyes, *Rap Music and Street Consciousness*.

44. Cross, *It's Not about a Salary*; World Class Wreckin' Crew, "Cabbage Patch," *Gold*, CD, SOH Distributors Network, 1994.

45. In spite of rising to hip-hop immortality, Dr. Dre struggled to live down his affiliation with the glittery electropop aesthetic of the World Class Wreckin' Cru. Following the breakup of NWA, Eazy-E openly mocked this chapter in Dr. Dre's career. See Carter Harris, "Eazy Street," *Source*, July 1994, 74–80, 89.

46. Davarian L. Baldwin, "Black Empires, White Desires: The Spatial Politics of Identity in the Age of Hip-Hop," in *That's the Joint!: The Hip-Hop Studies Reader*, ed. Murray Forman and Mark Anthony Neal (New York: Routledge, 2004), 182–202; Chang, *Can't Stop Won't Stop*; Cross, *It's Not about a Salary*; Quinn, *Nuthin' But a "G" Thang*.

47. NWA and the Posse, "Boyz-N-The-Hood," *N.W.A. and the Posse*, CD, Priority Records, 1987. Also see NWA and the Posse, "8 Ball," *N.W.A. and the Posse*; "A Bitch Iz a Bitch," *N.W.A. and the Posse*; "L.A. Is the Place," *N.W.A. and the Posse*.

48. For a provocative reading that identifies a homology between this track and an iconic violent episode from the early 1970s, see Chang, *Can't Stop Won't Stop*.

49. Cross, *It's Not about a Salary*; Davis, *City of Quartz*; Frantz Fanon, *The Wretched of the Earth*, trans. Constance Farrington (New York: Grove Press, 1963); Forman, *The 'Hood Comes First*; Schiesl, "Behind the Badge."

50. NWA, "Straight Outta Compton," *Straight Outta Compton*, CD, Priority Records, 1988.

51. On Manson and the cultural politics of the 1960s, see Greil Marcus, *The Doors: A Lifetime of Listening to Five Mean Years* (New York: PublicAffairs, 2011). On the black cultural backlash against NWA and other gangsta artists, see Chang, *Can't Stop Won't Stop*; Quinn, *Nuthin' But a "G" Thang*; Tricia Rose, *The Hip Hop Wars: What We Talk About When We Talk About Hip Hop—and Why It Matters* (New York: BasicCivitas, 2008).

52. "Jackin'" generally refers to larceny. "NWA—Straight Outta Compton," *Genius*, 2015, http://genius.com/Nwa-straight-outta-compton-lyrics/.

53. Cheryl L. Keyes, *Rap Music and Street Consciousness* (Urbana: University of Illinois Press, 2002); John W. Roberts, *From Trickster to Badman: The Black Folk Hero in Slavery and Freedom* (Philadelphia: University of Pennsylvania Press, 1990); Quinn, *Nuthin' But a "G" Thang*.

54. NWA, "Straight Outta Compton," music video, Ruthless Records, 1989.

55. Rose, *Black Noise*, 11.

56. Ed Guerrero, *Framing Blackness: The African American Image in Film* (Philadelphia: Temple University Press, 1993).

57. Michel de Certeau, *The Practice of Everyday Life* (Berkeley: University of Cali-

fornia Press, 1984), 96. Also see Robert J. Topinka, "Resisting the Fixity of Suburban Space: The Walker as Rhetorician," *Rhetoric Society Quarterly* 42 (2012): 65–84.

58. On *Straight Outta Compton*'s third track, "Gangsta, Gangsta," Ice Cube defiantly asks, "Do I look like a mutha fuckin' role model?" NWA, "Gangsta, Gangsta," *Straight Outta Compton*, CD, Priority Records, 1988.

59. NWA, "Fuck Tha Police," *Straight Outta Compton*, CD, Priority Records, 1988.

60. Jeffrey O. G. Ogbar, *Hip-Hop Revolution: The Culture and Politics of Rap* (Lawrence: University Press of Kansas, 2007).

61. Kimberlé Crenshaw, "Mapping the Margins: Intersectionality, Identity Politics, and Violence against Women of Color," *Stanford Law Review* 43 (1991): 1241–99.

62. See Rose, *Hip Hop Wars*.

63. Chandan Reddy, *Freedom with Violence: Race, Sexuality, and the US State* (Durham, NC: Duke University Press, 2011). Also see Perry, *Prophets of the Hood*.

64. D. Marvin Jones, *Race, Sex, and Suspicion: The Myth of the Black Male* (Westport, CT: Praeger, 2005), 58–59.

65. On Farrakhan and hip-hop, see Chang, *Can't Stop Won't Stop*; Mark Anthony Neal, *Soul Babies: Black Popular Culture and the Post-Soul Aesthetic* (New York: Routledge, 2002).

66. Karlyn Kohrs Campbell, "The Rhetoric of Black Nationalism: A Case Study in Self-Conscious Criticism," *Central States Speech Journal* 22 (1971): 151–60; Fanon, *Wretched of the Earth*; Patricia Hill Collins, *From Black Power to Hip Hop: Racism, Nationalism, and Feminism* (Philadelphia: Temple University Press, 2006).

67. Olive Woolley Burt, *American Murder Ballads and Their Stories* (New York: Oxford University Press, 1958), 201.

68. Guerrero, *Framing Blackness*.

69. Dorian Lynskey, *33 Revolutions per Minute: A History of Protest Songs, from Billie Holiday to Green Day* (New York: HarperCollins), 240.

70. Michael Veal, *Fela: The Life and Times of an African Music Icon* (Philadelphia: Temple University Press, 2000).

71. Juan Williams, "Fighting Words: Speaking Out against Racism, Sexism, and Gay-Bashing in Pop," *Washington Post*, October 15, 1989, LexisNexis Academic.

72. Matt Neufeld, "Lyrics Get Rap Group Cut from Cap Centre," *Washington Times*, August 22, 1989, LexisNexis Academic, para. 4.

73. Chang, *Can't Stop Won't Stop*.

74. Rose, *Black Noise*, 125.

75. Ibid., 135.

76. The letter is reprinted in its entirety in Chang, *Can't Stop Won't Stop*, 325.

77. See Richard Harrington, "The FBI as Music Critic; Letter on Rap Record Seen as Intimidation," *Washington Post*, October 4, 1989, LexisNexis Academic; David Marsh and Phyllis Pollack, "Wanted for Attitude," *Village Voice*, October 10, 1989, 33–37.

78. Marsh and Pollack, "Wanted for Attitude."

79. "'Cause my identity by itself causes violence" is from NWA's "Fuck Tha Police," *Straight Outta Compton*. Public Enemy's "Fight the Power" starts by seeming to aspire to nothing more than typical, catchy "song of the summer" status: "1989! / The number / Of another summer (get down) / Sound of the funky drummer / Music hittin' your heart cause I know you got soul / (Brothers and sisters, hey)" but quickly evolves into one of the late 1980s' most politically aware anthems of any genre ("Elvis was a hero to most / But he never meant shit to me you see / Straight up racist that sucker was / Simple and

plain / Mother fuck him and John Wayne/ 'Cause I'm Black and I'm proud / I'm ready and hyped plus I'm amped / Most of my heroes don't appear on no stamps").

80. See John Anderson and Hillary Hevenor, *Burning Down the House: MOVE and the Tragedy of Philadelphia* (New York: W. W. Norton, 1987); Chang, *Can't Stop Won't Stop*; Patricia J. Williams, *The Alchemy of Race and Rights: Diary of a Law Professor* (Cambridge, MA: Harvard University Press, 1991).

81. Chang, *Can't Stop Won't Stop*, 327.

82. On political popular music, see Michael Denning, *The Cultural Front: The Laboring of American Culture in the Twentieth Century* (London: Verso, 1998); Robin Denselow, *When the Music's Over: The Story of Political Pop* (London: Faber and Faber, 1989); Lynskey, *33 Revolutions per Minute*.

83. Christopher Holmes Smith, "'I Don't Like to Dream about Getting Paid': Representations of Social Mobility and the Emergence of the Hip-Hop Mogul," *Social Text* 77 (2003): 69–97.

84. Cross, *It's Not about a Salary*, 197.

85. Kheven Lee LaGrone, "From Minstrelsy to Gangsta Rap: The 'Nigger' as Commodity for Popular American Entertainment," *Journal of African American Men* 5 (2000): 125.

86. Denning, *Cultural Front*; Denselow, *When the Music's Over*; Lynskey, *33 Revolutions per Minute*.

87. See Neal, *Soul Babies*. Also see Alejandro A. Alonso, "Racialized Identities and the Formation of Black Gangs in Los Angeles," *Urban Geography* 25 (2004): 658–72; Chang, *Can't Stop Won't Stop*; Jeffrey O. G. Ogbar, *Black Power: Radical Politics and African American Identity* (Baltimore: Johns Hopkins University Press, 2004).

88. See Chang, *Can't Stop Won't Stop*; LaGrone, "From Minstrelsy to Gangsta Rap"; Quinn, *Nuthin' But a "G" Thang*; S. Craig Watkins, *Hip Hop Matters: Politics, Pop Culture, and the Struggle for the Soul of a Movement* (Boston: Beacon Press, 2005).

89. Bruner, "Carnivalesque Protest and the Humorless State." Also see Robin D. G. Kelley, *Freedom Dreams: The Black Radical Imagination* (Boston: Beacon Press, 2002).

90. Daniel Kreps, "Watch the Red-Band Trailer for N.W.A.'s Biopic 'Straight Outta Compton,'" *Rolling Stone*, February 9, 2015, http://www.rollingstone.com/movies/videos/watch-the-red-band-trailer-for-n-w-as-biopic-straight-outta-compton-20150209.

91. See Chang, *Can't Stop Won't Stop*; Cross, *It's Not about a Salary*, 204–17.

92. Chang, *Can't Stop Won't Stop*; Harris, "Eazy Street"; Ronin Ro, "Moving Target," *Source*, November 1992, 38–45, 61.

93. Chang, *Can't Stop Won't Stop*; The Derelict Todd B., Review of Eazy-E's *It's On (Dr. Dre 187) Killa*, *Source*, December 1993, 88; Pistol Pete, "Eazy Way Out," *Source*, June 1993, 16; Frank Williams, "Eazy-E: The Life, The Legacy," *Source*, June 1995, 52–62. Regarding NWA's financial motivations, see Cross, *It's Not about a Salary*.

94. Williams, "Eazy-E: The Life, The Legacy," 54. Also see "Rap Star Eazy-E Battles AIDS; Listed in Critical Condition in LA Hospital," *Jet*, April 3, 1995, LexisNexis Academic.

95. See C. Riley Snorton, *Nobody Is Supposed to Know: Black Sexuality on the Down Low* (Minneapolis: University of Minnesota Press, 2014).

Chapter 3

Epigraph. James Bernard, "Election '92: Are the Candidates Selling the Hip-Hop Nation Down the River?," *Source*, November 1992, 50.

1. *Do the Right Thing*, directed by Spike Lee (New York: 40 Acres and a Mule Film-works, 1989).

2. See Charles C. Johnson, "Lessons of *Sa-i-gu*," *City Journal*, April 27 2012, http://www.city-journal.org/2012/cjc0427cj.html; Seth Mydans, "Police Beating Trial Opens with Replay of Videotape," *New York Times*, March 6, 1992, http://www.nytimes.com/1992/03/06/us/police-beating-trial-opens-with-replay-of-videotape.html; *Understanding the Riots: Los Angeles before and after the Rodney King Case* (Los Angeles: Los Angeles Times, 1992).

3. While black merchants suffered major losses during the riots, Korean store own-ers bore a disproportionate amount of anger and violence during the events of what many of them call *sa-i-gu*, or April 29. This was partially due to law enforcement neglect dur-ing the riots, but also reflected long-standing tensions between LA's black and Korean residents. Ice Cube articulated some of these tensions in his extremely controversial 1991 track "Black Korea." Although deploying some of the worst examples of prejudicial lan-guage and violent posturing toward Korean residents, the forty-seven-second track gave expression to many African Americans' belief that Korean entrepreneurs in South Central and other disadvantaged urban sectors were exploiting black neighborhoods and racially profiling African American customers. The 1991 videotaped shooting of fifteen-year-old Latasha Harlins by fifty-one-year-old shopkeeper Soon Ja Du was a catalyst for these ten-sions. Du fatally shot the teenager based on the suspicion she was stealing orange juice from the store. Although Du was convicted of manslaughter, a sympathetic judge who be-lieved the businesswoman was reacting to rampant crime in and around her South Cen-tral store sentenced her to only five years of probation and four hundred hours of com-munity service. Many black Americans, including rap artists Ice Cube and Tupac Shakur, interpreted the sentence as one more example of the justice system's antipathy for African American life. Du's store was one of many burned to the ground during the 1992 riots. Jeff Chang, *Can't Stop Won't Stop: A History of the Hip-Hop Generation* (New York: Picador, 2005); Geoffrey Taylor Gibbs, "Can African-Americans Now Truly Believe in Judicial Fairness?," *Los Angeles Times*, November 24, 1991, http://articles.latimes.com/1991-11-24/opinion/op-115_1_black-life; Ice Cube, "Black Korea," *Death Certificate*, CD, Priority Re-cords, 1991; Tupac Shakur, "Keep Ya Head Up," music video, Interscope/Atlantic, 1993.

4. Chang, *Can't Stop Won't Stop*; Ice Cube, "We Had to Tear This Muthafucka Up," *The Predator*, CD, Priority Records, 1992. On sampling as evidence, see David Foster Wallace and Mark Costello, *Signifying Rappers* (New York: Little, Brown, 2013).

5. Chang, *Can't Stop Won't Stop*; Eithne Quinn, *Nuthin' But a "G" Thang: The Cul-ture and Commerce of Gangsta Rap* (New York: Columbia University Press, 2005).

6. Dr. Dre, "The Day the Niggaz Took Over," *The Chronic*, CD, Death Row Re-cords, 1992; Chang, *Can't Stop Won't Stop*, 420.

7. See Quinn, *Nuthin' But a "G" Thang*; S. Craig Watkins, *Hip Hop Matters: Politics, Pop Culture, and the Struggle for the Soul of a Movement* (Boston: Beacon Press, 2005).

8. Anthrax, "Bring the Noise," *Attack of the Killer B's*, CD, Island, 1991; Run-DMC, "Walk This Way," *Raising Hell*, CD, Profile/Arista, 1986.

9. Body Count, "Cop Killer," *Body Count*, CD, Sire, 1992.

10. See "Rapper Ice-T Defends Song against Spreading Boycott," *New York Times*, June 19, 1992, LexisNexis Academic; Dan Rather, "New Rap Song Makes the Police Un-easy Nationwide," *CBS Evening News*, June 11, 1992, LexisNexis Academic.

11. Jon Pareles, "Critic's Notebook; the Disappearance of Ice-T's 'Cop Killer,'" *New York Times*, July 30, 1992, LexisNexis Academic.

12. Heavy metal was also an object of public ire for promoting a so-called culture

of violence. For example, see Tipper Gore, "Protect Children from the Culture of Violence," *St. Petersburg Times* (Florida), March 15, 1988, LexisNexis Academic.

13. Quinn, *Nuthin' But a "G" Thang*, 110. Also see Jon Shecter, "'Cop Killer' Won't Die," *Source*, November 1992, 16. Notably, Dr. Dre claimed he planned to include a track titled "Mr. Officer" on *The Chronic*, but decided against it following the "Cop Killer" controversy. Akwanza, "The Doctor is in . . . Again," *Rap Pages*, June 1993, 12–16.

14. Sieving also argues that Ice-T and his supporters' emphasis on his First Amendment rights, rather than the politics of race and law at the song's core, further domesticated it and guaranteed its eventual removal from Body Count's album. See Christopher Sieving, "Cop Out? The Media, 'Cop Killer,' and the Deracialization of Black Rage," *Journal of Communication Inquiry* 22 (1998): 334–53.

15. In addition to appealing to public fears of racialized criminal threats, many of Clinton's policies on crime were motivated by the Oklahoma City bombing of 1995. Lance Selfa, *The Democrats: A Critical History* (Chicago: Haymarket Books, 2008); Jonathan Simon, *Governing through Crime: How the War on Crime Transformed American Democracy and Created a Culture of Fear* (Oxford: Oxford University Press, 2007).

16. Frank Newport, "Sixty-Nine Percent of Americans Support Death Penalty: Majority Say Death Penalty Is Applied Fairly," *Gallup News Service*, October 12, 2007, http://www.gallup.com/poll/101863/Sixtynine-Percent-Americans-Support-Death-Penalty.aspx; Tony Platt, "Reconstructing Race and Crime: The Racial Tradition Revisited," in *Racializing Justice, Disenfranchising Lives: The Racism, Criminal Justice, and Law Reader*, ed. Ian Seinberg, Manning Marable, and Keesha Middlemass (New York: Palgrave Macmillan, 2007), 35–42; Doris Marie Provine, "Creating Racial Disadvantage: The Case of Crack Cocaine," in *The Many Colors of Crime: Inequalities of Race, Ethnicity, and Crime in America*, ed. Ruth D. Peterson, Lauren J. Krivo, and John Hagan (New York: New York University Press, 2006), 277–94; Selfa, *Democrats*; Simon, *Governing through Crime*.

17. Robert Asen, *Visions of Poverty: Welfare Policy and the Political Imagination* (East Lansing: Michigan State University Press, 2002); Elaine Brown, "The Condemnation of Little B," in Seinberg, Marable, and Middlemass, *Racializing Justice, Disenfranchising Lives*, 43–8; Jane L. Collins and Victoria Mayer, *Both Hands Tied: Welfare Reform and the Race to the Bottom in the Low-Wage Labor Market* (Chicago: University of Chicago Press, 2010); David Harvey, *A Brief History of Neoliberalism* (Oxford: Oxford University Press, 2005).

18. Dana L. Cloud, "The Rhetoric of <Family Values>: Scapegoating, Utopia, and the Privatization of Social Responsibility," *Western Journal of Communication* 62 (1998): 387–419.

19. David Mills, "Sister Souljah's Call to Arms," *Washington Post*, May 13, 1992, LexisNexis Academic, para. 6.

20. Ibid., para. 5.

21. On the representational politics associated with the Denny video, see John Fiske, *Media Matters: Race and Gender in U.S. Politics* (Minneapolis: University of Minnesota Press, 1996). More recently, author Toni Morrison made a similar point in the context of activism responding to police violence against black individuals. Gaby Wood, "Toni Morrison Interview: On Racism, Her New Novel, and Marlon Brando," *Telegraph*, April 19, 2015, http://www.telegraph.co.uk/culture/books/authorinterviews/11532385/Toni-Morrison-interview-on-racism-her-new-novel-and-Marlon-Brando.html.

22. Thomas B. Edsall, "Clinton Stuns Rainbow Coalition," *Washington Post*, June 14, 1992, LexisNexis Academic, para. 3.

23. Ibid., para. 4.

24. David Roediger, *How Race Survived U.S. History: From Settlement and Slavery to the Obama Phenomenon* (London: Verso, 2008).

25. Gerald Bunting, "Why I Will Vote," *Source*, November 1992, 53.

26. Bernard, "Election '92." Also see Chang, *Can't Stop Won't Stop*.

27. Kierna Mayo, "A Souljah Story," *Source*, September 1992, 16.

28. Bernard, "Election '92," 57.

29. Quinn, *Nuthin' But a "G" Thang*.

30. Jennifer Rowland, "L.A. Police Say Gang Truce Works," *United Press International*, June 17, 1992, LexisNexis Academic.

31. On law enforcement responses to the truce, see Jesse Katz, "Police, Gangs Blame Each Other for Party Melees Violence," *Los Angeles Times*, June 9, 1992, http://articles.latimes.com/1992-06-09/local/me-263_1_law -enforcement; Rowland, "L.A. Police Say Gang Truce Works"; Richard A. Serrano and Jesse Katz, "LAPD Gang Task Force Deployed Despite Truce," *Los Angeles Times*, June 26, 1992, http://articles.latimes.com/1992-06-26/news/mn-973_1_ task-force. More recently, several Baltimore gangs entered into a truce in the wake of protests and rioting following the police killing of Freddie Gray and other black individuals. Similar to their LAPD counterparts during the 1990s, the Baltimore police interpreted the truce as an attempt to target law enforcement for violent retaliation. Justin Fenton, "Baltimore Police Say Gangs 'Teaming Up' to Take Out Officers," *Baltimore Sun*, April 27, 2015, http://www.baltimoresun.com/news/maryland/crime/blog/ bs-md-ci-freddie-gray-gang-threat-20150427-story.html.

32. Chang, *Can't Stop Won't Stop*, 389. Also see Lawrence Grossberg, *Caught in the Crossfire: Kids, Politics, and America's Future* (Boulder, CO: Paradigm Publishers, 2005); Manning Marable, "Racializing Justice, Disenfranchising Lives: Toward an Antiracist Criminal Justice," in Seinberg, Marable, and Middlemass, *Racializing Justice, Disenfranchising Lives: The Racism, Criminal Justice, and Law Reader*, 1–14.

33. Robin D. G. Kelley, *Race Rebels: Culture, Politics, and the Black Working Class* (New York: Free Press, 1994), 51. See also Adam Gussow, *Seems Like Murder Here: Southern Violence and the Blues Tradition* (Chicago: University of Chicago Press, 2002).

34. Robin D. G. Kelley, *Freedom Dreams: The Black Radical Imagination* (Boston: Beacon Press, 2002). See also James C. Scott, *Domination and the Arts of Resistance: Hidden Transcripts* (New Haven, CT: Yale University Press, 1990).

35. Barry Brummett, *A Rhetoric of Style*. Carbondale: Southern Illinois University Press, 2008.

36. Dick Hebdige, *Subculture: The Meaning of Style* (London: Routledge, 1979).

37. Monica L. Miller, *Slaves to Fashion: Black Dandyism and the Styling of Black Diasporic Identity* (Durham, NC: Duke University Press, 2009), 81.

38. Kelley, *Race Rebels*.

39. Style has always been a central component of gangsta rap and by no means begins with g funk. However, the political entailments of leisure and style in post-riot Los Angeles were particularly salient given their more explicit entrenchment in racialized discourses of criminality.

40. On Snoop Dogg's gang background, see dream hampton, "G-Down," *Source*, September 1993, 64–70.

41. Nelson George, *Buppies, B-Boys, Baps and Bohos: Notes on Post-Soul Black Culture* (New York: HarperCollins, 1992), 13.

42. Chang, *Can't Stop Won't Stop*; Kelley, *Race Rebels*; Quinn, *Nuthin' But a "G"*

Thang; Tricia Rose, *The Hip Hop Wars: What We Talk About When We Talk About Hip Hop—and Why It Matters* (New York: BasicCivitas, 2008).

43. Dr. Dre, "Rat-Tat-Tat-Tat," *The Chronic*, CD, Death Row Records, 1992; Gussow, *Seems Like Murder Here*; Quinn, *Nuthin' But a "G" Thang*.

44. Chang, *Can't Stop Won't Stop*; Quinn, *Nuthin' But a "G" Thang*; Chuck Phillips, "Snoop Doggy Dogg Leads the Pack," *Los Angeles Times*, December 2, 1993, http://articles.latimes.com/1993–12-02/entertainment/ca-63303_1_debut-album.

45. Josh Tyrangiel, "*The Chronic*," *Time*, January 22, 2010, http://entertainment.time.com/2006/11/02/the-all-time-100-albums/slide/the-chronic/.

46. Dr. Dre, "Fuck wit' Dre Day," *The Chronic*, CD, Death Row Records, 1992; Dr. Dre, "Nuthin' But a 'G' Thang," *The Chronic*.

47. Dr. Dre, "Nuthin' But a 'G' Thang."

48. Chang, *Can't Stop Won't Stop*; "Dr. Dre—Let Me Ride," *Genius*, 2015, http://genius.com/6050/Dr-dre-let-me-ride; Raegan Kelly, "Hip Hop Chicano: A Separate but Parallel Story," in Brian Cross, *It's Not about a Salary . . . Rap, Race and Resistance in Los Angeles* (London: Verso, 1993), 65–76.

49. Dr. Dre, "Let Me Ride."

50. Ibid.

51. Ibid.; "Penal Code Section 211–215," *California Penal Code*, January 1, 1873, http://www.leginfo.ca.gov/cgi-bin/displaycode?section=pen&group=00001–01000&file=211–215.

52. Dr. Dre, "Rat-Tat-Tat-Tat."

53. Dr. Dre, "Let Me Ride," *Chronic*.

54. Dr. Dre, "Let Me Ride," music video, directed by Dr. Dre (Death Row Records, 1994).

55. Dr. Dre, "Let Me Ride," *Chronic*.

56. Dr. Dre, "Let Me Ride," music video. See also Dr. Dre, "Nuthin' But a 'G' Thang," music video, directed by Dr. Dre (Death Row Records, 1992); Snoop Doggy Dogg, "Gin and Juice," music video, directed by Dr. Dre (Death Row Records, 1993); "Who Am I (What's My Name?)," music video, directed by Fab 5 Freddy (Death Row Records, 1993).

57. Kelley, *Freedom Dreams*, 32.

58. Ibid., 17. On science fiction and utopian yearning, see Fredric Jameson, *Archaeologies of the Future: The Desire Called Utopia and Other Science Fictions* (London: Verso, 2005). Maroon societies refer to communities formed by escaped slaves. See Richard Price, ed., *Maroon Societies: Rebel Slave Communities in the Americas* (Baltimore: Johns Hopkins University Press, 1979).

59. See Watkins, *Hip Hop Matters*.

60. Snoop Doggy Dogg, "Gin and Juice," *Doggystyle*, CD, Death Row Records, 1993.

61. Dr. Dre, "Murder Was the Case: The Movie."

62. Snoop Doggy Dogg, "Who Am I (What's My Name?)"

63. Snoop Doggy Dogg, "Serial Killa"; "Penal Code Section 187–199," *California Penal Code*, http://www.leginfo.ca.gov/.html/pen_table_of_contents.html.

64. Rob Fitzpatrick, "How Snoop's *Doggystyle* Changed Hip-Hop," *Guardian*, May 27, 2011, http://www.theguardian.com/culture/2011/may/28/snoops-doggystyle-hip-hop.

65. Snoop Doggy Dogg, "Who Am I (What's My Name?)"

66. Chang, *Can't Stop Won't Stop*; Gore, "Hate, Rape, and Rap," *Washington Post*, January 8, 1990, LexisNexis Academic; Gore, "Protect Children from the Culture of Violence." On the broader context of the culture wars, see Paul Gottfried, *The Conservative*

Movement (Independence, KY: Twayne, 1992); Andrew Hartman, *A War for the Soul of America: A History of the Culture Wars* (Chicago: University of Chicago Press, 2015).

67. Chang, *Can't Stop Won't Stop.*

68. Mark Anthony Neal, *What the Music Said: Black Popular Music and Black Public Culture* (New York: Routledge, 1999), 140.

69. Neal, *What the Music Said.* Also see Eric King Watts, *Hearing the Hurt: Rhetoric, Aesthetics, & Politics of the New Negro Movement* (Tuscaloosa: University of Alabama Press, 2012).

70. Neal, *What the Music Said.*

71. Quinn, *Nuthin' But a "G" Thang*; Rose, *Hip Hop Wars.*

72. Snoop Doggy Dogg, "Doggy Dogg World," music video, directed by Dr. Dre and Ricky Harris (Death Row Records, 1994). Also see George, *Buppies, B-Boys, Baps and Bohos.* On Blaxploitation, see Ed Guerrero, *Framing Blackness: The African American Image in Film* (Philadelphia: Temple University Press, 1993); Mark Anthony Neal, *Soul Babies: Black Popular Culture and the Post-Soul Aesthetic* (New York: Routledge, 2002).

73. Elka Worner, "Gangsta Rap—The Ongoing Debate," *United Press International*, May 28, 1994, LexisNexis Academic.

74. Anthony Violant, "Fighting Words; When Violent Music Finds Its Expression in Real Life, Real People Get Hurt," *Buffalo News* (New York), September 24, 1993.

75. Dr. Dre, "Let Me Ride," *Chronic.*

76. United States House of Representatives, Subcommittee on Commerce, Consumer Protection and Competitiveness, *Music Lyrics and Interstate Commerce*, February 11, 1994.

77. Chang, *Can't Stop Won't Stop.*

78. Joy Bennett Kinnon, "Does Rap Have a Future?," *Ebony*, June 1997, LexisNexis Academic.

79. Franki V. Ransom, "Black Women Launch Attack on 'Gangsta Rap'; Petition Drive Targets Record Firms," *Times-Picayune* (New Orleans, LA), December 23, 1993, LexisNexis Academic.

80. United States House of Representatives.

81. For a scholarly critique of these and other themes, see Steven Best and Douglas Kellner, "Rap, Black Rage, and Racial Difference," *Enculturation* 2 (1999), http://enculturation.gmu.edu/2_2/best-kellner.html.

82. Snoop Doggy Dogg, "Gin and Juice," *Doggystyle.*

83. United States House of Representatives.

84. "Old Stereotypes of Bad Rap," *Atlanta Journal-Constitution*, December 7, 1993, LexisNexis Academic.

85. John Leland, "Criminal Records; Gangsta Rap and the Culture of Violence," *Newsweek*, November 29, 1993, LexisNexis Academic.

86. United States Senate, Committee of the Judiciary, Juvenile Justice Subcommittee, *Shaping Our Responses to Violent and Demeaning Imagery in Popular Music*, February 23, 1994.

87. However, like NWA before them, a lack of radio play did little to hurt their ability to sell records. John Freeman, "'Gangsta Rap' Comes under Fire; Many Radio Stations Banning It, but Sales Still Soar," *San Diego Union-Tribune*, December 17, 1993, LexisNexis Academic; Robert Santiago, "Hold the Hallelujahs, Pulpit Victory over Rap Is Hollow One," *Plain Dealer*, December 16, 1993, LexisNexis Academic.

88. Howard Fineman, "An Older, Grimmer Jesse," *Newsweek*, January 10, 1994, LexisNexis Academic.

89. Cited in Chang, *Can't Stop Won't Stop*, 453.

90. See, for example, Jimmie L. Reeves and Richard Campbell, *Cracked Coverage: Television News, the Anti-Cocaine Crusade, and the Reagan Legacy* (Durham, NC: Duke University Press, 1994).

91. Chang, *Can't Stop Won't Stop*, 452.

92. Rose, *Hip Hop Wars*.

93. United States Senate.

94. Rose, *Hip Hop Wars*.

95. See Patricia Hill Collins, *Black Sexual Politics: African Americans, Gender, and the New Racism* (New York: Routledge, 2005); Kimberlé Crenshaw, "Mapping the Margins: Intersectionality, Identity Politics, and Violence against Women of Color," *Stanford Law Review* 43 (1991): 1241–99; Rose, *Hip Hop Wars*.

96. Kevin Powell, "Live from Death Row," in *Tupac Shakur*, ed. Alan Light (New York: Three Rivers Press, 1998), 71–77; Christopher Holmes Smith, "'I Don't Like to Dream about Getting Paid': Representations of Social Mobility and the Emergence of the Hip-Hop Mogul," *Social Text* 77 (2003): 69–97.

Chapter 4

1. dream hampton, "G-Down," *Source*, September 1993, 64.

2. Scott Brodeur, "The Misadventures of Slick Rick," *Source*, March 1995, 58–62; Jim DeRogatis, "Snoop's Album Debuts, Despite His Murder Rap," *Chicago Sun-Times*, November 25, 1993, LexisNexis Academic; dream hampton; "In the Joint," *Rap Pages*, March 1994, 13; Eisa Davis, "Trials and Tribulations," *Source*, January 1994, 46–52.

3. On rappers' legal entanglements as symptoms of racialized criminal justice, see Brodeur, "Misadventures of Slick Rick."

4. Richard Harrington, "Guns n' Rappers: 3 Arrested in Shootings," *Washington Post*, November 3, 1993, LexisNexis Academic.

5. Larry McShane, "Rap Violence Moves out of Recording Studio, into Street," *Charleston Gazette*, January 6, 1994. LexisNexis Academic; Lisa Respers, "Controversial Hard-Core Rappers Who Act Out Their Anti-Social Messages," *Buffalo News*, December 26, 1993, LexisNexis Academic.

6. John Leland, "Criminal Records; Gangsta Rap and the Culture of Violence," *Newsweek*, November 29, 1993, LexisNexis Academic.

7. See, for example, Cheryl R. Reed, "Playing Rapper, Boy Says; Fatal Shot Fired Doing Imitation," *Dayton Daily News*, February 16, 1994, LexisNexis Academic.

8. Michael Eric Dyson, *Holler If You Hear Me: Searching for Tupac Shakur* (New York: Basic Civitas Books, 2001), 106.

9. *Tupac: Resurrection*, directed by Lauren Lazin (Los Angeles: Paramount Pictures, 2003). For more on Shakur's legacy in the hip-hop nation, see Murray Forman, "Tupac Shakur: (O)Stensibly (G)One," conference paper presented at *All Eyez on Me: Tupac Shakur and the Search for the Modern Folk Hero* (Harvard University, Cambridge, MA, 2003); Vanessa Satten, "Still: Fifteen Years since Tupac's Death, His Influence Is as Big as Ever," *XXL*, September 2011, 40–44.

10. William H. Grier and Price M. Cobbs, *Black Rage* (New York: Basic Books, 1969).

11. bell hooks, *Killing Rage: Ending Racism* (New York: Henry Holt, 1995). See also Audre Lorde, *Sister Outsider* (Berkeley, CA: Crossing Press, 1984); Cornel West, *Race Matters* (Boston: Beacon Press, 2001).

12. Paul Harris, *Black Rage Confronts the Law* (New York: New York University Press, 1997), 37.

13. Kevin Powell, "This Thug's Life," in *Tupac Shakur*, ed. Alan Light (New York: Three Rivers Press, 1998), 21–31. See also Seth Rosenfeld, *Subversives: The FBI's War on Student Radicals, and Reagan's Rise to Power* (New York: Farrar, Straus and Giroux, 2012).

14. *Tupac: Resurrection.*

15. Tupac Shakur, "Dear Mama," *Me Against the World*, CD (Atlantic/Interscope Records, 1995).

16. Ibid.

17. Powell, "This Thug's Life."

18. *Tupac: Resurrection.*

19. Martin Luther King Jr., "I Have a Dream," in *Speeches That Changed the World* (London: Smith-Davies Publishing, 2005), 150–53.

20. Powell, "This Thug's Life"; *Tupac: Resurrection.*

21. *Tupac: Resurrection.*

22. Danyel Smith, "Introduction," in Light, *Tupac Shakur*, 15–19.

23. *Tupac: Resurrection.*

24. Tupac Shakur, "Trapped," *2Pacalypse Now*, CD, Interscope Records, 1991.

25. Marsha Mitchell, "Strictly Straight Up," *Rap Pages*, June 1993, 44–45.

26. Powell, "This Thug's Life," 29.

27. *Tupac: Resurrection.*

28. Ibid.

29. Robin D. G. Kelley, *Race Rebels: Culture, Politics, and the Black Working Class* (New York: Free Press, 1994); Mark Anthony Neal, *What the Music Said: Black Popular Music and Black Public Culture* (New York: Routledge, 1999).

30. Also see Mitchell, "Strictly Straight Up."

31. On the politics of the "street" Malcolm, see Kelley, *Race Rebels.*

32. ThugLifeArmyNews, "Tupac at Malcolm X Grassroots Movement," *YouTube*, April 15, 2008, http://www.youtube.com/watch?v=3m2OUSZ5WR8.

33. Shakur, "Trapped."

34. Dyson, *Holler If You Hear Me*, 115.

35. James Darsey, *The Prophetic Tradition and Radical Rhetoric in America* (New York: New York University Press, 1997).

36. *Tupac: Resurrection.*

37. Ibid.

38. Frank Williams, "The Living End," *Source*, November 1996, 106.

39. Mitchell, "Strictly Straight Up," 44.

40. Shakur, "Holla If Ya Hear Me," *Strictly 4 My N.I.G.G.A.Z.*, CD, Atlantic/Interscope Records, 1993.

41. Ibid.

42. Shakur, "I Get Around." See Dorian Lynskey, *33 Revolutions per Minute: A History of Protest Songs, from Billie Holiday to Green Day* (New York: HarperCollins, 2011).

43. See Eithne Quinn, *Nuthin' But a "G" Thang: The Culture and Commerce of Gangsta Rap* (New York: Columbia University Press, 2005); Tricia Rose, *The Hip Hop Wars:*

What We Talk About When We Talk About Hip Hop—and Why It Matters (New York: BasicCivitas, 2008).

44. *Tupac: Resurrection.*

45. Powell, "This Thug's Life"; Ronald Smothers, "Rapper Charged in Shootings of Off-Duty Officers," *New York Times*, November 2, 1993, http://www.nytimes.com/1993/11/02/us/rapper-charged-in-shootings-of-off-duty-officers.html; "Thug Life: Where Do the Children Play?" *Billboard*, September 28, 1996, LexisNexis Academic.

46. Williams, "Living End."

47. Dyson, *Holler If You Hear Me.*

48. See Ronald L. Jackson III, *Scripting the Black Masculine Body: Identity, Discourse, and Racial Politics in Popular Media* (Albany: State University of New York Press, 2006); D. Marvin Jones, *Race, Sex, and Suspicion: The Myth of the Black Male* (Westport, CT: Praeger, 2005).

49. Tupac Shakur, "Ambitionz Az a Ridah," *All Eyez on Me*, CD, Death Row Records, 1996.

50. Dyson, *Holler If You Hear Me*, 162. Also see D. L. Cummings, "Black Steel," *Source*, September 1995, 81–102.

51. The same issue published an opposing perspective by a writer who claimed, "After reading Tupac's accuser's account of the events that night, I am fully convinced that Shakur is a man who sees women as sexual objects to satisfy his desires and then pimp to his boys." "Mail," *Vibe*, September 1995, 33.

52. See Kimberlé Crenshaw, "Mapping the Margins: Intersectionality, Identity Politics, and Violence against Women of Color," *Stanford Law Review* 43 (1991): 1241–99.

53. See Jeff Chang, *Can't Stop Won't Stop: A History of the Hip-Hop Generation* (New York: Picador, 2005); Quinn, *Nuthin' But a "G" Thang.*

54. Tim Dog's invective came as a response to NWA's work, while Dr. Dre used "Nuthin' But a G Thang" as a vehicle to attack former 2 Live Crew member and producer Luther "Luke" Campbell. Campbell returned Dr. Dre's dis with his own "Cowards of Compton," released on his 1993 album *In the Nude*. Murray Forman, *The 'Hood Comes First: Race, Space, and Place in Rap and Hip-Hop* (Middletown, CT: Wesleyan University Press, 2002).

55. For example, a 1986 gang brawl at a Run-DMC show in Long Beach resulted in forty injuries. Quinn, *Nuthin' But a "G" Thang.*

56. Cheo Hodari Coker, "How the West Was Won," in Light, *Tupac Shakur*, 39; Selwyn Seyfu Hinds, "Don of the Westside," *Source*, May 1996, 52.

57. Forman, *The 'Hood Comes First*; Allison Samuels and John Leland, "Trouble Man," *Newsweek*, September 23, 1996, LexisNexis Academic; Powell, "Live from Death Row," in Light, *Tupac Shakur*, 71–77.

58. This is not to suggest that East Coast artists abstained completely from the rivalry. For example, the New York rap duo Mobb Deep released two diss tracks at the height of tensions, 1996's "Drop a Gem on 'Em" and "L.A., L.A." Also, at the 1995 filming of Tha Dogg Pound's "New York, New York" video, shots were fired at the West Coast artist's trailer in New York City. The Blackspot, "Stakes Is High," in Light, *Tupac Shakur*, 106–11; Forman, *The 'Hood Comes First*; Miles Marshall Lewis, "Bicoastalism," *Source*, August 1996, 56.

59. The Blackspot, "Stakes Is High"; Cory Johnson, "Sweatin' Bullets," in Light, *Tupac Shakur*, 41; Lewis, "Bicoastalism"; *Tupac: Resurrection*; "Untitled," in Light, *Tupac Shakur*, 59.

60. *Tupac: Resurrection.*

61. Shakur, "California Love," *2Pac: Greatest Hits*, CD, Death Row Records, 1998. See also Jon Pareles, "Tupac Shakur, 25, Rap Performer Who Personified Violence, Dies," *New York Times*, September 14, 1996, http://www.nytimes.com/1996/09/14/arts/tupac-shakur -25-rap-performer-who-personified-violence-dies.html?pagewanted=all&src=pm; Powell, "Live from Death Row."

62. Jeffrey Jolson-Colburn, "Soul Train Founder Denies Rapper Was Armed at Awards Show," *BPI Entertainment News Wire*, April 2, 1996, LexisNexis Academic.

63. Rob Marriott, "Last Testament," in Light, *Tupac Shakur*, 126.

64. As Forman notes, record companies became more cautious in signing and distributing rap acts. Prominent figures like Nation of Islam leader Louis Farrakhan, as well as hip-hop veterans like Chuck D of Public Enemy and Ice-T, sought to heal the rift between the two camps. There was a palpable sense that nothing less than the soul of the hip-hop nation was at stake. See Forman, *The 'Hood Comes First*; Lewis, "Bicoastalism"; Danyel Smith, "Staying Power," in Light, *Tupac Shakur*, 105.

65. Shakur, "California Love".

66. On disputes between Suge Knight and his artists, see Rob Marriott, "All That Glitters," in Light, *Tupac Shakur*, 130–35.

67. Shakur, "Hit 'Em Up," *2Pac: Greatest Hits*, CD, Death Row Records, 1998. See Chang, *Can't Stop Won't Stop*; Cheryl L. Keyes, *Rap Music and Street Consciousness* (Urbana: University of Illinois Press, 2002); Quinn, *Nuthin' But a "G" Thang*. Contrary to Shakur's mockery, Bad Boy Entertainment was a hugely successful record company during the 1990s. In particular, Biggie's debut album, *Ready to Die*, received extremely positive reviews and is widely regarded as one of hip-hop's greatest recordings. See Cheo H. Coker, "The Notorious B.I.G.: *Ready to Die*," *Rolling Stone*, November 3, 1994, http://web .archive.org/web/20090114112549/http://www.rollingstone.com/artists/notoriousbig/ albums/album/192664/review/5946007/ready_to_die; "Got Five on It," *Source*, March 2002, 176; Shortie, "The Notorious B.I.G.: *Ready to Die*," *Source*, October 1994, 79.

68. On hand signals and other nonverbal dimensions of gang communication, see Dwight Conquergood, "Homeboys and Hoods: Gang Communication and Cultural Space," in *Cultural Struggles: Performance, Ethnography, and Praxis*, ed. E. Patrick Johnson (Ann Arbor: University of Michigan Press, 2013), 224–63.

69. Shakur, "Ambitionz Az a Ridah."

70. Chang, *Can't Stop Won't Stop*.

71. Shakur, "California Love."

72. Shakur, "2 of Amerikaz Most Wanted," *All Eyez on Me*. See The Blackspot, "Stakes Is High."

73. Dyson, *Holler If You Hear Me*.

74. Shakur, "2 of Amerikaz Most Wanted," music video, directed by Gobi M. Rahimi (Death Row Records, 1996).

75. Shakur, "Life Goes On," *All Eyez on Me*. Also see Shakur, "I Ain't Mad Atcha."

76. Shakur, "To Live and Die in L.A.," *The Don Killuminati: The Seven Day Theory*, CD, Death Row Records, 1996.

77. Kenneth Burke, *A Rhetoric of Motives* (Berkeley: University of California Press, 1969).

78. See Eric Hobsbawm, *Bandits* (New York: New Press, 2000); Fredric Jameson, "Reification and Utopia in Mass Culture," in his *Signatures of the Visible* (New York: Routledge, 1992), 9–34.

79. Rob Marriott, "Ready to Die," in Light, *Tupac Shakur*, 116–23.

80. Mark Steyn, "Bozo in the Hood; Tupac Shakur's Short, Violent, Misogynist Life," *American Spectator*, November 1996, LexisNexis Academic, para. 8.

81. Michelle Dearmond, "Rap Star Tupac Shakur Dies of Wounds," *Chicago Sun-Times*, September 14, 1996, http://www.highbeam.com/doc/1P2-4352107.html, para. 1.

82. Sheila Simmons, "Fans Not Surprised by Rapper's Death," *Plain Dealer*, September 20, 1996, Access World News, para. 11.

83. Robert Reinhold, "In the Middle of L.A.'s Gang Wars," *New York Times*, May 22, 1988, http://www.nytimes.com/1988/05/22/magazine/in-the-middle-of-la-s-gang-wars.html?pagewanted=all&src=pm.

84. Pareles, "Tupac Shakur, 25, Rap Performer Who Personified Violence, Dies."

85. Pamela Constable, "Rapper Dies of Wounds from Shooting; Drive-by Assault in Las Vegas Ends Tupac Shakur's Short, Violent Life," *Washington Post*, September 14, 1996, LexisNexis Academic, para. 8.

86. Esther Iverem, "A Death as Real as It Gets; Tupac Shakur's Gangsta Image Was the Rapper's Fatal Flaw," *Washington Post*, September 14, 1996, LexisNexis Academic, para. 1.

87. Neal, *What the Music Said*.

88. Robin Moppins, "The Legacy of Tupac Shakur," *Plain Dealer*, October 7, 1996, Access World News, para. 1, 7.

89. Darrell Dawsey, "No Time for Tears: A Eulogy for Tupac," *Essence*, December 1996, LexisNexis Academic, para. 7.

90. "Harlem Mosque Sets Rap Peace Meeting," *New York Times*, September 18, 1996, http://www.nytimes.com/1996/09/18/nyregion/harlem-mosque-sets-rap-peace-meeting.html, para. 2.

91. "Farrakhan to Sponsor D.C. Events," *Billboard*, August 23, 1997, LexisNexis Academic.

92. See Dana L. Cloud, "The Rhetoric of <Family Values> Scapegoating, Utopia, and the Privatization of Social Responsibility," *Western Journal of Communication* 62 (1998): 387–419; Erica R. Meiners, *Right to Be Hostile: Schools, Prisons, and the Making of Public Enemies* (New York: Routledge, 2007).

93. Kenneth Carroll, "Tupac's Squandered Gift; Shakur Forfeited His Poetic License by Exploiting Mayhem," *Washington Post*, September 22, 1996, LexisNexis Academic, para. 3.

94. Nikki Giovanni, "Dedication For Tupac Shakur (1971–1996)," *Love Poems* (New York: William Morrow, 1997), 5. See Felicia R. Lee, "At Home With: Nikki Giovanni; Defying Evil, and Mortality," *New York Times*, August 1, 1996, LexisNexis Academic; Denise Barnes, "Nikki Giovanni: Always Well-Versed on Subjects," *Washington Times*, June 30, 1998, LexisNexis Academic.

95. Tyrone Beason, "Survival of the Baddest: Poet and Activist Nikki Giovanni Keeps Her '60s Spirit Intact for a New Generation," *Seattle Times*, January 15, 2004, Access World News, para. 4.

96. Christine Harold and Kevin Michael DeLuca, "Behold the Corpse: Violent Images and the Case of Emmett Till," *Rhetoric and Public Affairs* 8 (2005): 263–86; Dyson, *Holler If You Hear Me*; Mark Lelinwalla, "Beautiful Struggle," *XXL*, September 2011, 85; Manning Marable, *Malcolm X: A Life of Reinvention* (New York: Viking, 2011).

97. See Mike Davis, *City of Quartz: Excavating the Future in Los Angeles* (London: Verso, 2006); Ed Guerrero, *Framing Blackness: The African American Image in Film*

(Philadelphia: Temple University Press, 1993); Hobsbawm, *Bandits*; Peter Linebaugh, *The London Hanged: Crime and Civil Society in the Eighteenth Century* (Cambridge: Cambridge University Press, 1992); John W. Roberts, *From Trickster to Badman: The Black Folk Hero in Slavery and Freedom* (Philadelphia: University of Pennsylvania Press, 1990).

98. See Quinn, *Nuthin' But a "G" Thang*.

99. Kevin Powell, "Ready to Live" in Light, *Tupac Shakur*, 51.

100. Cited in Morton G. Wenger and Thomas A. Bonomo, "Crime, the Crisis of Capitalism, and Social Revolution," in *Crime and Capitalism: Readings in Marxist Criminology*, ed. David F. Greenberg (Philadelphia: Temple University Press, 1993), 675–76. See also Linebaugh, *London Hanged*.

101. Powell, "Live from Death Row," 77.

Conclusion

Epigraph 1. Tupac Shakur, "2 of Amerikaz Most Wanted," *All Eyez on Me*, CD, Death Row Records, 1996.

Epigraph 2. Geraldo Rivera, "Geraldo Rivera: Trayvon Martin Would Be Alive but for His Hoodie," *Fox News Latino*, March 23, 2012, http://latino.foxnews.com/latino/politics/2012/03/23/trayvon-martins-hoodie-and-george-zimmerman-share-blame/, para. 7.

1. For various takes on these questions, see Barbara A. Biesecker, "The Obligation to Theorize, Today," *Western Journal of Communication* 77 (2013): 518–22; Stephen John Hartnett, "Communication, Social Justice, and Joyful Commitment," *Western Journal of Communication* 74 (2010): 68–93; Christopher Swift, "Academic Engagement," *Quarterly Journal of Speech* 96 (2010): 443–49.

2. Fox Butterfield, "Charles Stuart's Brother Indicted in Murder Case," *New York Times*, September 27, 1991, http://www.nytimes.com/1991/09/27/us/charles-stuart-s-brother-indicted-in-murder-case.html.

3. Bill Hewitt, "Tears of Hate and Pity," *People*, March 13, 1994, http://www.people.com/people/archive/article/0,,20105269,00.html.

4. "Cops: McCain Worker Made Up Attack Story," *CBS News*, October 24, 2008, http://www.cbsnews.com/news/cops-mccain-worker-made-up-attack-story/.

5. Dilip Parameshwar Gaonkar, "Toward New Imaginaries: An Introduction," *Public Culture* 14 (2002): 1.

6. See, for example, Katheryn Russell-Brown, *The Color of Crime* (New York: New York University Press, 2009).

7. Al Baker and Colin Moynihan, "Two Officers Speak to Grand Jury on Killing of Unarmed Black Man," *New York Times*, March 6, 2007, http://www.nytimes.com/2007/03/06/nyregion/06grand.html; Jane Fritsch, "The Diallo Verdict," *New York Times*, February 26, 2000, http://www.nytimes.com/2000/02/26/nyregion/diallo-verdict-overview-4-officers-diallo-shooting-are-acquitted-all-charges.html?pagewanted=all&src=pm.

8. See Tony Briscoe, "Protesters Plan 'Black Christmas' March along Mag Mile," *Chicago Tribune*, December 23, 2015, http://www.chicagotribune.com/news/local/breaking/ct-laquan-mcdonald-city-hall-protest-20151222-story.html; Dana Ford and Ed Payne, "Grand Jury Decides against Indictments in Sandra Bland's Death," *CNN*, December 23, 2015, http://www.cnn.com/2015/12/21/us/sandra-bland-no-indictments/; Oliver Laughland, Kayla Epstein, and Jessica Glenza, "Eric Garner Protests Continue in Cities across America through Second Night," *Guardian*, December 5, 2014, http://www.theguardian

.com/us-news/2014/dec/05/eric-garner-case-new-york-protests-continue-through-second-night; Mark Puente, "After Freddie Gray Death, U.S. Starts Civil Rights Probe of Baltimore Police," *Baltimore Sun*, May 8, 2015, http://www.baltimoresun.com/news/maryland/baltimore-city/bs-md-justice-announce-20150508-story.html#page=1; Michael Sherer and Elizabeth Dias, "As Zimmerman Trial Ends, What's Next," *Time*, July 29, 2013, http://content.time.com/time/magazine/article/0,9171,2147718,00.html; Ashley Southall and C. J. Hughes, "Dozens Arrested during Brooklyn Bridge Protest against Police Violence," *New York Times*, April 14, 2015, http://www.nytimes.com/2015/04/15/nyregion/protesters-arrested-as-brooklyn-bridge-is-snarled.html; Steven W. Thrasher, "What Next for Black Lives Matter in Ferguson after City's Police Shooting?," *Guardian*, March 13, 2015, http://www.theguardian.com/us-news/2015/mar/13/black-lives-matter-ferguson-police-shooting; Kai Wright, "Why Alton Sterling and Philando Castile Are Dead," *Nation*, July 7, 2016, https://www.thenation.com/article/why-alton-sterling-and-philando-castile-are-dead/.

9. "The Last Tweets of Obama's 'Son' Trayvon Martin," *US Action News*, March 27, 2012, http://usactionnews.com/2012/03/the-last-tweets-of-obamas-no_limit_nigga-trayvon-martin/; David Martosko, "Second Trayvon Martin Twitter Feed Identified," *Daily Caller*, March 29, 2012, http://dailycaller.com/2012/03/29/second-trayvon-martin-twitter-feed-identified/; Amanda Sloane and Graham Winch, "Judge Allows Evidence of Trayvon Martin's Marijuana Use," *CNN*, July 9, 2013, http://www.cnn.com/2013/07/08/justice/zimmerman-trial; "Trayvon Martin Case: He Was Suspended Three Times and Caught with 'Burglary Tool,'" *Mail Online*, March 26, 2012, http://www.dailymail.co.uk/news/article-2120504/Trayvon-Martin-case-He-suspended-times-caught-burglary-tool.html; "The Trayvon Martin Our Government-Subsidized Media Won't Let You See," *Sad Hill News*, March 25, 2012, http://sadhillnews.com/2012/03/25/the-trayvon-martin-our-government-subsidized-media-wont-let-you-see.

10. Matt Gutman, Seni Tienabesco, and Ben Forer, "George Zimmerman Tells Trayvon Martin's Parents 'I Am Sorry,'" *ABC News*, April 20, 2012, http://abcnews.go.com/US/george-zimmerman-case-exclusive-photo-shows-bloodied-back/story?id=16177849#.T5FqDGLLx5j.

11. "Willie Horton (National Security PAC, 1988)," *Living Room Candidate*, 2012, http://www.livingroomcandidate.org/commercials/1988/willie-horton.

12. Yamiche Alcindor, "Trayvon Martin's Father Says He Warned Son about Stereotypes," *USA Today*, April 19, 2012, http://usatoday30.usatoday.com/news/nation/story/2012-04-14/african-american-parents-talk-to-sons-about-race/54258448/1; Edgar Sandoval and Helen Kennedy, "'Million Hoodie' March Takes Union Square in Protest of Trayvon Martin's Fatal Shooting," *New York Daily News*, March 21, 2012, http://www.nydailynews.com/new-york/million-hoodie-march-takes-union-square-protest-trayvon-martin-murder-article-1.1048522.

13. Howard Fineman, "An Older, Grimmer Jesse," *Newsweek*, January 10, 1994, LexisNexis Academic.

14. Lizette Alvarez, "Trayvon Martin Texts Are Released," *New York Times*, May 23, 2013, http://www.nytimes.com/2013/05/24/us/zimmermans-lawyers-release-text-messages-of-trayvon-martin.html?_r=0.

15. Lizette Alvarez and Cara Buckley, "Zimmerman Is Acquitted in Trayvon Martin Killing," *New York Times*, July 13, 2013, http://www.nytimes.com/2013/07/14/us/george-zimmerman-verdict-trayvon-martin.html?pagewanted=all. Two important preludes to the Martin-Zimmerman case are the arrest of Harvard's Henry Louis Gates Jr. for trying to enter his own house and the massive mobilization surrounding the arrest and prose-

cution of the so-called Jena 6 in Louisiana. See "After Beers, Professor, Officer Plan to Meet Again," *CNN.com*, July 31, 2009, http://www.cnn.com/2009/POLITICS/07/30/harvard.arrest.beers/; "Race, Violence . . . Justice?," *National Public Radio*, August 30, 2011, http://www.npr.org/2011/08/30/140058680/race-violence-justice-looking-back-at-jena-6.

16. I have also explored these issues in the broader historical context of the black radical tradition. See Bryan J. McCann, "On Whose Ground? Racialized Violence and the Prerogative of 'Self-Defense' in the Trayvon Martin Case," *Western Journal of Communication* 78 (2014): 480–99.

17. For example, when radio host Don Imus referred to the black members of Rutgers University's women's basketball team as a group of "nappy headed hoes" in 2007, he claimed his words were no worse than what black male rappers said about black women in their music. In 2015, after the circulation of a video showing white members of a fraternity at the University of Oklahoma singing a racist chant, some commentators argued that gangsta rap had helped make the racial epithets the students uttered more socially acceptable. See William Banfield, *Cultural Codes: Makings of a Black Music Philosophy* (Lanham, MD: Scarecrow Press, 2010); Philip Bump, "'Morning Joe' Misses the Mark on Rap Music and the SAE Chants," *Washington Post*, March 11, 2015, http://www.washingtonpost.com/blogs/the-fix/wp/2015/03/11/morning-joe-blames-rap-music-for-the-oklahoma-sae-chants-not-quite/.

18. United States Senate, Committee of the Judiciary, Juvenile Justice Subcommittee, *Shaping Our Responses to Violent and Demeaning Imagery in Popular Music*, February 23, 1994.

19. On conceptualizing the United States as an "incarceration nation," see Stephen J. Hartnett, *Incarceration Nation: Investigative Prison Poems of Hope and Terror* (Walnut Creek, CA: AltaMira, 2003).

20. See Eithne Quinn, *Nuthin' But a "G" Thang: The Culture and Commerce of Gangsta Rap* (New York: Columbia University Press, 2005); Tricia Rose, *The Hip Hop Wars: What We Talk About When We Talk About Hip-Hop—and Why It Matters* (New York: BasicCivitas, 2008).

21. Common, "I Used to Love H.E.R.," *Resurrection*, CD, Relativity Records, 1994.

22. Lauryn Hill, "Lost Ones," *The Miseducation of Lauryn Hill*, CD, Ruffhouse Records, 1998.

23. For more on the need for dialogue within the hip-hop nation, see Rose, *Hip Hop Wars*.

24. Quinn, *Nuthin' But a "G" Thang*, 190–91.

25. See Amy Goodman and Juan Gonzalez, "Hip Hop Artist M-1 of Dead Prez," *Democracy Now!*, October 26, 2006, http://www.democracynow.org/2006/10/26/hip_hop_artist_m_1_of; "Yasiin Bey and Dead Prez Prep Trayvon Martin Tribute," *BET*, April 6, 2012, http://www.bet.com/news/music/2012/04/06/yasiin-bey-and-dead-prez-prep-trayvon-martin-tribute.html.

26. dead prez, "Hell Yeah (Pimp the System)," *RBG: Revolutionary But Gangsta*, CD, Sony Music Entertainment, 2004.

27. Ibid.

28. Woody Guthrie, "Pretty Boy Floyd," *The Best of Woody Guthrie, Vol. 1*, CD, Prestige Elite, 2007.

29. NWA, "Fuck Tha Police," *Straight Outta Compton*, CD, Priority Records, LLC, 1988.

30. Peter Travers, "Straight Outta Compton," *Rolling Stone*, August 13, 2015, http://www.rollingstone.com/movies/reviews/straight-outta-compton-20150813, para. 4.

31. Nisha, "Exclusive: Director F. Gary Gray Talks N.W.A. Biopic 'Straight Outta Compton,'" *Source*, August 8, 2015, http://thesource.com/2015/08/08/exclusive-f-gary-gray-talks-n-w-a-biopic-straight-outta-compton/, para. 11.

32. Daniel Kreps, "Watch the Red-Band Trailer for N.W.A.'s Biopic 'Straight Outta Compton,'" *Rolling Stone*, February 9, 2015, http://www.rollingstone.com/movies/videos/watch-the-red-band-trailer-for-n-w-as-biopic-straight-outta-compton-20150209.

33. See Dee Barnes, "Here's What's Missing from *Straight Outta Compton*: Me and the Other Women Dr. Dre Beat Up," *Gawker*, August 18, 2015, http://gawker.com/heres-whats-missing-from-straight-outta-compton-me-and-1724735910

34. Dean E. Robinson, *Black Nationalism in American Politics and Thought* (Cambridge: Cambridge University Press, 2001).

35. Michelle Alexander, *The New Jim Crow: Mass Incarceration in the Age of Colorblindness* (New York: New Press, 2010).

36. See Eldridge Cleaver, *Soul on Ice* (New York: Delta, 1992).

37. On racially disproportionate arrest and conviction rates, see Alexander, *New Jim Crow*.

38. Rory Carroll, "Christopher Dorner: Cabin Fire Was Not Intentional, Say Police," *Guardian*, February 14, 2013, http://www.theguardian.com/world/2013/feb/14/christopher-dorner-fire-police; Dana Ford, "Renegade Ex-Cop Dorner Died from Single Gunshot to Head," *CNN*, February 16, 2013, http://www.cnn.com/2013/02/15/us/california-dorner-death/index.html?hpt=hp_t1.

39. See Michael Martinez and Paul Vercammen, "Rogue Ex-Cop Is Heavily Armed, Trained and Out There Somewhere," *CNN.com*, February 9, 2013, http://www.cnn.com/2013/02/08/us/lapd-attacks/index.html?hpt=hp_t1.

40. @Sir_Pope_L, Twitter post, February 12, 2013, 8:47 p.m., https://twitter.com/Sir_POPE_L/status/301522841990483968/photo/1.

41. @TheLawson_1, Twitter post, February 12, 2013, 11:36 p.m., https://twitter.com/TheLawson_1/status/301565524524032000/photo/1.

42. @TrulyKins, Twitter post, February 12, 2013, 6:13 p.m., https://twitter.com/TrulyKins/status/301484224639299586.

43. @rostro86, Twitter post, February 12, 2013, 4:49 p.m., https://twitter.com/rostro86/statuses/301463056691650561.

44. @sk1zm, Twitter post, May 27, 2013, 3:38 p.m., https://twitter.com/sk1zm/status/339118456890871808.

45. The rap group Ab-Soul also invoked Dorner in a visceral track about white supremacy and empire titled "Christopher DRONEr." Claire Lobenfeld, "Ab-Soul – 'Christopher DRONEr,'" *Stereogum*, August 7, 2013, http://www.stereogum.com/1429492/ab-soul-christopher-droner/mp3s/.

46. @sean_jay_89, Twitter post, February 12, 2013, 5:14 p.m., https://twitter.com/sean_jay_89/statuses/301469319936765953; @TrulyKins.

47. See, for example, Mark Landler and Michael D. Shear, "President Offers a Personal Take on Race in U.S.," *New York Times*, July 19, 2013, http://www.nytimes.com/2013/07/20/us/in-wake-of-zimmerman-verdict-obama-makes-extensive-statement-on-race-in-america.html?hp&_r=1.

48. "Christopher Dorner's Manifesto (Disturbing Content and Language)," *KTLA*

5, February 12, 2013, http://ktla.com/2013/02/12/read-christopher-dorners-so-called-manifesto/, para. 5.

49. Ibid., para. 38.

50. Ibid.

51. Ibid., para. 59, 69.

52. See "Blog," *Black Lives Matter*, n.d., http://blacklivesmatter.com/blog/; Ta-Nehisi Coates, "Nonviolence as Compliance," *Atlantic*, April 27, 2015, http://www.theatlantic.com/politics/archive/2015/04/nonviolence-as-compliance/391640/; David Von Drehle, "In the Line of Fire," *Time*, April 9, 2015, http://time.com/3814970/in-the-line-of-fire-2/.

53. Deborah Gould, "On Affect and Protest," in *Political Emotions: New Agendas in Communication*, ed. Ann Cvetkovich, Ann Reynolds, and Janet Staiger (New York: Routledge, 2010), 18–24.

Bibliography

Abu-Jamal, Mumia. *Live from Death Row*. New York: HarperCollins, 1996.

"After Beers, Professor, Officer Plan to Meet Again." *CNN.com*, July 31, 2009. http://www.cnn.com/2009/POLITICS/07/30/harvard.arrest.beers/.

Ahmed, Sara. *The Cultural Politics of Emotion*. 2nd ed. New York: Routledge, 2015.

Akwanza. "The Doctor is in . . . Again." *Rap Pages*, June 1993.

Alcindor, Yamiche. "Trayvon Martin's Father Says He Warned Son about Stereotypes." *USA Today*, April 19, 2012. http://usatoday30.usatoday.com/news/nation/story/2012-04-14/african-american-parents-talk-to-sons-about-race/54258448/1.

Alexander, Bryant Keith. *Performing Black Masculinity: Race, Culture, and Queer Identity*. Lanham, MD: Altamira, 2006.

Alexander, Michelle. *The New Jim Crow: Mass Incarceration in the Age of Colorblindness*. New York: New Press, 2010.

Allsopp, Fred W. *Folklore of Romantic Arkansas*. Vol. 1. New York: Grolier Society, 1931.

Alonso, Alejandro A. "Racialized Identities and the Formation of Black Gangs in Los Angeles." *Urban Geography* 25 (2004): 658–72.

Alvarez, Lizette. "Trayvon Martin Texts Are Released." *New York Times*, May 23, 2013. http://www.nytimes.com/2013/05/24/us/zimmermans-lawyers-release-text-messages-of-trayvon-martin.html?_r=0.

Alvarez, Lizette, and Cara Buckley. "Zimmerman Is Acquitted in Trayvon Martin Killing." *New York Times*, July 13, 2013. http://www.nytimes.com/2013/07/14/us/george-zimmerman-verdict-trayvon-martin.html?pagewanted=all.

Anderson, John, and Hillary Hevenor. *Burning Down the House: MOVE and the Tragedy of Philadelphia*. New York: W. W. Norton, 1987.

Anthrax. *Attack of the Killer B's*. CD. Island, 1991.

Apel, Dora. *Imagery of Lynching: Black Men, White Women, and the Mob*. New Brunswick, NJ: Rutgers University Press, 2004.

Arendt, Hannah. *Crises of the Republic*. New York: Harcourt Brace Jovanovich, 1972.

Asen, Robert. *Visions of Poverty: Welfare Policy and the Political Imagination*. East Lansing: Michigan State University Press, 2002.

Asenas, Jennifer, Bryan J. McCann, Kathleen Feyh, and Dana Cloud. "Saving Kenneth Foster: Speaking with Others in the Belly of the Beast of Capital Punishment." In *Communication Activism*. Vol. 3, *Struggling for Social Justice Amidst Difference*, edited by Lawrence R. Frey and Kevin M. Carragee, 264–90. New York: Hampton Press, 2012.

Attali, Jacques. *Noise: The Political Economy of Music*. Translated by Brian Massumi. Minneapolis: University of Minnesota Press, 1985.

Austin, Curtis J. *Up Against the Wall: Violence in the Making and Unmaking of the Black Panther Party*. Fayetteville: University of Arkansas Press, 2006.

Baker, Al, and Colin Moynihan. "Two Officers Speak to Grand Jury on Killing of Unarmed Black Man." *New York Times*, March 6, 2007. http://www.nytimes.com/2007/03/06/nyregion/06grand.html.

Baker, Carol. "L.A. Cops Drop 'Hammer' on Gangs." *United Press International*. July 10, 1989. LexisNexis Academic.

Baldwin, Davarian L. "Black Empires, White Desires: The Spatial Politics of Identity in the Age of Hip-Hop." In *That's the Joint!: The Hip-Hop Studies Reader*, edited by Murray Forman and Mark Anthony Neal, 182–202. New York: Routledge, 2004.

Baldwin, James. *Nobody Knows My Name: More Notes of a Native Son*. New York: Dell, 1961.

Banfield, William. *Cultural Codes: Makings of a Black Music Philosophy*. Lanham, MD: Scarecrow Press, 2010.

Barnes, Dee. "Here's What's Missing from *Straight Outta Compton*: Me and the Other Women Dr. Dre Beat Up." *Gawker*, August 18, 2015. http://gawker.com/heres-whats-missing-from-straight-outta-compton-me-and-1724735910.

Barnes, Denise. "Nikki Giovanni: Always Well-Versed on Subjects." *Washington Times*, June 30, 1998. LexisNexis Academic.

Bartels, Larry M. *Unequal Democracy: The Political Economy of the Gilded Age*. Princeton, NJ: Princeton University Press, 2010.

Barthes, Roland. *Image, Music, Text*. New York: Hill and Wang, 1977.

Bauer, Raymond A., and Alice H. Bauer. "Day to Day Resistance to Slavery." *Journal of Negro History* 27 (1942): 388–419.

Bazerman, Charles. "Speech Acts, Genres, and Activity Systems: How Texts Organize Activity and People." In *What Writing Does and How It Does It*, edited by Charles Bazerman and Paul Prior, 309–40. Mahwah, NJ: Lawrence Erlbaum Associates, 2004.

Beason, Tyrone. "Survival of the Baddest: Poet and Activist Nikki Giovanni Keeps Her '60s Spirit Intact for a New Generation." *Seattle Times*, January 15, 2004. Access World News.

Berger, Dan. *Captive Nation: Black Prison Organizing in the Civil Rights Era*. Chapel Hill: University of North Carolina Press, 2014.

Bernard, James. "Election '92: Are the Candidates Selling the Hip-Hop Nation Down the River?" *Source*, November 1992.

Bernstein, Lee. *America Is the Prison: Arts and Politics in Prison in the 1970s*. Chapel Hill: University of North Carolina Press, 2010.

Best, Steven, and Douglas Kellner. "Rap, Black Rage, and Racial Difference." *Enculturation* 2 (1999).

Biesecker, Barbara. "The Obligation to Theorize, Today." *Western Journal of Communication* 77 (2013): 518–22.

The Birth of a Nation. Directed by D. W. Griffith. 1915. Chatsworth, CA: Image Entertainment, 1998. DVD.

The Blackspot. "Stakes Is High." In Light, *Tupac Shakur*, 106–11.

"Blog." *Black Lives Matter*, n.d. http://blacklivesmatter.com/blog/.

Bloom, Joshua, and Waldo E. Martin Jr. *Black against Empire: The History and Politics of the Black Panther Party.* Berkeley: University of California Press, 2014.

Body Count. *Body Count.* CD. Sire, 1992.

Boone, Pat. *Moody River / Great! Great! Great!* CD. Sepia Records, 2012.

Briscoe, Tony. "Protesters Plan 'Black Christmas' March along Mag Mile." *Chicago Tribune*, December 23, 2015. http://www.chicagotribune.com/news/local/breaking/ct -laquan-mcdonald-city-hall-protest-20151222-story.html.

Brodeur, Scott. "The Misadventures of Slick Rick." *Source*, March 1995.

Brown, Cecil. *Stagolee Shot Billy.* Cambridge, MA: Harvard University Press, 2004.

Brown, Elaine. "The Condemnation of Little B." In Seinberg, Marable, and Middlemass, *Racializing Justice, Disenfranchising Lives*, 43–48.

Brown, Michael K., Marin Carnoy, Elliott Currie, Troy Duster, David B. Oppenheimer, Marjorie M. Shultz, and David Wellman. *White-Washing Race: The Myth of a Color-Blind Society.* Berkeley: University of California Press, 2003.

Brummett, Barry. *A Rhetoric of Style.* Carbondale: Southern Illinois University Press, 2008.

Buhle, Paul. *Robin Hood: People's Outlaw and Forest Hero; A Graphic Guide.* Oakland, CA: PM Press, 2011.

Bump, Philip. "'Morning Joe' Misses the Mark on Rap Music and the SAE Chants." *Washington Post*, March 11, 2015. http://www.washingtonpost.com/blogs/the-fix/wp/2015/ 03/11/morning-joe-blames-rap-music-for-the-oklahoma-sae-chants-not-quite/.

Bunting, Gerald. "Why I Will Vote." *Source*, November 1992.

Burke, Kenneth. *Counter-Statement.* Berkeley: University of California Press, 1968.

———. *Language as Symbolic Action.* Berkeley: University of California Press, 1966.

———. *A Rhetoric of Motives.* Berkeley: University of California Press, 1969.

Burt, Olive Woolley. *American Murder Ballads and Their Stories.* New York: Oxford University Press, 1958.

Butterfield, Fox. "Charles Stuart's Brother Indicted in Murder Case." *New York Times*, September 27, 1991. http://www.nytimes.com/1991/09/27/us/charles-stuart-s-brother -indicted-in-murder-case.html.

Campbell, Karlyn Kohrs. "The Rhetoric of Black Nationalism: A Case Study in Self-Conscious Criticism." *Central States Speech Journal* 22 (1971): 151–60.

Campbell, Karlyn Kohrs, and Kathleen Hall Jamieson. "Form and Genre in Rhetorical Criticism: An Introduction." In *Form and Genre: Shaping Rhetorical Action*, edited by Karlyn Kohrs Campbell and Kathleen Hall Jamieson, 9–32. Falls Church, VA: Speech Communication Association, 1978.

Carroll, Kenneth. "Tupac's Squandered Gift; Shakur Forfeited His Poetic License by Exploiting Mayhem." *Washington Post*, September 22, 1996. LexisNexis Academic, accessed September 14, 2013.

Carroll, Rory. "Christopher Dorner: Cabin Fire Was Not Intentional, Say Police." *The Guardian*, February 14, 2013. http://www.theguardian.com/world/2013/feb/14/ christopher-dorner-fire-police.

Carson, E. Ann, and William J. Sabol. *Prisoners in 2011*. Washington, DC: US Department of Justice, 2012. Accessed July 3, 2013. http://www.bjs.gov/content/pub/pdf/p11.pdf.

Carter, David A. "The Industrial Workers of the World and the Rhetoric of Song." *Quarterly Journal of Speech* 66 (1980): 365–74.

Certeau, Michel de. *The Practice of Everyday Life*. Berkeley: University of California Press, 1984.

Chang, Jeff. *Can't Stop Won't Stop: A History of the Hip-Hop Generation*. New York: Picador, 2005.

Chin, Gabriel J. "The New Civil Death: Rethinking Punishment in the Era of Mass Conviction." *University of Pennsylvania Law Review* 160 (2012): 1789–833.

"Christopher Dorner's Manifesto (Disturbing Content and Language)." *KTLA 5*, February 12, 2013. http://ktla.com/2013/02/12/read-christopher-dorners-so-called-manifesto/.

Churchill, Ward, and Jim Vander Wall. *The COINTELPRO Papers: Documents from the FBI's Secret Wars against Dissent in the United States*. Cambridge, MA: South End Press, 1990.

Cleaver, Eldridge. *Soul on Ice*. New York: Delta, 1992.

Cloud, Dana L. "The Rhetoric of <Family Values>: Scapegoating, Utopia, and the Privatization of Social Responsibility." *Western Journal of Communication* 62 (1998): 387–419.

Coates, Ta-Nehisi. "Nonviolence as Compliance." *Atlantic*, April 27, 2015. http://www.theatlantic.com/politics/archive/2015/04/nonviolence-as-compliance/391640/.

Coker, Cheo H. "The Notorious B.I.G.: *Ready to Die*." *Rolling Stone*, November 3, 1994. http://web.archive.org/web/20090114112549/http://www.rollingstone.com/artists/notoriousbig/albums/album/192664/review/5946007/ready_to_die.

Coker, Cheo Hodari. "How the West Was Won." In Light, *Tupac Shakur*, 39.

Collins, Jane L., and Victoria Mayer. *Both Hands Tied: Welfare Reform and the Race to the Bottom in the Low-Wage Labor Market*. Chicago: University of Chicago Press, 2010.

Common. "I Used to Love H.E.R." *Resurrection*. CD. Relativity Records, 1994.

Condit, Celeste Michelle, and John Louis Lucaites. *Crafting Equality: America's Anglo-African Word*. Chicago: University of Chicago Press, 1993.

Conquergood, Dwight. "Homeboys and Hoods: Gang Communication and Cultural Space." In *Cultural Struggles: Performance, Ethnography, and Praxis*, edited by E. Patrick Johnson, 224–63. Ann Arbor: University of Michigan Press, 2013.

Constable, Pamela. "Rapper Dies of Wounds from Shooting; Drive-by Assault in Las Vegas Ends Tupac Shakur's Short, Violent Life." *Washington Post*, September 14, 1996. LexisNexis Academic.

Cooper, Alexia D., Matthew R. Durose, and Howard N. Snyder. "Recidivism of Prisoners Released in 30 States in 2005: Patterns from 2005 to 2010." *Bureau of Justice Statistics*, April 22, 2014. http://www.bjs.gov/index.cfm?ty=pbdetail&iid=4987.

"Cops: McCain Worker Made Up Attack Story." *CBS News*, October 24, 2008. http://www.cbsnews.com/news/cops-mccain-worker-made-up-attack-story/.

Corrigan, Lisa M. "Writing Resistance and Heroism: Guerilla Strategies from Castro's Gulag." *Communication Quarterly* 59 (2011): 61–81.

Crenshaw, Kimberlé. "Mapping the Margins: Intersectionality, Identity Politics, and Violence against Women of Color." *Stanford Law Review* 43 (1991): 1241–99.

Cross, Brian. *It's Not about a Salary . . . Rap, Race, and Resistance in Los Angeles*. London: Verso, 1993.

Cummings, D. L. "Black Steel." *Source*, September 1995.

Cummins, Eric. *The Rise and Fall of California's Radical Prison Movement*. Stanford, CA: Stanford University Press, 1994.

Cuomo, Mario Matthew. "1984 Democratic National Convention Keynote Address." *American Rhetoric*," July 16, 1984. http://www.americanrhetoric.com/speeches/mariocuomo1984dnc.htm.

Darsey, James. *The Prophetic Tradition and Radical Rhetoric in America*. New York: New York University Press, 1997.

Davis, Angela Y. *Are Prisons Obsolete?* New York: Seven Stories Press, 2003.

———. *Blues Legacies and Black Feminism: Gertrude "Ma" Rainey, Bessie Smith, and Billie Holiday*. New York: Pantheon Books, 1998.

Davis, Kimberly Chabot. *Beyond the White Negro: Empathy and Anti-Racist Reading*. Urbana: University of Illinois Press, 2014.

Davis, Mike. *City of Quartz: Excavating the Future in Los Angeles*. London: Verso, 2006.

———. *Planet of Slums*. London: Verso, 2006.

Dawsey, Darrell. "No Time for Tears: A Eulogy for Tupac." *Essence*, December 1996. LexisNexis Academic.

dead prez. *RBG: Revolutionary but Gangsta*. CD. Sony Music Entertainment, 2004.

Dearmond, Michelle. "Rap Star Tupac Shakur Dies of Wounds." *Chicago Sun-Times*, September 14, 1996. http://www.highbeam.com/doc/1P2-4352107.html.

De Coster, Stacy, and Karen Heimer. "Crime at the Intersections: Race, Class, Gender, and Violent Offending." In *The Many Colors of Crime: Inequalities of Race, Ethnicity, and Crime in America*, edited by Lauren J. Krivo, Ruth D. Peterson, and John Hagan, 138–56. New York: New York University Press, 2006.

Deleuze, Gilles. "Lecture Transcripts on Spinoza's Concept of *Affect*." January 24, 1978. http://www.webdeleuze.com/php/texte.php?cle=14&groupe=Spinoza&langue=2.

Denning, Michael. *The Cultural Front: The Laboring of American Culture in the Twentieth Century*. London: Verso, 1998.

Denselow, Robin. *When the Music's Over: The Story of Political Pop*. London: Faber and Faber, 1989.

The Derelict Todd B. Review of Eazy-E's *It's On (Dr. Dre 187) Killa*. *Source*, December 1993.

DeRogatis, Jim. "Snoop's Album Debuts, Despite His Murder Rap." *Chicago Sun-Times*, November 25, 1993. LexisNexis Academic.

Do the Right Thing. Directed by Spike Lee. New York: 40 Acres and A Mule Filmworks, 1989.

Dolemite. Directed by D'Urville Martin. Los Angeles: Dimension Pictures, 1975.

Dubber, Markus Dirk. "Criminal Justice Process and War on Crime." In *The Blackwell Companion to Criminology*, edited by Colin Sumner, 49–67. Malden, MA: Blackwell Publishing, 2004.

Du Bois, W. E. B. *Black Reconstruction in America, 1860–1880*. New York: Free Press, 1998.

———. *The Philadelphia Negro*. Philadelphia: University of Pennsylvania Press, 1899.

———. "The Spawn of Slavery: The Convict-Lease System in the South." In *Race, Crime, and Justice: A Reader*, edited by Shaun L. Gabbidon and Helen Taylor Greene, 3–8. New York: Routledge, 2005.

Duggan, Lisa. *The Twilight of Equality?: Neoliberalism, Cultural Politics, and the Attack on Democracy*. Boston: Beacon Press, 2003.

"Dr. Dre—Let Me Ride." *Genius*, 2015. http://genius.com/6050/Dr-dre-let-me-ride.

Dr. Dre. *The Chronic*. CD. Death Row Records, 1992.

———. "Let Me Ride." Music video. Directed by Dr. Dre. Death Row Records, 1994.

———. "Murder Was the Case: The Movie." Death Row Records, 1995.

———. "Nuthin' But a 'G' Thang." Music video. Directed by Dr. Dre. Death Row Records, 1992.

Dyson, Michael Eric. *Holler If You Hear Me: Searching for Tupac Shakur*. New York: Basic Civitas Books, 2001.

———. *I May Not Get There with You: The True Martin Luther King, Jr.* New York: Touchstone, 2000.

Engels, Jeremy. *Enemyship: Democracy and Counter-Revolution in the Early Republic*. East Lansing: Michigan State University Press, 2010.

Fanon, Frantz. *The Wretched of the Earth*. Translated by Constance Farrington. New York: Grove Press, 1963.

"Farrakhan to Sponsor D.C. Events." *Billboard*, August 23, 1997. LexisNexis Academic.

Fenton, Justin. "Baltimore Police Say Gangs 'Teaming Up' to Take Out Officers." *Baltimore Sun*, April 27, 2015. http://www.baltimoresun.com/news/maryland/crime/blog/bs-md-ci-freddie-gray-gang-threat-20150427-story.html.

Fineman, Howard. "An Older, Grimmer Jesse." *Newsweek*, January 10, 1994. LexisNexis Academic.

Fisher, Walter R. "Reaffirmation and Subversion of the American Dream." *Quarterly Journal of Speech* 59 (1973): 131–39.

Fiske, John. *Media Matters: Race and Gender in U.S. Politics*. Minneapolis: University of Minnesota Press, 1996.

Fitzpatrick, Rob. "How Snoop's *Doggystyle* Changed Hip-Hop." *Guardian*, May 27, 2011. http://www.theguardian.com/culture/2011/may/28/snoops-doggystyle-hip-hop.

Ford, Dana. "Renegade Ex-Cop Dorner Died from Single Gunshot to Head." *CNN*, February 16, 2013. http://www.cnn.com/2013/02/15/us/california-dorner-death/index.html?hpt=hp_t1.

Ford, Dana, and Ed Payne. "Grand Jury Decides against Indictments in Sandra Bland's Death." *CNN*, December 23, 2015. http://www.cnn.com/2015/12/21/us/sandra-bland-no-indictments/.

Forman, Murray. *The 'Hood Comes First: Race, Space, and Place in Rap and Hip-Hop*. Middletown, CT: Wesleyan University Press, 2002.

———. "Tupac Shakur: (O)Stensibly (G)One." Conference paper presented at *All Eyez on Me: Tupac Shakur and the Search for the Modern Folk Hero*. Harvard University, Cambridge, MA, 2003.

Foucault, Michel. *Discipline and Punish: The Birth of the Prison*. Translated by Alan Sheridan. New York: Vintage Books, 1977.

Francesconi, Robert. "Free Jazz and Black Nationalism: A Rhetoric of Musical Style." *Critical Studies in Mass Communication* 3 (1986): 36–49.

Freeman, John. "'Gangsta Rap' Comes under Fire; Many Radio Stations Banning It, but Sales Still Soar." *San Diego Union-Tribune*, December 17, 1993. LexisNexis Academic.

Friedman, Milton. *Capitalism and Freedom*. 40th anniversary ed. Chicago: University of Chicago Press, 2002.

Fritsch, Jane. "The Diallo Verdict." *New York Times*, February 26, 2000. http://www.nytimes.com/2000/02/26/nyregion/diallo-verdict-overview-4-officers-diallo-shooting-are-acquitted-all-charges.html?pagewanted=all&src=pm.

Gaonkar, Dilip Parameshwar. "Toward New Imaginaries: An Introduction." *Public Culture* 14 (2002): 1–19.

Gates, Henry Louis, Jr. *The Signifying Monkey: A Theory of African-American Literary Criticism*. New York: Oxford University Press, 1988.

Gehrke, Pat J. *The Ethics and Politics of Speech: Communication and Rhetoric in the Twentieth Century*. Carbondale: Southern Illinois University Press, 2009.

Gibbs, Geoffrey Taylor. "Can African-Americans Now Truly Believe in Judicial Fairness?" *Los Angeles Times*, November 24, 1991. http://articles.latimes.com/1991-11-24/opinion/op-115_1_black-life.

Gilroy, Paul. *The Black Atlantic: Modernity and Double Consciousness*. Cambridge, MA: Harvard University Press, 1993.

———. "It Ain't Where You're From, It's Where You're At . . . The Dialectics of Diasporic Identification." *Third Text* 5 (1991): 3–16.

Giovanni, Nikki. *Love Poems*. New York: William Morrow, 1997.

Goff, Phillip Atiba, Jennifer L. Eberhardt, Melissa J. Williams, and Matthew Christian Jackson. "Not Yet Human: Implicit Knowledge, Historical Dehumanization, and Contemporary Consequences." *Journal of Personality and Social Psychology* 94 (2008): 292–306.

"Goldwater's 1964 Acceptance Speech." *WashingtonPost.com*, May 1998. http://www.washingtonpost.com/wp-srv/politics/daily/may98/goldwaterspeech.htm.

Goltz, Dustin Bradley. "Frustrating the 'I': Critical Dialogic Reflexivity with Personal Voice." *Text and Performance Quarterly* 31 (2011): 386–405.

Goodale, Greg. *Sonic Persuasion: Reading Sound in the Recorded Age*. Urbana: University of Illinois Press, 2011.

———. "The Sonorous Envelope and Political Deliberation." *Quarterly Journal of Speech* 99 (2013): 218–24.

Goodman, Amy, and Juan Gonzalez. "Hip Hop Artist M-1 of Dead Prez." *Democracy Now!*, October 26, 2006. http://www.democracynow.org/2006/10/26/hip_hop_artist_m_1_of.

Gore, Tipper. "Hate, Rape, and Rap." *Washington Post*, January 8, 1990. LexisNexis Academic.

———. "Protect Children from the Culture of Violence." *St. Petersburg Times* (Florida), March 15, 1988. LexisNexis Academic.

"Got Five on It." *Source*, March 2002.

Gottfried, Paul. *The Conservative Movement*. Independence, KY: Twayne, 1992.

Gottschalk, Marie. *The Prison and the Gallows: The Politics of Mass Incarceration in America*. Cambridge: Cambridge University Press, 2006.

Gould, Deborah. "On Affect and Protest." In *Political Emotions: New Agendas in Communication*, edited by Ann Cvetkovich, Ann Reynolds, and Janet Staiger, 18–24. New York: Routledge, 2010.

Grandmaster Flash and The Furious Five. *The Message*. CD. Sugar Hill Records, 1982.

The Grateful Dead. *Shakedown Street*. LP. Grateful Dead Productions, 1978.

Grossberg, Lawrence. *Caught in the Crossfire: Kids, Politics, and America's Future*. Boulder, CO: Paradigm, 2005.

———. *Cultural Studies in the Future Tense*. Durham, NC: Duke University Press, 2010.

———. "Does Cultural Studies Have Futures? Should It? (Or What's the Matter with New York?): Cultural Studies, Contexts, and Conjunctures." *Cultural Studies* 20 (2006): 1–32.

———. "Rock, Territoriality, and Power." In his *Dancing in Spite of Myself: Essays on Popular Culture*, 89–101. Durham, NC: Duke University Press, 1997.

Guerrero, Ed. *Framing Blackness: The African American Image in Film*. Philadelphia: Temple University Press, 1993.

Guillaumin, Colette. *Racism, Sexism, Power and Ideology*. London: Routledge, 1995.

Gunn, Joshua. "Gothic Music and the Inevitability of Genre." *Popular Music and Society* 23 (1999): 31–50.

———. "Maranatha." *Quarterly Journal of Speech* 98 (2012): 359–85.

Gunn, Joshua, Greg Goodale, Mirko M. Hall, and Rosa A. Eberly. "Auscultating Again: Rhetoric and Sound Studies." *Rhetoric Society Quarterly* 43 (2013): 475–89.

Gunn, Joshua, and Mirko M. Hall, "Stick It in Your Ear: The Psychodynamics of iPod Enjoyment." *Communication and Critical/Cultural Studies* 5 (2008): 135–57.

Gunn, Joshua, and John Louis Lucaites. "The Contest of Faculties: On Discerning the Politics of Social Engagement in the Academy," *Quarterly Journal of Speech* 96 (2010): 404–12.

Gussow, Adam. *Seems Like Murder Here: Southern Violence and the Blues Tradition*. Chicago: University of Chicago Press, 2002.

Guthrie, Woody. *The Asch Recordings*. Vol. 2. CD. Smithsonian Folkways, 1999.

———. *The Best of Woody Guthrie*. Vol. 1. CD. Prestige Elite, 2007.

Gutman, Matt, Seni Tienabesco, and Ben Forer. "George Zimmerman Tells Trayvon Martin's Parents 'I Am Sorry.'" *ABC News*, April 20, 2012. http://abcnews.go.com/US/george-zimmerman-case-exclusive-photo-shows-bloodied-back/story?id=16177849#.T5FqDGLLx5j.

Haas, Jeffrey. *The Assassination of Fred Hampton: How the FBI and the Chicago Police Murdered a Black Panther*. Chicago: Lawrence Hill Books, 2010.

Hall, Rachel. *Wanted: The Outlaw in American Visual Culture*. Charlottesville: University of Virginia Press, 2009.

Hall, Stuart, Chas Critcher, Tony Jefferson, John Clarke, and Brian Roberts. *Policing the Crisis: Mugging, the State, and Law and Order*. Hampshire, UK: Palgrave Macmillan, 1978.

hampton, dream. "G-Down." *Source*, September 1993.

"Harlem Mosque Sets Rap Peace Meeting." *New York Times*, September 18, 1996. http://www.nytimes.com/1996/09/18/nyregion/harlem-mosque-sets-rap-peace-meeting.html.

Harold, Christine, and Kevin Michael DeLuca. "Behold the Corpse: Violent Images and the Case of Emmett Till." *Rhetoric and Public Affairs* 8 (2005): 263–86.

Harrington, Richard. "The FBI as Music Critic; Letter on Rap Record Seen as Intimidation." *Washington Post*, October 4, 1989. LexisNexis Academic.

———. "Guns n' Rappers: 3 Arrested in Shootings." *Washington Post*, November 3, 1993. LexisNexis Academic.

Harris, Carter. "Eazy Street." *Source*, July 1994.

Harris, Paul. *Black Rage Confronts the Law*. New York: New York University Press, 1997.

Hartman, Andrew. *A War for the Soul of America: A History of the Culture Wars*. Chicago: University of Chicago Press, 2015.

Hartman, Saidiya V. *Scenes of Subjection: Terror, Slavery, and Self-Making in Nineteenth-Century America*. New York: Oxford University Press: 1997.

Hartnett, Stephen John. "The Annihilating Public Policies of the Prison-Industrial Complex; or, Crime, Violence, and Punishment in an Age of Neoliberalism." *Rhetoric and Public Affairs* 11 (2008): 491–515.

———. "Communication, Social Justice, and Joyful Commitment." *Western Journal of Communication* 74 (2010): 68–93.

———. *Executing Democracy*. Vol. 1, *Capital Punishment and the Making of America, 1683–1807*. East Lansing: Michigan State University Press, 2010.

———. *Executing Democracy*. Vol. 2, *Capital Punishment and the Making of America, 1835–1843*. East Lansing: Michigan State University Press, 2012.

———. "Lincoln and Douglas Meet the Abolitionist David Walker as Prisoners Debate Slavery: Empowering Education, Applied Communication, and Social Justice." *Journal of Applied Communication Research* 26 (1998): 232–53.

———. "Prisons, Profit, Crime, and Social Control: A Hermeneutic of the Production of Violence." In *Race, Class, and Community Identity*, edited by Andrew Light and Meck Nagel, 199–221. New York: Humanities Press, 2000.

Hartnett, Stephen John, ed. *Challenging the Prison-Industrial Complex: Activism, Arts, and Educational Alternatives*. Urbana: University of Illinois Press, 2011.

Hartnett, Stephen John, and Daniel Larson. "'Tonight Another Man Will Die': Crime, Violence, and the Master Tropes of Contemporary Arguments about the Death Penalty." *Communication and Critical/Cultural Studies* 3 (2006): 263–87.

Harnett, Stephen John, Eleanor Novek, and Jennifer K. Wood, eds. *Working for Justice: A Handbook of Prison Education and Advocacy*. Urbana: University of Illinois Press, 2013.

Hartnett, Stephen John, Jennifer K. Wood, and Bryan J. McCann. "Turning Silence into Speech and Action: Prison Activism and the Pedagogy of Empowered Citizenship." *Communication and Critical/Cultural Studies* 8 (2011): 331–52.

Harvey, David. *A Brief History of Neoliberalism*. Oxford: Oxford University Press, 2005.

Hasian, Marouf, Jr., and Lisa A. Flores. "Mass Mediated Representations of the Susan Smith Trial." *Howard Journal of Communication* 11 (2000): 163–78

Hauser, Gerard A. *Prisoners of Conscience: Moral Vernaculars of Political Agency*. Columbia: University of South Carolina Press, 2012.

Hawhee, Debra. *Moving Bodies: Kenneth Burke at the Edges of Language*. Columbia: University of South Carolina Press, 2009.

Hayek, F. A. *The Road to Serfdom*. Abingdon, UK: Routledge, 2001.

Hebdige, Dick. *Subculture: The Meaning of Style*. London: Routledge, 1979.

Hill, Lauryn. *The Miseducation of Lauryn Hill*. CD. Ruffhouse Records, 1998.

Hill Collins, Patricia. *Black Sexual Politics: African Americans, Gender, and the New Racism*. New York: Routledge, 2005.

———. *From Black Power to Hip Hop: Racism, Nationalism, and Feminism*. Philadelphia: Temple University Press, 2006.

Hinds, Selwyn Seyfu. "Don of the Westside." *Source*, May 1996.

Hobsbawm, Eric. *Bandits*. New York: New Press, 2000.

hooks, bell. *Killing Rage: Ending Racism*. New York: Henry Holt, 1995.

———. *We Real Cool: Black Men and Masculinity*. New York: Routledge, 2004.

Hughes, Langston. *The Best of Simple*. New York: Hill and Wang, 1961.

Hunt, Darnell. "Introduction: Dreaming of Black Los Angeles." In *Black Los Angeles: American Dreams and Racial Realities*, edited by Darnell Hunt and Ana-Christina Ramón, 1–17. New York: New York University Press, 2010.

Ice Cube. *Death Certificate*. CD. Priority Records, 1991.

———. *The Predator*. CD. Priority Records, 1992.

Iverem, Esther. "A Death as Real as It Gets; Tupac Shakur's Gangsta Image Was the Rapper's Fatal Flaw." *Washington Post*, September 14, 1996. LexisNexis Academic.

Jackson, George. *Soledad Brother: The Prison Letters of George Jackson*. Chicago: Lawrence Hill Books, 1994.

Jackson, Ronald L., III. *Scripting the Black Masculine Body: Identity, Discourse, and Racial Politics in Popular Media*. Albany: State University of New York Press, 2006.

James, Joy. *Imprisoned Intellectuals: America's Political Prisoners Write on Life, Liberation, and Rebellion*. Lanham, MD: Rowman and Littlefield, 2003.

Jameson, Fredric. *Archaeologies of the Future: The Desire Called Utopia and Other Science Fictions*. London: Verso, 2005.

——. "Reification and Utopia in Mass Culture." In *Signatures of the Visible*, 9–34. New York: Routledge, 1992.

Jamieson, Kathleen Hall. *Dirty Politics: Deception, Distraction, and Democracy*. New York: Oxford University Press, 1993.

Jav'lin. "Walk with Me." *YouTube*, February 8, 2007. https://www.youtube.com/watch?v=UaJdrxT8hiY.

Johnson, Charles C. "Lessons of Sa-i-gu." *City Journal*, April 27, 2012. http://www.city-journal.org/2012/cjc0427cj.html.

Johnson, Cory. "Sweatin' Bullets." In Light, *Tupac Shakur*, 41.

Johnson, E. Patrick. *Appropriating Blackness: Performance and the Politics of Authenticity*. Durham, NC: Duke University Press, 2003.

Johnson, Lyndon B. "Special Message to the Congress on Crime and Law Enforcement, March 9, 1966." *American Presidency Project*. http://www.presidency.ucsb.edu/ws/?pid=27478.

Jolson-Colburn, Jeffrey. "Soul Train Founder Denies Rapper Was Armed at Awards Show." *BPI Entertainment News Wire*, April 2, 1996. LexisNexis Academic.

Jones, D. Marvin. *Race, Sex, and Suspicion: The Myth of the Black Male*. Westport, CT: Praeger, 2005.

Jordan-Zacherys, Julia. "The Female Bogeyman: Political Implications of Criminalizing Black Women." In Seinberg, Marable, and Middlemass, *Racializing Justice, Disenfranchising Lives*, 101–22.

Jorgenson, Carl. "Black in the 60s: A Centennial Reprise." *Social Text* (Spring–Summer 1984): 313–17.

Kelley, Robin D. G. *Freedom Dreams: The Black Radical Imagination*. Boston: Beacon Press, 2002.

——. *Race Rebels: Culture, Politics, and the Black Working Class*. New York: Free Press, 1994.

Kelly, Casey. "Neocolonialism and the Global Prison in National Geographic's Locked Up Abroad." *Critical Studies in Media Communication* 29 (2012): 331–47.

Keyes, Cheryl L. *Rap Music and Street Consciousness*. Urbana: University of Illinois Press, 2002.

King, Martin Luther, Jr. "I Have a Dream." In *Speeches That Changed the World*, 150–53. London: Smith-Davies, 2005.

Kinnon, Joy Bennett. "Does Rap Have a Future?" *Ebony*, June 1997. LexisNexis Academic.

Kirschner, Tony. "Studying Rock: Toward a Materialist Ethnography." In *Mapping the Beat: Popular Music and Contemporary Theory*, edited by Thomas Swiss, John M. Sloop, and Andrew Herman, 247–68. Malden, MA: Blackwell, 1998.

Klein, Naomi. *The Shock Doctrine: The Rise of Disaster Capitalism*. New York: Picador, 2007.

Kreps, Daniel. "Watch the Red-Band Trailer for N.W.A.'s Biopic 'Straight Outta Compton.'" *Rolling Stone*, February 9, 2015. http://www.rollingstone.com/movies/videos/watch-the-red-band-trailer-for-n-w-as-biopic-straight-outta-compton-20150209.

Krugman, Paul. *The Conscience of a Liberal*. New York: W. W. Norton, 2007.

LaGrone, Kheven Lee. "From Minstrelsy to Gangsta Rap: The 'Nigger' as Commodity for Popular American Entertainment." *Journal of African American Men* 5 (2000): 117–31.

Landler, Mark, and Michael D. Shear. "President Offers a Personal Take on Race in U.S." *New York Times*, July 19, 2013. http://www.nytimes.com/2013/07/20/us/in-wake-of -zimmerman-verdict-obama-makes-extensive-statement-on-race-in-america.html?hp& _r=1.

Lang, Brent. "'Straight Outta Compton' Final Box Office Soars to $60.2 Million." *Variety*, August 17, 2015. http://variety.com/2015/film/news/straight-outta-compton -box-office-opening-final-1201571387/.

Larson, Daniel Mark. "Killing Democracy; or, How the Drug War Drives the Prison-Industrial Complex." In *Challenging the Prison Industrial Complex: Activism, Arts, and Educational Alternatives*, edited by Stephen John Hartnett, 73–104. Urbana: University of Illinois Press, 2011.

"The Last Tweets of Obama's 'Son' Trayvon Martin," *US Action News*, March 27, 2012, http://usactionnews.com/2012/03/the-last-tweets-of-obamas-no_limit_nigga-trayvon -martin/

Laughland, Oliver, Kayla Epstein, and Jessica Glenza. "Eric Garner Protests Continue in Cities across America through Second Night." *Guardian*, December 5, 2014. http:// www.theguardian.com/us-news/2014/dec/05/eric-garner-case-new-york-protests -continue-through-second-night.

Lee, Felicia R. "At Home With: Nikki Giovanni; Defying Evil, and Mortality." *New York Times*, August 1, 1996. LexisNexis Academic.

Leland, John. "Criminal Records; Gangsta Rap and the Culture of Violence." *Newsweek*, November 29, 1993. LexisNexis Academic.

Lena, Jennifer C. "Voyeurism and Resistance in Rap Music Videos." *Communication and Critical/Cultural Studies* 5 (2008): 264–79.

Lewis, Miles Marshall. "Bicoastalism." *Source*, August 1996.

Lewis, William F. "Telling America's Story: Narrative Form and the Reagan Presidency." *Quarterly Journal of Speech* 73 (1987): 280–302.

Light, Alan, ed. *Tupac Shakur*. New York: Three Rivers Press, 1998.

Linebaugh, Peter. *The London Hanged: Crime and Civil Society in the Eighteenth Century*. Cambridge: Cambridge University Press, 1992.

Linebaugh, Peter, and Marcus Rediker. *The Many-Headed Hydra: Sailors, Slaves, Commoners, and the Hidden History of the Revolutionary Atlantic*. Boston: Beacon Press, 2000.

Lipsitz, George. *Dangerous Crossroads: Popular Music, Postmodernism, and the Poetics of Place*. London: Verso, 1994.

———. "Turning Hegemony on Its Head: The Insurgent Knowledge of Américo Paredes." *Journal of American Folklore* 125 (2012): 111–25.

Logue, Josh. "Latina/o/x." *Inside Higher Ed*, December 8, 2015. https://www.insidehighered .com/news/2015/12/08/students-adopt-gender-nonspecific-term-latinx-be-more -inclusive.

Lorde, Audre. *Sister Outsider*. Berkeley, CA: Crossing Press, 1984.

Lundberg, Christian. "Enjoying God's Death: *The Passion of the Christ* and the Practices of an Evangelical Public." *Quarterly Journal of Speech* 95 (2009): 387–411.

Lynskey, Dorian. *33 Revolutions per Minute: A History of Protest Songs, from Billie Holiday to Green Day*. New York: HarperCollins, 2011.

MacAskill, Ewan, Julian Borger, and Glenn Greenwald. "The National Security Agency: Surveillance Giant with Eyes on America." *Guardian*, June 6, 2013. http://www.guardian.co.uk/world/2013/jun/06/national-security-agency-surveillance.

Macek, Steve. *Urban Nightmares: The Media, the Right, and the Moral Panic over the City.* Minneapolis: University of Minnesota Press, 2006.

Marable, Manning. *Malcolm X: A Life of Reinvention.* New York: Viking, 2011.

———. "Racializing Justice, Disenfranchising Lives: Toward an Antiracist Criminal Justice." In Seinberg, Marable, and Middlemass, *Racializing Justice, Disenfranchising Lives*, 1–14.

Marcus, Greil. *The Doors: A Lifetime of Listening to Five Mean Years.* New York: PublicAffairs, 2011.

———. *Mystery Train: Images of America in Rock 'n' Roll Music.* 5th ed. New York: Plume, 2008.

Marriott, Rob. "All That Glitters," In Light, *Tupac Shakur*, 130–35.

———. "Last Testament." In Light, *Tupac Shakur*, 124–26.

———. "Ready to Die." In Light, *Tupac Shakur*, 116–23.

Marsh, David, and Phyllis Pollack. "Wanted for Attitude." *Village Voice*, October 10, 1989, 33–37.

Martinez, Michael, and Paul Vercammen. "Rogue Ex-Cop Is Heavily Armed, Trained and Out There Somewhere." *CNN.com*, February 9, 2013. http://www.cnn.com/2013/02/08/us/lapd-attacks/index.html?hpt=hp_t1.

Martosko, David. "Second Trayvon Martin Twitter Feed Identified." *Daily Caller*, March 29, 2012. http://dailycaller.com/2012/03/29/second-trayvon-martin-twitter-feed-identified/.

Massumi, Brian. *Parables for the Virtual: Movement, Affect, Sensation.* Durham, NC: Duke University Press, 2002.

Matula, Theodore. "Contextualizing Musical Rhetoric: A Critical Reading of the Pixies' 'Rock Music.'" *Communication Studies* 51 (2000): 218–37.

Mauer, Marc. *Race to Incarcerate.* New York: New Press, 2006.

Mauer, Marc, and Medea Chesney-Lind, eds. *Invisible Punishment: The Collateral Consequences of Mass Imprisonment.* New York: New Press, 2002.

Mayo, Kierna. "A Souljah Story." *Source*, September 1992.

McCann, Bryan J. "Genocide as Representative Anecdote: Crack Cocaine, the CIA, and the Nation of Islam in Gary Webb's 'Dark Alliance.'" *Western Journal of Communication* 74 (2010): 396–416.

———. "On Whose Ground? Racialized Violence and the Prerogative of 'Self-Defense' in the Trayvon Martin Case." *Western Journal of Communication* 78 (2014): 480–99.

———. "Redemption in the Neoliberal and Radical Imaginations: The Saga of Stanley 'Tookie' Williams." *Communication, Culture, and Critique* 7 (2014): 92–111.

———. "Therapeutic and Material <Victim>hood: Ideology and the Struggle for Meaning in the Illinois Death Penalty Controversy." *Communication and Critical/Cultural Studies* 4 (2007): 382–401.

McCartin, Joseph A. "The Strike That Busted Unions." *New York Times*, August 2, 2011. http://www.nytimes.com/2011/08/03/opinion/reagan-vs-patco-the-strike-that-busted-unions.html.

McCulloch, Derek, and Shepherd Hendrix. *Stagger Lee.* Berkeley, CA: Image Comics, 2006.

McDermott, Terry. "Parental Advisory: Explicit Lyrics." In *Da Capo Best Music Writing 2003: The Year's Finest Writing on Rock, Pop, Jazz, Country, and More*, vol. 4, edited by Matt Groening and Paul Bresnick, 9–34. Cambridge, MA: Da Capo Press.

McHale, John P. "Unreasonable Doubt: Using Video Documentary to Promote Justice." In *Communication Activism*. Vol. 2, *Media and Performance Activism*, edited by Lawrence R. Frey and Kevin M. Carragee, 195–222. New York: Hampton Press, 2007.

McKittrick, Katherine, and Clyde Woods. "No One Knows the Mysteries at the Bottom of the Ocean." In *Black Geographies and the Politics of Place*, edited by Katherine McKittrick and Clyde Woods, 1–13. Toronto: Between the Lines; Cambridge, MA: South End Press, 2007.

McShane, Larry. "Rap Violence Moves out of Recording Studio, into Street." *Charleston Gazette*, January 6, 1994. LexisNexis Academic.

Medina, Jennifer. "California Sheds Prisoners but Grapples with Courts." *New York Times*, January 21, 2013. http://www.nytimes.com/2013/01/22/us/22prisons.html?_r=0.

Meiners, Erica R. *Right to Be Hostile: Schools, Prisons, and the Making of Public Enemies*. New York: Routledge, 2007.

Mercer, Kobena. "Reading Racial Fetishism." In *Representation: Cultural Representations and Signifying Practices*, edited by Stuart Hall, 285–90. London: Sage Publications, 1997.

Meyer, Richard E. "The Outlaw: A Distinctive American Folktype." *Journal of the Folklore Institute* 17 (1980): 94–124.

Miller, Carolyn R. "Genre as Social Action." *Quarterly Journal of Speech* 70 (1984): 151–67.

Miller, Monica L. *Slaves to Fashion: Black Dandyism and the Styling of Black Diasporic Identity*. Durham, NC: Duke University Press, 2009.

Mills, David. "Sister Souljah's Call to Arms." *Washington Post*, May 13, 1992. http://pqasb.pqarchiver.com/washingtonpost/access/74018923.html?dids=23:23&FMT=ABS.

Mitchell, Marsha. "Strictly Straight Up." *Rap Pages*, June 1993.

Moppins, Robin. "The Legacy of Tupac Shakur." *Plain Dealer*, October 7, 1996. LexisNexis Academic, accessed December 31, 2013.

Morris, Charles E., III. "Context's Critic, Invisible Traditions, and Queering Rhetorical History." *Quarterly Journal of Speech* 101 (2015): 225–43

Morrison, Toni. *Beloved*. New York: Plume, 1988.

Moten, Fred. *In the Break: The Aesthetics of the Black Radical Tradition*. Minneapolis: University of Minnesota Press, 2003.

Muhammad, Khalil Gibran. *The Condemnation of Blackness: Race, Crime, and the Making of Modern Urban America*. Cambridge, MA: Harvard University Press, 2010.

Mydans, Seth. "Police Beating Trial Opens with Replay of Videotape." *New York Times*, March 6, 1992. http://www.nytimes.com/1992/03/06/us/police-beating-trial-opens-with-replay-of-videotape.html.

Nisha. "Exclusive: Director F. Gary Gray Talks N.W.A. Biopic 'Straight Outta Compton.'" *Source*, August 8, 2015. http://thesource.com/2015/08/08/exclusive-f-gary-gray-talks-n-w-a-biopic-straight-outta-compton/.

Neal, Mark Anthony. *Soul Babies: Black Popular Culture and the Post-Soul Aesthetic*. New York: Routledge, 2002.

———. *What the Music Said: Black Popular Music and Black Public Culture*. New York: Routledge, 1999.

"News Conference," August 12, 1986. *Ronald Reagan Presidential Foundation and Library*. 2010. http://www.reaganfoundation.org/reagan-quotes-detail.aspx?tx=2079.

Neufeld, Matt. "Lyrics Get Rap Group Cut from Cap Centre." *Washington Times*, August 22, 1989. LexisNexis Academic.

Newport, Frank. "Sixty-Nine Percent of Americans Support Death Penalty: Majority Say Death Penalty Is Applied Fairly." *Gallup News Service*, October 12, 2007. http://www.gallup.com/poll/101863/Sixtynine-Percent-Americans-Support-Death-Penalty.aspx.

Newton, Huey P. "Patrolling." In *The Huey P. Newton Reader*, edited by David Hilliard and Donald Weise, 53–66. New York: Seven Stories Press, 2002.

Nick Cave and the Bad Seeds. *Murder Ballads*. CD. Mute Records, 1996.

Nielson, Erik, and Michael Render (a.k.a. Killer Mike). "Rap's Poetic (In)justice: Column." *USA Today*, December 1, 2014. http://www.usatoday.com/story/opinion/2014/11/28/poetic-injustice-rap-supreme-court-lyrics-violence-trial-column/19537391/.

Nixon, Richard M. "9—Annual Message to the Congress on the State of the Union." January 22, 1970. *American Presidency Project*. http://www.presidency.ucsb.edu/ws/?pid=2921.

———. "Nixon's Acceptance of the Republican Party Nomination for President." *Republican National Convention*. Miami Beach, August 8, 1968.

"Nixon's Plan for Health Reform, in His Own Words." *Kaiser Health News*, September 3, 2009. http://www.kaiserhealthnews.org/stories/2009/september/03/nixon-proposal.aspx.

Novak, Daniel A. *The Wheel of Servitude: Black Forced Labor after Slavery*. Lexington: University Press of Kentucky, 1978.

"NWA—Straight Outta Compton." *Genius*, 2015. http://genius.com/Nwa-straight-outta-compton-lyrics/.

NWA. *Straight Outta Compton*. CD. Priority Records, 1988.

———. "Straight Outta Compton." Music video. Directed by Rupert Wainwright. Ruthless Records, 1989.

NWA and the Posse. *N.W.A. and the Posse*. CD. Priority Records, 1987.

Office Space. Motion Picture. Directed by Mike Judge. Los Angeles: Twentieth-Century Fox Film Corporation, 1999.

Ogbar, Jeffrey O. G. *Black Power: Radical Politics and African American Identity*. Baltimore: Johns Hopkins University Press, 2004.

———. *Hip-Hop Revolution: The Culture and Politics of Rap*. Lawrence: University Press of Kansas, 2007.

"Old Stereotypes of Bad Rap." *Atlanta Journal-Constitution*, December 7, 1993. LexisNexis Academic.

Owen, A. Susan, and Peter Ehrenhaus. "Looking at Lynching: Spectacle, Resistance and Contemporary Transformations." *Quarterly Journal of Speech* 97 (2011): 100–113.

Padilla, Felix M. *The Street Gang as an American Enterprise*. New Brunswick, NJ: Rutgers University Press, 1992.

Pager, Devah. *Marked: Race, Crime, and Finding Work in an Era of Mass Incarceration*. Chicago: University of Chicago Press, 2007.

Pareles, Jon. "Critic's Notebook; the Disappearance of Ice-T's 'Cop Killer.'" *New York Times*, July 30, 1992. LexisNexis Academic.

———. "Tupac Shakur, 25, Rap Performer Who Personified Violence, Dies." *New York Times*, September 14, 1996. http://www.nytimes.com/1996/09/14/arts/tupac-shakur-25-rap-performer-who-personified-violence-dies.html?pagewanted=all&src=pm.

Parenti, Christian. *Lockdown America: Police and Prisons in the Age of Crisis*. London: Verso, 1999.

PCARE. "Fighting the Prison-Industrial Complex: A Call to Communication and Cultural Studies Scholars to Change the World." *Communication and Critical/Cultural Studies* 4 (2007): 402–20.

Pearson, Kyra. "The Trouble with Aileen Wuornos, Feminism's 'First Serial Killer.'" *Communication and Critical/Cultural Studies* 4 (2007): 256–75.

Perkinson, Robert. *Texas Tough: The Rise of America's Prison Empire*. New York: Metropolitan Books, 2010.

Perlstein, Rick. *Nixonland: The Rise of a President and the Fracturing of America*. New York: Scribner, 2008.

Perry, Imani. *Prophets of the Hood: Politics and Poetics in Hip Hop*. Durham, NC: Duke University Press, 2004.

Pete, Pistol. "Eazy Way Out." *Source*, June 1993.

Phillips, Chuck. "Snoop Doggy Dogg Leads the Pack." *Los Angeles Times*, December 2, 1993. http://articles.latimes.com/1993–12-02/entertainment/ca-63303_1_debut-album.

Phillips, Scott. "Racial Disparities in the Capital of Capital Punishment." *Houston Law Review* 45 (2008). LexisNexis Academic Universe.

Picart, Caroline Joan S. "Rhetorically Reconfiguring Victimhood and Agency: The Violence against Women Act's Civil Rights Clause." *Rhetoric and Public Affairs* 6 (2003): 97–125.

Pickett, Wilson. *Pick It Wilson*. CD. Rhino Entertainment, 2007.

Platt, Tony. "Reconstructing Race and Crime: The Racial Tradition Revisited." In Seinberg, Marable, and Middlemass, *Racializing Justice, Disenfranchising Lives*, 35–42.

"Police Arrest Hundreds in L.A. Gangland Areas." *Washington Post*, August 21, 1989. LexisNexis Academic.

Powell, Kevin. "Live from Death Row." In Light, *Tupac Shakur*, 71–77.

———. "Ready to Live." In Light, *Tupac Shakur*, 45–51.

———. "This Thug's Life." In Light, *Tupac Shakur*, 21–31.

Price, Lloyd. *Lloyd Price Greatest Hits: The Original ABC-Paramount Recordings*. CD. UMG Recordings, 1994.

Price, Richard, ed. *Maroon Societies: Rebel Slave Communities in the Americas*. Baltimore: Johns Hopkins University Press, 1979.

Provine, Doris Marie. "Creating Racial Disadvantage: The Case of Crack Cocaine." In *The Many Colors of Crime: Inequalities of Race, Ethnicity, and Crime in America*, edited by Ruth D. Peterson, Lauren J. Krivo, and John Hagan, 277–94. New York: New York University Press, 2006.

Public Enemy. "Fight the Power." *Music from Do the Right Thing*. CD. Motown, 1989.

Puente, Mark. "After Freddie Gray Death, U.S. Starts Civil Rights Probe of Baltimore Police." *Baltimore Sun*, May 8, 2015. http://www.baltimoresun.com/news/maryland/baltimore-city/bs-md-justice-announce-20150508-story.html#page=1.

Quinn, Eithne. *Nuthin' But a "G" Thang: The Culture and Commerce of Gangsta Rap*. New York: Columbia University Press, 2005.

Quinn, Michael. "'Never Shoulda Been Let out the Penitentiary': Gangsta Rap and the Struggle over Racial Identity." *Cultural Critique* 34 (1996): 65–89.

"Race, Violence . . . Justice?" *National Public Radio*, August 30, 2011. http://www.npr.org/2011/08/30/140058680/race-violence-justice-looking-back-at-jena-6.

Raines, Howell. "Reagan Wins by a Landslide, Sweeping at Least 48 States; G.O.P. Gains Strength in House." *New York Times,* November 7, 1984. http://www.nytimes.com/1984/11/07/politics/07REAG.html?pagewanted=1.

Rand, Erin J. *Reclaiming Queer: Activist and Academic Rhetorics of Resistance.* Tuscaloosa: University of Alabama Pres, 2014.

Rankine, Claudia. *Citizen: An American Lyric.* Minneapolis: Graywolf Press, 2014.

Ransom, Franki V. "Black Women Launch Attack on 'Gangsta Rap'; Petition Drive Targets Record Firms." *Times-Picayune* (New Orleans, LA), December 23, 1993. LexisNexis Academic.

"Rap Star Eazy-E Battles AIDS; Listed in Critical Condition in LA Hospital." *Jet,* April 3, 1995. LexisNexis Academic.

"Rapper Ice-T Defends Song against Spreading Boycott." *New York Times,* June 19, 1992. LexisNexis Academic.

Rather, Dan. "New Rap Song Makes the Police Uneasy Nationwide." *CBS Evening News,* June 11, 1992. LexisNexis Academic.

Reagan, Ronald. "Address before a Joint Session of Congress on the State of the Union." February 6, 1985.

———. *An American Life: The Autobiography.* New York: Simon and Schuster, 1990.

Reddy, Chandan. *Freedom with Violence: Race, Sexuality, and the US State.* Durham, NC: Duke University Press, 2011.

Reed, Cheryl L. "Playing Rapper, Boy Says; Fatal Shot Fired Doing Imitation." *Dayton Daily News,* February 16, 1994. LexisNexis Academic.

Reed, Ishmael. *Mumbo Jumbo: A Novel.* New York: Open Road, 2013.

Reeves, Jimmie L., and Richard Campbell. *Cracked Coverage: Television News, the Anti-Cocaine Crusade, and the Reagan Legacy.* Durham, NC: Duke University Press, 1994.

Reinhold, Robert. "In the Middle of L.A.'s Gang Wars." *New York Times,* May 22, 1988. http://www.nytimes.com/1988/05/22/magazine/in-the-middle-of-la-s-gang-wars.html?pagewanted=all&src=pm.

Report on the National Advisory Commission on Civil Disorders. New York: Bantam Books, 1968.

Respers, Lisa. "Controversial Hard-Core Rappers Who Act Out Their Anti-Social Messages." *Buffalo News,* December 26, 1993. LexisNexis Academic.

Rice, Jenny Edbauer. "The New 'New': Making a Case for Critical Affect Studies." *Quarterly Journal of Speech* 94 (2008): 200–212.

Rickert, Thomas J. *Ambient Rhetoric: The Attunements of Rhetorical Being.* Pittsburgh: University of Pittsburgh Press, 2013.

Rivera, Geraldo. "Geraldo Rivera: Trayvon Martin Would Be Alive but for His Hoodie." *Fox News Latino,* March 23, 2012. http://latino.foxnews.com/latino/politics/2012/03/23/trayvon-martins-hoodie-and-george-zimmerman-share-blame/.

Ro, Ronin. "Moving Target." *Source,* November 1992.

———. "Pulp Fiction." *Source,* March 1995.

Roberts, John W. *From Trickster to Badman: The Black Folk Hero in Slavery and Freedom.* Philadelphia: University of Pennsylvania Press, 1990.

Robinson, Cyril D. "The Production of Black Violence in Chicago." In *Crime and Capitalism: Readings in Marxist Criminology,* edited by David F. Greenberg, 279–333. Philadelphia: Temple University Press, 1993.

Robinson, Dean E. *Black Nationalism in American Politics and Thought.* Cambridge: Cambridge University Press, 2001.

Robinson, Paul. "Race, Space, and the Evolution of Black Los Angeles." In *Black Los Angeles: American Dreams and Racial Realities*, edited by Darnell Hunt and Ana-Christina Ramón, 21–59. New York: New York University Press, 2010.

Rodríguez, Dylan. *Forced Passages: Imprisoned Radical Intellectuals and the U.S. Prison Regime*. Minneapolis: University of Minnesota Press, 2006.

Roediger, David R. *How Race Survived U.S. History: From Settlement and Slavery to the Obama Phenomenon*. London: Verso, 2008.

Romero, Anthony, and Mark V. Holden. "A New Beginning for Criminal Justice Reform." *Politico*, July 7, 2015. http://www.politico.com/magazine/story/2015/07/a-new -beginning-for-criminal-justice-reform-119822.

Rose, Tricia. *Black Noise: Rap Music and Black Culture in Contemporary America*. Middletown, CT: Wesleyan University Press, 1994.

——. *The Hip Hop Wars: What We Talk About When We Talk About Hip Hop—and Why It Matters*. New York: BasicCivitas, 2008.

Rosenfeld, Seth. *Subversives: The FBI's War on Student Radicals, and Reagan's Rise to Power*. New York: Farrar, Straus and Giroux, 2012.

Rowland, Jennifer. "L.A. Police Say Gang Truce Works." *United Press International*, June 17, 1992. LexisNexis Academic.

Run-DMC. *Raising Hell*. CD. Profile/Arista, 1986.

Samuels, Allison, and John Leland. "Trouble Man." *Newsweek*, September 23, 1996. LexisNexis Academic.

Sandoval, Edgar, and Helen Kennedy. "'Million Hoodie' March Takes Union Square in Protest of Trayvon Martin's Fatal Shooting." *New York Daily News*, March 21, 2012. http://www.nydailynews.com/new-york/million-hoodie-march-takes-union-square -protest-trayvon-martin-murder-article-1.1048522.

Santiago, Roberto. "Hold the Hallelujahs, Pulpit Victory over Rap Is Hollow One." *Plain Dealer*, December 16, 1993. LexisNexis Academic.

Satten, Vanessa. "Still: Fifteen Years since Tupac's Death, His Influence Is as Big as Ever," *XXL*, September 2011.

Schiappa, Edward. *Defining Reality: Definitions and the Politics of Meaning*. Carbondale: Southern Illinois University Press, 2003.

Schiesl, Martin J. "Behind the Badge: The Police and Social Discontent in Los Angeles since 1950." In *20th Century Los Angeles: Power, Promotion, and Social Conflict*, edited by Norman M. Klein and Martin J. Schiesl, 153–94. Claremont, CA: Regina Books, 1989.

Schlosser, Eric. "The Prison-Industrial Complex." *Atlantic Monthly*, December 1998. http://www.theatlantic.com/issues/98dec/pris2.htm.

Scott, James C. *Domination and the Arts of Resistance: Hidden Transcripts*. New Haven, CT: Yale University Press, 1990.

Seigworth, Gregory J., and Melissa Gregg. "An Inventory of Shimmers': Affect, for Now." In *The Affect Theory Reader*, edited by Gregory J. Seigworth and Melissa Gregg, 1–25. Durham, NC: Duke University Press, 2012.

Seinberg, Ian, Manning Marable, and Keesha Middlemass, eds. *Racializing Justice, Disenfranchising Lives: The Racism, Criminal Justice, and Law Reader*. New York: Palgrave Macmillan, 2007.

Selfa, Lance. *The Democrats: A Critical History*. Chicago: Haymarket Books, 2008.

Sellin, Thorstein. "The Negro Criminal: A Statistical Note." *Annals of the American Academy of Political and Social Science* 140 (1928): 52–64

Sellnow, Deanna, and Timothy Sellnow. "'The Illusion of Life' Rhetorical Perspective: An Integrated Approach to the Study of Music as Communication." *Critical Studies in Media Communication* 18 (2001): 395–415.

The Sentencing Project. *Incarcerated Women.* September 2012. http://www.sentencin gproject.org/doc/publications/cc_Incarcerated_Women_Factsheet_Sep24sp.pdf.

Shailor, Jonathan. *Performing New Lives: Prison Theatre.* London: Jessica Kingsley Publishers, 2011.

Shakur, Tupac. *All Eyez on Me.* CD. Death Row Records, 1996.

———. *The Don Killuminati: The Seven Day Theory.* CD. Death Row Records, 1996.

———. "Keep Ya Head Up." Music video. Interscope/Atlantic, 1993.

———. *Me Against the World.* CD. Atlantic/Interscope Records, 1995.

———. *Strictly 4 My N.I.G.G.A.Z.* CD. Atlantic/Interscope Records, 1993.

———. "2 of Amerikaz Most Wanted." Music video. Directed by Gobi M. Rahimi. Death Row Records, 1996.

———. *2Pac: Greatest Hits.* CD. Death Row Records, 1998.

———. *2Pacalypse Now.* CD. Interscope Records, 1991.

Shecter, Jon. "'Cop Killer' Won't Die." *Source,* November 1992.

Sherer, Michael, and Elizabeth Dias. "As Zimmerman Trial Ends, What's Next." *Time,* July 29, 2013. http://content.time.com/time/magazine/article/0,9171,2147718,00.html.

Shortie. "The Notorious B.I.G.: Ready to Die." *Source,* October 1994.

Sieving, Christopher. "Cop Out? The Media, 'Cop Killer,' and the Deracialization of Black Rage." *Journal of Communication Inquiry* 22 (1998): 334–53.

Simmons, Sheila. "Fans Not Surprised by Rapper's Death." *Plain Dealer,* September 20, 1996. LexisNexis Academic.

Simon, Jonathan. *Governing through Crime: How the War on Crime Transformed American Democracy and Created a Culture of Fear.* Oxford: Oxford University Press, 2007.

Simon, Roger. "How a Murderer and Rapist Became the Bush Campaign's Most Valuable Player." *Baltimore Sun,* November 11, 1990. http://articles.baltimoresun.com/1990 -11–11/features/1990315149_1_willie-horton-fournier-michael-dukakis.

Sloane, Amanda, and Graham Winch. "Judge Allows Evidence of Trayvon Martin's Marijuana Use." *CNN.com,* July 9, 2013. http://www.cnn.com/2013/07/08/justice/ zimmerman-trial.

Sloop, John M. *The Cultural Prison: Discourse, Prisoners, and Punishment.* Tuscaloosa: University of Alabama Press, 1996.

Smith, Christopher Holmes. "'I Don't Like to Dream about Getting Paid': Representations of Social Mobility and the Emergence of the Hip-Hop Mogul." *Social Text* 77 (2003): 69–97.

Smith, Danyel. "Introduction." In Light, *Tupac Shakur,* 15–19.

———. "Staying Power." In Light, *Tupac Shakur,* 105.

Smothers, Ronald. "Rapper Charged in Shootings of Off-Duty Officers." *New York Times,* November 2, 1993. http://www.nytimes.com/1993/11/02/us/rapper-charged-in-shootings -of-off-duty-officers.html.

Snoop Doggy Dogg. "Doggy Dogg World." Music video. Directed by Dr. Dre and Ricky Harris. Death Row Records, 1994.

———. *Doggystyle.* CD. Death Row Records, 1993.

———. "Gin and Juice." Music video. Directed by Dr. Dre. Death Row Records, 1993.

———. "Who Am I (What's My Name?)." Music video. Directed by Fab 5 Freddy. Death Row Records, 1993.

Snorton, C. Riley. *Nobody Is Supposed to Know: Black Sexuality on the Down Low*. Minneapolis: University of Minnesota Press, 2014.

Soja, Edward W. "Taking Los Angeles Apart: Towards a Postmodern Geography." In his *Postmodern Geographies: The Reassertion of Space in Critical Social Theory*. London: Verso, 1989.

Sorkin, Michael. "Explaining Los Angeles." In *California Counterpoint: New West Coast Architecture 1982*, edited by Kenneth Frampton and Silvia Kolbowski, 8–21. New York: Rizzoli, 1982.

Southall, Ashley, and C. J. Hughes. "Dozens Arrested during Brooklyn Bridge Protest against Police Violence." *New York Times*, April 14, 2015. http://www.nytimes.com/2015/04/15/nyregion/protesters-arrested-as-brooklyn-bridge-is-snarled.html.

Stabile, Carol A. *White Victims, Black Villains: Gender, Race, and Crime News in US Culture*. New York: Routledge, 2006.

"Stackalee." In *A Treasury of American Folklore: Stories, Ballads, and Traditions of the People*, edited by B. A. Botkin, 122–30. New York: Crown Publishers, 1944.

Steyn, Mark. "Bozo in the Hood; Tupac Shakur's Short, Violent, Misogynist Life." *American Spectator*, November 1996. LexisNexis Academic.

Street, John. *Music and Politics*. Malden, MA: Polity Press, 2012.

Swift, Christopher. "Academic Engagement." *Quarterly Journal of Speech* 96 (2010): 443–49.

Terry, David P. "Once Blind, Now Seeing: Problematics of Confessional Performance." *Text and Performance Quarterly* 26 (2006): 209–28.

Thompson, Heather Ann. "Why Mass Incarceration Matters: Rethinking Crisis, Decline, and Transformation in Postwar American History." *Journal of American History* 98 (2010): 703–34.

"Thug Life: Where Do the Children Play?" *Billboard*, September 28, 1996. LexisNexis Academic.

ThugLifeArmyNews. "Tupac at Malcolm X Grassroots Movement." *YouTube*, April 15, 2008. http://www.youtube.com/watch?v=3m2OUSZ5WR8.

Thrasher, Steven W. "What Next for Black Lives Matter in Ferguson after City's Police Shooting?" *Guardian*, March 13, 2015. http://www.theguardian.com/us-news/2015/mar/13/black-lives-matter-ferguson-police-shooting.

Tierney, John. "The Rational Choices of Crack Addicts." *New York Times*, September 16, 2013. http://www.nytimes.com/2013/09/17/science/the-rational-choices-of-crack-addicts.html?pagewanted=all&_r=1.

Topinka, Robert J. "Resisting the Fixity of Suburban Space: The Walker as Rhetorician." *Rhetoric Society Quarterly* 42 (2012): 65–84.

Travers, Peter. "Straight Outta Compton." *Rolling Stone*, August 13, 2015. http://www.rollingstone.com/movies/reviews/straight-outta-compton-20150813.

"Trayvon Martin Case: He Was Suspended Three Times and Caught with 'Burglary Tool.'" *Mail Online*, March 26, 2012. http://www.dailymail.co.uk/news/article-2120504/Trayvon-Martin-case-He-suspended-times-caught-burglary-tool.html.

"The Trayvon Martin Our Government-Subsidized Media Won't Let You See." *Sad Hill News*, March 25, 2012. http://sadhillnews.com/2012/03/25/the-trayvon-martin-our-government-subsidized-media-wont-let-you-see.

"Trials and Tribulations." *Source*, January 1994.

Troy, Gil. *Morning in America: How Ronald Reagan Invented the 1980s*. Princeton, NJ: Princeton University Press, 2005.

Tupac: Resurrection. Directed by Lauren Lazin. Los Angeles: Paramount Pictures, 2003.

Tyrangiel, Josh. "The Chronic." *Time*, January 22, 2010. http://entertainment.time.com/
2006/11/02/the-all-time-100-albums/slide/the-chronic/.

Understanding the Riots: Los Angeles before and after the Rodney King Case. Los Angeles:
Los Angeles Times, 1992.

United States House of Representatives, Subcommittee on Commerce, Consumer Protection and Competitiveness. *Music Lyrics and Interstate Commerce*, February 11, 1994.

United States Senate, Committee of the Judiciary, Juvenile Justice Subcommittee. *Shaping
Our Responses to Violent and Demeaning Imagery in Popular Music*, February 23, 1994.

"Untitled." In Light, *Tupac Shakur*, 59–61.

Veal, Michael. *Fela: The Life and Times of an African Music Icon*. Philadelphia: Temple
University Press, 2000.

Violant, Anthony. "Fighting Words; When Violent Music Finds Its Expression in Real
Life, Real People Get Hurt." *Buffalo News* (New York), September 24, 1993. LexisNexis
Academic.

Von Drehle, David. "In the Line of Fire." *Time*, April 9, 2015. http://time.com/3814970/
in-the-line-of-fire-2/.

Wallace, David Foster, and Mark Costello. *Signifying Rappers*. New York: Little, Brown,
2013.

Warren, Jennifer. *One in 100: Behind Bars in America*. Washington, DC: Pew Charitable
Trusts, 2008. http://www.pewtrusts.org/uploadedFiles/wwwpewtrustsorg/Reports/
sentencing_and_corrections/one_in_100.pdf.

Watkins, S. Craig. *Hip Hop Matters: Politics, Pop Culture, and the Struggle for the Soul of
a Movement*. Boston: Beacon Press, 2005.

Watts, Eric King. "Border Patrolling and 'Passing' in Eminem's *8 Mile*." *Critical Studies
in Media Communication* 22 (2005): 187–206.

———. "An Exploration of Spectacular Consumption: Gangsta Rap as Cultural Commodity." *Communication Studies* 48 (1997): 42–58.

———. *Hearing the Hurt: Rhetoric, Aesthetics, and Politics of the New Negro Movement*.
Tuscaloosa: University of Alabama Press, 2012.

Wenger, Morton G., and Thomas A. Bonomo. "Crime, the Crisis of Capitalism, and Social Revolution." In *Crime and Capitalism: Readings in Marxist Criminology*, edited
by David F. Greenberg, 674–88. Philadelphia: Temple University Press, 1993.

West, Cornel. *Race Matters*. Boston: Beacon Press, 2001.

"What Is the PIC? What Is Abolition?" *Critical Resistance*, 2015. http://criticalresistance
.org/about/not-so-common-language/.

Williams, Frank. "Eazy-E: The Life, The Legacy." *Source*, June 1995.

———. "The Living End." *Source*, November 1996.

Williams, Juan. "Fighting Words: Speaking Out against Racism, Sexism, and Gay-Bashing
in Pop." *Washington Post*, October 15, 1989. LexisNexis Academic.

Williams, Patricia J. *The Alchemy of Race and Rights: Diary of a Law Professor*. Cambridge, MA: Harvard University Press, 1991.

"Willie Horton (National Security PAC, 1988)." *Living Room Candidate*. 2012. http://
www.livingroomcandidate.org/commercials/1988/willie-horton.

Wood, Gaby. "Toni Morrison Interview: On Racism, Her New Novel, and Marlon Brando."
Telegraph, April 19, 2015. http://www.telegraph.co.uk/culture/books/authorinterviews/
11532385/Toni-Morrison-interview-on-racism-her-new-novel-and-Marlon-Brando.html.

Wood, Jennifer K. "Justice as Therapy: The Victim Rights Clarification Act." *Communication Quarterly* 51 (2003): 296–311.

World Class Wreckin' Crew. *Gold*. CD. SOH Distributors Network, 1994.

Worner, Elka. "Gangsta Rap—The Ongoing Debate." *United Press International*, May 28, 1994. LexisNexis Academic.

Wright, Kai. *Why Alton Sterling and Philando Castile Are Dead*. Nation, July 7, 2016. https://www.thenation.com/article/why-alton-sterling-and-philando-castile-are-dead/.

Wright, Richard. *Native Son*. New York: Signet, 1961.

"Yasiin Bey and Dead Prez Prep Trayvon Martin Tribute." *BET*, April 6, 2012. http://www.bet.com/news/music/2012/04/06/yasiin-bey-and-dead-prez-prep-trayvon-martin-tribute.html, accessed December 27, 2013.

Young, Cynthia A. *Soul Power: Culture, Radicalism, and the Making of a U.S. Third World Left*. Durham, NC: Duke University Press 2006.

Yousman, Bill. *Prime Time Prisons on U.S. TV: Representation of Incarceration*. New York: Peter Lang, 2009.

Zinn, Howard. *A People's History of the United States: 1492–Present*. New York: HarperCollins, 1999.

Index